Innovation, Technology, and Knowledge Management

Series Editor

Elias G. Carayannis, George Washington University, Washington, WA, USA

This series highlights emerging research and practice at the dynamic intersection of innovation, technology, and knowledge management, where individuals, organizations, industries, regions, and nations are harnessing creativity and invention to achieve and sustain growth. Volumes in the series explore the impact of innovation at the "macro" (economies, markets), "meso" (industries, firms), and "micro" levels (teams, individuals), drawing from such related disciplines as finance, organizational psychology, R&D, science policy, information systems, and strategy, with the underlying theme that in order for innovation to be useful it must involve the sharing and application of knowledge.

This book series is indexed in Scopus.

Francisco Sagasti

Knowledge is Power

The Twilight of Sir Francis Bacon's Epoch and the Prospects for Humanity

Springer

Francisco Sagasti
Universidad del Pacífico
Lima, Peru

ISSN 2197-5698 ISSN 2197-5701 (electronic)
Innovation, Technology, and Knowledge Management
ISBN 978-3-032-20667-1 ISBN 978-3-032-20668-8 (eBook)
https://doi.org/10.1007/978-3-032-20668-8

This Springer imprint is published by the registered company Springer Nature Switzerland AG
The registered company address is: Gewerbestrasse 11, 6330 Cham, Switzerland

This book is dedicated to the memory of
Geoffrey Oldham O.B.E.
Friend, mentor, colleague, and companion of many decades

Preface

"Knowledge is power" stated Sir Francis Bacon 430 years ago. Intrigued by the ideas of this philosopher-statesman, in 1980, I began to study his life and works. Soon I came across German philosopher Hans Jonas' account of what he called the Baconian Program: "to aim knowledge at power over nature, and to utilize power over nature for the improvement of the human lot" (Jonas, 1984, p. 140). This seemed more an objective than a program and launched me on a quest to find a more satisfactory definition.

After repeated incursions into the vast literature on Bacon and his writings, I could not find an explicit description of the Baconian Program and its content. This prompted a decades-long effort to understand what this far-thinking philosopher-statesman meant, how were his ideas received, and what were their consequences. I attempted to retrospectively frame what he had in mind, looking for scattered clues in the 14 volumes of his complete works. It soon became obvious that the statements I was culling and stitching together could not be understood without reference to his complex life.

Sir Francis Bacon, philosopher, lawyer, and statesman died of suffocation on April 9, 1626, reportedly after venturing out of his carriage to study the effects of extremely cold conditions on the preservation of bodies. His legacy has shaped the four centuries during which his views on dominating nature through understanding were gradually and successfully put into practice. Yet, success came at a high price: unforeseen and undesirable consequences that ended up exhausting the Baconian Program and compromising its success.

We are now witnessing the twilight of Bacon's epoch. Uncertainty, bewilderment, and anxiety accompany the encroaching darkness. Similar upheavals characterized the emergence of the modern world during the sixteenth and seventeenth centuries, when geographic discoveries changed our conceptions of the world and its peoples, the Earth was found not to be the center of the universe, and experimental science, a revolutionary way of generating knowledge, empowered humanity to an extent scarcely imagined at the time (Heller, 1978).

Epochal transitions challenge established habits of thought. They call for narratives that help reappraise the historical processes that led us to where we are now, assess their consequences, and explore their implications for the future.

The life and works of Sir Francis Bacon (1561–1626) provide both a starting point and a conducting thread for this book. He put forward a set of proposals to generate and mobilize scientific knowledge as the means to understand and master natural phenomena, and for using this knowledge to improve the human condition. What would eventually be defined as the Baconian Program was only implicitly articulated by this outstanding philosopher-statesman. Unfolding gradually from the mid-1600s to the late-1900s, it would inspire thinkers and doers before being deliberately deployed with extraordinary success during the twentieth century. But the remarkable achievements of Bacon's program ended up questioning its premises and undermining its foundations. The twilight of the Baconian epoch is launching humanity on an uncertain journey into uncharted territory, full of dangers and threats to the survival of our species but also of opportunities and new ways of exercising human faculties.

The first part of this book focuses on Sir Francis Bacon's life and legacy. Chapter 1 contains a concise biography of Sir Francis Bacon whose eventful life, full of contradictions and inconsistencies, of disappointments and triumphs, prefigures the epoch that would bear his name. Bacon did not express his views and proposals in the form of an explicit and comprehensive set of prescriptions. However, dispersed in his numerous and diverse writings, it is possible to find statements that can be viewed as an implicit program for humanity. Chapter 2 reviews the reactions to Bacon's work and life during the centuries that witnessed the unfolding, deployment, and success of his implicit program, which testifies to its enduring relevance. Chapter 3 offers a retrospective interpretation of his proposals to explicitly articulate the components of the Baconian Program: method, purpose, direction, focus, and institutions.

The second part describes the unfolding, deployment, and success of Bacon's program from the seventeenth to the twentieth centuries, tracing the interactions between knowledge, techniques, and production during the Scientific Revolution, the Enlightenment, and the Industrial Revolution. It then highlights the emergence of science-based technologies that would become the engine of economic growth and social development during the twentieth century. During this period, scientific knowledge was gradually but inexorably placed at the service of economic and political objectives, to the extent that the consequences of the deliberate deployment and success of Bacon's implicit program ended up questioning its premises and content. As a result, the foundations on which it initially stood have shifted; they can no longer provide, on their own, adequate and fruitful guidance for the future.

The third part of the book examines the twilight of Bacon's epoch and what may follow it. Chapter 9 explores the emerging context for human endeavors, analyzes changes in worldviews, examines the emergence of a paradoxical fractured global order, and argues that the extraordinary advances in information sciences and technologies have created new realms for the exercise of human faculties—cyberspace and virtual reality—that transcend the Cartesian mind/matter duality that prevailed during the Baconian epoch. Chapter 10 assesses the ambiguous success of Bacon's implicit program, examining how each of its components—method, purpose, direction, focus, and institutions—has been altered since they were first formulated. Chapter 11 ends the third part with tentative hints about the shape of post-Baconian times.

The epilogue centers on the myth of Prometheus, which has been retold many times through history and was interpreted by Bacon in his *Wisdom of the Ancients* (Bacon, 2011). A brief review of accounts of the Promethean myth precedes a reading that reflects human concerns at the twilight of Bacon's epoch: Does twilight mean dusk or dawn for humanity? If dusk, can we find out how long, dark, and nightmarish the night may be? Is there anything we could do to make the impending night as short—and the eventual dawn as luminous—as possible?

Bacon's memorable injunction on knowledge and power has stood the test of time. It has done so intellectually and in practice. This book summarizes my reflections on Sir Francis Bacon's life, work, and times, on what happened with his ideas during 400 years, and what may come next. The result, dear reader, is what you have in your hands or on your screen.

Lima, Peru — Francisco Sagasti

References

Bacon, F. (2011). Wisdom of the ancients. In J. Spedding, R. Ellis, & D. D. Heath (Eds.), *The works of Francis Bacon: Vol. 6: Literary and professional works 1*. Cambridge University Press.

Heller, A. (1978). *Renaissance man*. Schocken Books.

Jonas, H. (1984). *The imperative of responsibility: In search of an ethics for the technological age*. University of Chicago Press.

A Note on Sources, References, and Bibliography

The text that follows draws on a very large number of sources and quotes literally the writings of Francis Bacon and of authors that have referred to his work, as well as material from books and articles from other writers that illustrate the points made and the arguments put forward. Rather that adhering strictly to a style that puts the year and page number of the publications referred to in the main text, which would have made it unwieldy, the reader will find this information in the notes at the end of each chapter.

Acknowledgments

This book has been written over a long time. I began to think about Sir Francis Bacon and the Baconian Program in the early 1980s, and prepared several working papers, reports, and articles on the subject since then. My views on Bacon's works, life, and the impact of his ideas evolved as I delved deeper into his writings. While doing so, I have had the support from three generations of younger colleagues—they were always more than research assistants—who helped me to identify and process a large amount of background and source material.

The first crop of younger colleagues, who worked with me during the 1980s and 1990s include Carlos Eduardo Paredes, Gonzalo Garland, Alberto Pascó Font, Gonzalo Alcalde, Carla Sáenz, Eliana Chrem, Úrsula Casabonne, Fernando Hesse, Úrsula de Bary, Mario Bazán, Fernando Prada, Rafel Castillo, Juana Kuramoto, Michael Colby, Javier Escobal, Gregorio Arévalo, Carlos Contreras, and Onelia Cardettini. They helped me to prepare several working papers that provided inputs for the chapters in Part II of the book. A second group of younger colleagues included Lucía Málaga and Romeld Bustamante, who diligently helped me to review and summarize material included in Parts II and III.

Amanda Sagasti Charpentier deserves a special recognition, for she spent several months reviewing and summarizing hundreds of papers, articles, and monographs that gave shape to the chapters in Part III. Without her help, it would have not been possible to develop a reasonable view of the twilight of Bacon's epoch. Meyllyn de la Cruz Ponciano provided invaluable and diligent help with the notes, references, and bibliography.

Paraphrasing one of the most illustrious early scientists, "if I have seen further, it is because I stood on the shoulders of my younger colleagues." I am deeply grateful to all of them.

Several friends and senior colleagues provided comments and suggestions on the various papers, presentations, draft chapters, and the final manuscript. I am indebted to Carl Smith, Alberto Cordero, Pepi Patrón, Max Hernández, Michael Colby, Colin Bradford, Martin Albrow, Uno Svedin, Rosemary Rizo Patrón, Jurgen Schuldt, Ricardo Charpentier, Marie Louise Rowley, Vanessa Timmer, David Bes, Carlota

Pérez, and Keith Oldham, who read parts of the manuscript and whose reactions helped me to sharpen the arguments.

Special thanks to Keith Bezanson who revised the final manuscript several times and gave me most valuable comments and suggestions, and to Silvia Charpentier, who offered continuous encouragement and support, especially during the difficult times I spent holding high office. At an operational level, the daily assistance of my decades-long collaborators, Esther Aquiño and Washington Moreno, avoided distractions and allowed me to focus attention on intellectual pursuits.

Several agencies and foundations provided financial support at different stages of my work on *Knowledge is Power*. The Swedish Agency for Research Cooperation (SAREC) awarded me the first grant to begin working on the manuscript in the early 1980s and I am thankful to Lennart Båge for his support. The Canadian International Development Research Centre (IDRC), an institution with which I have had a long and fruitful association, provided financial support at several stages of my work during several decades. I want to express my thanks to its former presidents David Hopper, Keith Bezanson, and Maureen O'Neil, as well as to Ruth Zagorin, Pierre Beemans, James Mullin, Rohinton Medhora, and Tony Tillet for their unwavering faith in my finishing this book.

Patricia Rosenfield and Akin Adubifa of the Carnegie Corporation of New York helped with financial support in the early 2000s at a critical time when I found my research on the Baconian Program quite challenging. David Hamburg, the President of the Carnegie Corporation of New York, invited me to become a member of the Task Force on Science and Technology for Development of the Carnegie Commission on Science and Technology, co-chaired by Dr. Rodney Nichols and President Jimmy Carter, and I was able to exchange views with and obtain ideas from the members of the Commission.

A project sponsored by the United Nations University, coordinated jointly with Jean-Jacques Salomon and Cèline Sachs-Jeantet provided an opportunity to work with a select number of high-level experts in the preparation of a textbook on science and technology for development which fed into the second part of the book. Sesh Velamoor of the Foundation for the Future awarded me a grant that allowed me to explore ideas that would be incorporated into Part III of this book. The Rockefeller Foundation financed a meeting and provided a grant to work on the subjects covered in Chap. 10, and I am grateful to Janet Maugham for her interest and support for my research. A brief stay at the Institute for Advanced Sustainability Studies (IASS) in Potsdam at the invitation of Constantin von Barlowen provided an opportunity to test my ideas with a group of highly qualified researchers.

Special thanks are due to the Rockefeller Bellagio Center. My stay during April 2014 gave me the opportunity to define the structure and the main lines of argument of the book. Shortly thereafter, I became engaged in the political life of my country, which kept me away from my Baconian pursuits for a decade. After leaving high office, I revised and updated most of the manuscript. A second stay at Bellagio in April 2025 allowed me to complete the last three chapters. I am most grateful to Pilar Palacia and Elena Galosa, the directors of the Bellagio Center in 2014 and 2025, respectively, for the unique intellectual environment they created, and to

Sarah Geisenheimer of the Rockefeller Foundation for the opportunity to advance my work on *Knowledge is Power*. A stay at The New Institute in Hamburg during May–June 2025 allowed me to review and complete the whole manuscript, for which I am thankful to Britta Padberg, Anna Kastman, and Erck Rickmers. In both places, my colleagues were most helpful and the support staff were superb.

But my deepest gratitude for the interest and encouragement to work on the twilight of Sir Francis Bacon goes to Geoffrey Oldham, friend, mentor, advisor, and companion for many years since the early 1970s. This book is dedicated to him. Together with Keith Bezanson, Geoff continuously prodded me to complete a manuscript that took a long time to write. Without their constant and nagging encouragement, this book may have never been finished.

Contents

About the Author

Francisco Sagasti is a professor at the Graduate School of the Universidad del Pacífico, where he holds a UNESCO Chair on Knowledge and Innovation for Social Transformation. He is also a senior affiliated researcher at the Instituto de Estudios Peruanos (IEP) in Lima, Peru. Dr. Sagasti has been President of the Republic of Peru and member of Congress, where he headed the parliamentary caucus of his party and chaired the Science, Technology, and Innovation Committee.

Dr. Sagasti has been a fellow at the Woodrow Wilson Center for International Scholars, a Perry World House Distinguished Global Leader at the University of Pennsylvania, a Fellow at the Rockefeller Bellagio Center and at The New Institute in Hamburg, a professor of strategic planning at management at the Pacífico Business School, at the Universidad del Pacífico in Lima, Peru, and former Executive Director of the think-tank FORO Nacional Internacional. He has advised private corporations, international organizations, foundations, and public sector agencies on strategy and governance issues.

Dr. Sagasti has been chairman of the Board of the Science and Technology Program at the Prime Minister's Office in Peru; member of the Board of Governors of the Canadian International Development Research Centre (IDRC), of the International Advisory Board of the Lemelson Foundation, of the Governing Board of the International Institute for Environment and Development (IIED), and of the Advisory Board of the United Nations University. He has also been Chief of

Strategic Planning and Senior Advisor at the World Bank; chairman of the United Nations Advisory Committee on Science and Technology for Development; Senior Advisor at the Department of Scientific Affairs of the Organization of American States and the Community of Andean Nations; and advisor to numerous international organizations. Dr. Sagasti has been a Silberberg visiting professor at the Wharton School of Finance, University of Pennsylvania; a visiting professor at the University for Peace in Costa Rica and at the Instituto de Empresa in Madrid; and an associate researcher at the Institute of Development Studies, University of Sussex. He is a member of the "Club de Madrid" that gathers a hundred former democratic Heads of State and Prime Ministers.

In Peru, his native country, Dr. Sagasti has been founder and executive director of GRADE, a leading Peruvian policy-oriented think-tank; advisor to the ministers of Foreign Affairs, Education, Industry, and the Prime Minister; advisor to the Chief of the National Planning Institute; member of the board of the National Council for Science and Technology; and member of the board of the Industrial Technology and Standards Institute. He has also taught at the Pontificia Universidad Católica del Perú and the ESAN Business School, and has been consultant to numerous private, public, and international civil society organizations.

He holds engineering degrees from the National Engineering University in Lima, Peru, an MSc in industrial engineering from Penn State University, and a Ph.D. in operations research and social systems sciences from the University of Pennsylvania. He has been a visiting lecturer at universities in various regions of the world, delivered keynote speeches at scores of academic events, and holds an honorary doctorate from the Universidad Continental in Lima.

In 2017, Dr. Sagasti received the Robert K. Merton Award of the International Sociological Association for his academic and professional achievements in the field of social studies of science and technology. Previously, he received the Paul Hoffman Award created in memory of the Administrator of the Marshall Plan and first Executive Director of the United Nations Development Programme.

Dr. Sagasti has published more than 25 books including: *Incertidumbre: cinco Ensayos para entender nuestro tiempo*, Lima, Editorial Planeta, 2024; *Decisiones en tiempos turbulentos: medio siglo en ciencias de sistemas, planeamiento, gestión y gobernanza* Lima/Mexico, Fondo Editorial de la Universidad del Pacífico/Fondo de Cultura Económica, 2024; *Arte y tecnología: coreografía por computadoras*, Lima, Fondo Editorial de la Pontificia Universidad Católica del Perú, 2024; *Tecnología, ingeniería Desarrollo*, Lima, Fondo Editorial de la Universidad Nacional de Ingeniería, 2024; *Gobernar en tiempos de crisis—Política e ideas en el Gobierno de Trasnsición y Emergencia*, Lima, Editorial Planeta, 2023; *Discursos del Bicentenario*, Lima, Editorial Planeta, 2022; *Imaginemos un Perú mejor … y hagámoslo realidad*, Lima, Editorial Planeta, 2021; *Un desafío persistente: políticas de ciencia, tecnología e innovación en el Perú del siglo 21* (with Lucía Málaga), Lima/Mexico, Fondo de Cultura Económica, 2017; *Looking Back to Move Forward: a 40 Year Retrospective of the STPI Project,* Lima, FORO Nacional Internacional, 2015; *Ciencia, Tecnología, Innovación: Políticas para América Latina*, Lima/Mexico, Fondo de Cultura Económica, 2011 (2014); Power, Purse and Numbers: A Diagnostic Study of the UN Budget and Finance Process and Structure (with Ursula Casabonne and Fernando Prada), Stockholm, The Four Nations Initiative, October 2007; *The Future of Development Financing: Challenges and Strategic Choices* (with K. Bezanson and F. Prada), London, Palgrave Macmillan, 2005; *Knowledge and Innovation for Development: The Sisyphus Challenge of the 21st Century*, Cheltenham, Edward Elgar, 2004; *Financing and Providing Global Public Goods: Expectations and Prospects* (with K. Bezanson), Stockholm, Ministry for Foreign Affairs, 2001; *Democracy and Good Government* (with Pepi Patrón, Max Hernández and Nicolás Lynch), third edition, Lima, Editorial APOYO/Agenda: PERÚ, 2001; *Development Cooperation in a Fractured Global Order* (with G. Alcalde), Ottawa, IDRC, 1999; He coordinated the publication of *Development Strategies for the 21st Century: The Case of Peru*, Lima, Peru Report, 2001 (2014); and edited (with Céline Sachs and Jean-Jacques Salomon) *The Uncertain Quest: Science, Technology and Development*,

Tokyo, United Nations University Press, 1994, with translations into Spanish and French.

He is also the author of more than 250 academic articles, working papers, and book chapters (complete list of publications available on request); contributes to newspapers and magazines in Lima, Peru, has been member of the Editorial Boards of *Foresight, World Development, Technological Forecasting and Social Change,* and *El Trimestre Económico*. He has also directed a nine-part TV series *Abriendo Caminos* on social and economic change in Peru. For additional information, please see: www.franciscosagasti.com

Part I
Sir Francis Bacon's Life and Legacy

Introduction to Part I

The world as we know it has been largely shaped by a controversial genius of questionable reputation. A brilliant mind and political ambition combined to make Sir Francis Bacon, Lord Verulam and Viscount of St. Albans, a pivotal figure in the rise of knowledge as a driving force for progress. Yet, his intellectual achievements, political vicissitudes, and personal shortcomings have been the subject of heated debate for centuries.

Scientific pioneer or mediocre researcher? Lucid visionary or interpreter of ancient myths? Sober statesman or unscrupulous courtesan? Legal reformer or venal judge? Bacon's complex life and works defy attempts to provide simple answers and lead to further questions: Was he a keen secularist or a fervent Christian? Did he staunchly defend royal privilege or the rights of common people? Was he a practitioner of the occult or champion of modern knowledge? More than four and a half centuries after his birth, we are still trying to interpret his legacy and to assess the impact of his ideas.

Periods of profound change and upheavals give rise to individuals whose virtues and weaknesses reflect the character of their times. Sir Francis Bacon (1561–1626) is an emblematic figure in the long transition from Medieval and Renaissance to modern times. Bacon lived in England during the reign of Elizabeth I of England (1559–1603) and James I of Scotland, England, and Ireland (1603–1625). These were decades of geographic discoveries, technical progress, and advances in the arts, which, together with religious struggles, political unrest, and intermittent wars, provided the background for major socioeconomic and cultural transformations.

Bacon's earnest dedication to intellectual pursuits coexisted with an active participation in politics and the administrative affairs of the Crown. At different times, he was Member of Parliament, judge, litigant, holder of high office, and counselor to the Queen, King, and their favorites. An incessant search for recognition and royal favors went hand in hand with a chronic lack of financial resources. Bacon courted the high and mighty for appointments to secure a level of income required to engage in intellectual pursuits without hassle. A recurrent shortage of funds was aggravated by domestic aloofness, which allowed servants and other associates to take advantage of carelessness in the administration of his household.

Firmly planted between two ages, Bacon built on—but also questioned and transcended—scholastic thinking, Aristotelian philosophy, contemplative speculation, natural magic, alchemy, and Christian dogma. Straddling the intellectual and political realms, he articulated a new approach for generating knowledge and understanding nature, stating clearly that it should be used to "better man's estate." Sir Francis Bacon wrote extensively, often in an aphoristic and cryptic style; his ideas were widely disseminated starting in the mid-seventeenth century and soon acquired a life of their own. Successive waves of interpretation gave rise to various strands of Baconianism that, taken as a whole, unleashed a quest for scientific and applied knowledge that transformed humanity and its habitat.

The first chapter provides a concise biography of Sir Francis Bacon, highlighting the diversity of his public, professional, and intellectual roles. Chapter two shows the inconsistencies of Bacon's life and the richness of his works, which allowed many of his critics and supporters to select some aspects of particular interest to them, and to portray the man and his program in partial and often skewed ways. Prompted by a desire to understand what Bacon had in mind, I delved into his works and soon realized that he did not articulate his views as a set of clearly organized prescriptions. Chapter three offers a retrospective interpretation of his scattered proposals, structuring them into what I think he would have done if he had put forward a fleshed-out "Baconian Program."

Chapter 1
Bacon's Unsettled Life and Extraordinary Works

Bacon's life was a bundle of contradictions.

Lisa Jardine and Alan Stewart

Sir Francis Bacon's *Essays*, the first of his books I read, made me realize that it is not possible to understand his ideas without considering his complex life. Pursuing both intellectual and political aims in Elizabeth I and James I times was no mean feat. He had to achieve a precarious balance between philosophical musings and power machinations; however separate he claimed them to be, they leveraged each other.

Bacon was born in January 1561 to Sir Nicholas Bacon, highly respected Keeper of the Royal Seal during the reign of Queen Elizabeth I, and to his second wife Ann Cooke, a well-connected and spirited Calvinist, related through her sister's marriage to Lord Burghley, the Queen's High Treasurer. Bacon had an elder brother, Anthony, and four half-brothers and sisters from his father's first marriage.

Sir Nicholas was recruited for public service by Thomas Cromwell, Henry VIII's influential minister, and was one of the few court officials who survived his fall in 1540 to serve with Queen Elizabeth. A believer in the need to cautiously reform the English commonweal and in following a balanced, middle-of-the-road path in discharging his official functions, Sir Nicholas instilled the idea of royal service in Francis' mind and sought to prepare him for it. His mother, a headstrong Protestant unusually well cultivated for her times, supervised the early education of her two children, retained highly competent teachers, and made sure they were instructed in religious matters. A comfortable and well-tutored boyhood allowed the precocious Francis to display his wit during frequent court visits, to the extent that Queen Elizabeth used to call him the "young Lord Keeper."

When he was 12 years old, Francis joined his elder brother Anthony at Cambridge University. He already knew Latin, and stayed there for two and a half years, studying Greek and Roman historical and literary texts, while cultivating gentlemanly manners under the strict tutorship of the Master of Trinity College. Later in his life, Bacon would recall that his aversion to Aristotelian methods, which he saw as

F. Sagasti, *Knowledge is Power*, Innovation, Technology, and Knowledge Management, https://doi.org/10.1007/978-3-032-20668-8_1

"barren of the production of works for the benefit of the life of man" (Rawley, 2011, p. 4), emerged during his period at Cambridge. Both brothers' health was rather frail and required constant ministering, which may have spurred Francis' lifelong interest in ways of conserving and prolonging life.

Bacon was admitted to Gray's Inn to study law in 1576, but when Sir Amias Paulet was named ambassador to France his father arranged for Francis to join him as one of his secretaries. Bacon's duties involved helping the ambassador to prepare detailed reports on the political situation, religious intrigues, and court events. He became proficient in the use of ciphers and codes, and on more than one occasion traveled to London to deliver dispatches to the Queen and high government officials. Foreign ambassadors usually followed the French court's internal displacements and Bacon accompanied Paulet to Blois, Tours, and Poitiers. Toward the end of his Parisian stay, Bacon left the embassy residence and moved to the house of a civil lawyer, where he was able to observe French civil law in action.

Meticulous note-taking and writing discipline were work habits acquired by Bacon during his time in France. Sir Amias Paulet was a dedicated official who prepared frequent and comprehensive dispatches in code; working with him Bacon learned to value the accuracy, usefulness, and timeliness of information. While in France, Bacon also freelanced for Thomas Bodley, founder of the Bodleian Library in Oxford, who sought and purveyed intelligence to various clients and patrons. Bacon was asked to write assessments of the "strength, riches, traffics, havens, shipping, commodities, vent, and the wants and disadvantages of places … their buildings, furnitures, their entertainments; all their husbandry, and ingenious inventions … for multiplying their commodities, encouraging arts and manufactures, or of worth in any kind."[1] He was also supposed to obtain information on royal alliances, treaties, conquests, wars, laws, magistrates, discontents, and disorders. The young assistant diplomat's proficiency in compiling data, gathering evidence and organizing the supply of information would become useful in his political and intellectual endeavors.

His father's death in February 1579 forced Bacon's return to England, where he found that no arrangements had been made by Sir Nicholas to ensure his financial future. After settling estates on his elder sons and leaving his widow as life tenant in the country house inherited by Francis' brother Anthony, he had nothing to bequeath to his youngest son. Bacon faced the choice of living with his mother or attending Gray's Inn in London, where he had been admitted 3 years earlier. Choosing the latter, he followed in the footsteps of his elder brothers, although none of them had great interest in the law and did not complete their studies.

[1] Letter from Thomas Bodley to Francis Bacon, published as letter written by Bacon for Essex and directed to the Earl of Rutland, see (Bacon, 2011c, vol. 9, p. 17). More information about the letter, whose authorship is fiercely debated in Jardine and Stewart (1999).

Working Hard and Begging Favors

Bacon earned his living by practicing law but continuously sought ways of lessening his dependence on the legal profession. In 1580, he requested his uncle, Lord Burghley, the High Treasurer, to intercede with the Queen in obtaining an honorary legal appointment with enough income to achieve a degree of financial independence. This did not materialize during Elizabeth's reign and Bacon was forced to keep on practicing law. He rose rapidly through the ranks at Gray's Inn, probably with some help from his uncle and a good word from the Queen. An increasingly visible role as Member of Parliament, starting with a brief stint in 1581 and continuing from 1584 onward through the mid-1590s, complemented his legal activities.

At this time, Bacon was identified with leading figures in the Puritan movement who, against the Queen's wishes, promoted Church reform. The young Parliamentarian and lawyer faced a quandary. In addition to contravening his father's teaching of loyally serving the monarch, this undermined his chances of royal patronage to achieve high office. Bacon gradually shifted his allegiance to moderate factions, aligned himself with senior officials primarily dedicated to serving the Queen, and was given the task of investigating Catholic and Jesuit plots against the Crown.

Bacon did not abandon intellectual pursuits during the 1580s; he read widely, prepared his legal cases carefully, and became a leading parliamentary orator. During this period, he worked on a manuscript that highlighted the limitations of received philosophical ideas and practices, boldly asserting a new dawn in the history of humanity was imminent. Initially titled *The Magnificent Birth of Opportunity*, it would be published after Bacon's death as *The Masculine Birth of Time*.

While serving in Parliament and working as a lawyer in the early 1590s, Bacon continued his forays into intellectual and political battlegrounds with *An Advertisement Touching the Controversies of the Church of England* and *On Tribute*. In the first of these works, he called for the cessation of hostilities between the Church of England establishment that demanded allegiance to official liturgy, stressed the authority of bishops, and repressed dissent, and the reformist Protestants who eschewed elaborate rituals, opposed a church hierarchy seen too close to Catholicism, and preached rebellion. The second was a play with four characters: fortitude, love, knowledge, and the sovereign. The longest segment praises the policies and personal qualities of Queen Elizabeth and was undoubtedly written to gain royal favor. The part on knowledge outlines two recurrent themes in Bacon's work: a critique of ways of knowing received from Greek philosophers and alchemists, and the importance of inventions to master nature.

A clear statement of Bacon's ambitious lifetime objectives is found in a letter to Lord Burghley, written in 1592 when Bacon was 31 years old: "I have vast contemplative ends, as I have moderate civil ends: for I have taken all knowledge to be my province." He aimed at purging knowledge of "frivolous disputations" and "verbosities," as well as of "blind experiments" and verbally transmitted "traditions and impostures," in order to reach "industrious observations, grounded conclusions, and profitable inventions and discoveries."[2] Bacon's emphasis on contemplative ends must be taken with a pinch of salt, for he relinquished worldly aims only in the last years of his life after being disgraced, and even then not completely.

The last decade of Elizabeth's reign was a turbulent period for Bacon. The lukewarm support received from Lord Burghley to further his career made him search for other patrons, and in the late 1580s, he found one in Robert Devereaux, Earl of Essex and the Queen's favorite. Through the good offices of Burghley and with the support of Essex, Bacon was granted the clerkship of the Star Chamber in 1589, but the actual position and the income associated with it materialized only two decades later. The Earl of Essex repeatedly asked the Queen to appoint Bacon as Attorney General. She refused and appointed Edward Coke instead, a lifelong adversary of Bacon who would eventually be instrumental in his downfall.

Despite efforts from his mother and other supporters, Bacon's political career did not flourish during Elizabeth's reign. The Queen was displeased with Bacon's behavior in the 1593 sitting of the House of Commons, in which he had been a member of the committee that dealt with a request for subsidies from the English monarch and the House of Lords. Bacon supported the request but asserted the House of Commons' privilege to first offer the subsidy to the Upper House, rather than responding to a demand from the latter. Also, instead of a triple subsidy to be paid over 4 years, Bacon proposed it be spread over 6 years, arguing that otherwise it would be difficult to collect and could lead to popular unrest.

The subsidy was eventually agreed as requested, but Bacon's standing with the Queen and his prospects in the Elizabethan court were sorely damaged. He tried to justify his behavior claiming to have spoken "only to satisfy my conscience," without attempting "to sway the cause," and because of "duty and zeal towards her Majesty and her service."[3] Elizabeth chose not to elevate Bacon to high office possibly with the additional justification that he was rather young for the positions he aspired to, and because of her reluctance to appear pliant to Essex's increasingly strident advocacy of his protégé. Nonetheless, the Queen and the Privy Council continued to employ Bacon's legal services, trusting him with sensitive security cases and giving him a warrant to use torture when examining prisoners charged with treason.

The Earl of Essex was a brilliant but arrogant and impulsive man, who frequently disregarded royal orders in spite of Bacon's moderating counsel. Essex's recurrent quarrels and reconciliations with the Queen punctuated a stormy relationship that came to a head after her favorite led a disastrous campaign in Ireland. Essex lost three-quarters of his army, wasted a large amount of funds, negotiated a truce and returned to England against Elizabeth's wishes. The Queen ordered Essex to be detained and tried and asked Bacon to join the prosecution team. The Earl was sentenced, dismissed from all his official positions, and confined to house arrest in June

[2] Letter to William Cecil, 1st Baron Burghley, 1592 in Bacon (2011b, vol. 8).

[3] A letter to the Lord Treasurer Burghley in excuse of his Speech in Parliament against the Triple Subsidy, 1593 (Bacon, 2011b, vol. 8, p. 234).

1600, although he was soon set free and retired to Oxfordshire. During that summer, Bacon unsuccessfully attempted to reconcile his benefactor with Elizabeth.

The impetuous Earl returned to his London house in the autumn of 1600 and made halfhearted attempts to appease the Queen, who pointedly ignored them. Frustrated and angry, Essex mobilized allies and supporters to storm the royal palace, seize the monarch, force her to dismiss her senior officials and appoint Essex loyalists. In February 1601, the plan was put in motion with hundreds of his followers gathering at his house, but after a day of marches and skirmishes with royalist troops, the conspirator and dozens of his men were surrounded at Essex House and arrested.

The Earl was declared a traitor and sent to prison. His patron's rebellion put Bacon in an awkward situation; he and his brother Anthony were close to Essex and owed him many favors, even though Francis had always advised him to treat the sovereign with respect. Placing his concern for the security of the monarch above everything else, and openly exhibiting his allegiance to the Queen, Bacon played a leading role in prosecuting his former patron. The trial of Essex and his associates was not handled well by the Attorney General, Sir Edward Coke, and Bacon intervened several times to set the trial back on course and secure a guilty verdict.

Bacon pleaded with the Queen to show mercy, but to no avail. Essex was beheaded in the Tower of London and several of his co-conspirators were executed in the following days. The Queen ordered Bacon to prepare an official version of the events but displeased with the respectful way in which he referred to the disgraced Earl, she ordered changes to be introduced. The prominent role that Bacon played in the trial of his close friend and benefactor, including writing an account of the proceedings, has been held against him ever since as proof of faulty character.

During the 1590s, Bacon assiduously courted royal favor and was also fully engaged in lawyerly and parliamentarian pursuits. Nonetheless, he also managed to write elaborate plays performed at Gray's Inn, speeches and notebooks of quotations, and numerous legal and state briefs. His most notable work from this period is the 1597 first edition of the *Essays*, largely derived from personal experience, which would be revised and expanded in 1612 and 1625. Bacon's lifestyle and carelessness with money led to burdensome debts that briefly imprisoned him in 1598, but by the mid-1601, he had managed to extricate himself from them and would only again see prison during a brief stint two decades later.

Intellectual Gratification and Burdensome Political Rewards

Queen Elizabeth died in March 1603 after reigning more than 44 years, all of Bacon's lifetime. At 42 years of age, he was bereft of what had been a permanent, but highly fickle, referent for his personal advancement efforts. Bacon lost no time in approaching the new monarch, King James I of England, Scotland, and Ireland. Together with 300 other gentlemen, Bacon was knighted during the celebrations to mark the new king's accession to the throne and was officially asked to continue providing legal advice to the monarch, much as he had done to Queen Elizabeth.

The accession of King James I marked the beginning of a long period of active legal and political work for Bacon, which he managed to combine with a prodigious amount of writing. During 1603–1604, he produced and revised many texts in English and Latin, some of which would not be published till after his death. These include *A Confession of Faith*, *On the True Greatness of Britain*, *Preface of the Interpretation of Nature*, and *Certain Considerations Touching the Better Pacification and Edification of the Church of England*. Another text from this period, "A Brief Discourse touching the Happy Union of the Kingdoms of England and Scotland," drew a parallel between the "rules of nature" and the "rules of policy," a recurrent time in his work, and outlined the need for collaboration in unveiling the secrets of nature and making them useful to men. Bacon's uneasiness with the role he played in prosecuting the Earl of Essex, his former friend and patron, motivated him to write a short *Apology, on certain imputations concerning the late earl of Essex*, in which he attempted to cast his involvement in the affair in a favorable light.

Even though in the mid-1603 Bacon had stated: "my ambition now I shall only put upon my pen, whereby I shall be able to obtain memory and merit of the times succeeding,"[4] he became an active member of Parliament four times during 1604–1610, was involved in many legal cases, and continued pursuing royal favor. The periods between meetings of Parliament in 1603–1605 gave Bacon time away from political duties, allowing him to complete the most far-reaching work he had written as yet, *Of the Proficiency and Advancement of Learning, Divine and Humane*, published in September 1605.

The *Advancement of Learning* argues that the generation and acquisition of knowledge is important in its own right, describes the errors incurred by unwary intellectual practitioners, justifies the search for and usefulness of knowledge in both religious and secular terms, and outlines his plans for the reformation of knowledge. The first volume is devoted to "the excellence of learning and knowledge" and to the "merit and true glory in the augmentation and propagation thereof," while the second deals with "the particular acts and works … embraced and undertaken for the advancement of learning." For Bacon "fruitful natural philosophy hath a double scale or ladder, … ascending from experiments to the invention of causes, and descending from causes to the invention of new experiments" (Bacon, 2011a, vol. 3, pp. 263–264, 351–352), both of which are necessary in the conduct of scientific inquiry. He also viewed the mechanical arts and the technical inventions of craftsmen as a rich source of material to further the advancement of learning. Natural philosophy was the term widely used since ancient times until the nineteenth century for what is now called science.

The extensive references to ancient texts and Bacon's liberal use of Latin quotations suggest that he had been keeping notes for the *Advancement of Learning* for a long time. The book offers a detailed classification of the different types of

[4] Letter to Robert, Lord Cecil, 1603 (Bacon, 2011d, vol. 10, p. 80).

knowledge, a discussion of research methods, and an interpretation of the errors, vices, and foibles that discredit intellectual endeavors. A key idea Bacon put forward is that knowledge can be continuously improved and expanded, and that the process of generating knowledge is itself amenable to improvement. He firmly believed that new discoveries and inventions alleviate human suffering, improve the human condition, and contribute to the greatness of kingdoms, which made them worthy of receiving state support and royal patronage. *The Advancement of Learning* would become the first of his planned six-part *Great Instauration*, of which the *Novum Organum*, published in 1620, was to be the second.

"To the King" was the simple dedication in the cover of the *Advancement of Learning*. Declaring himself amazed at King James' intellectual virtues and faculties, faithfulness of memory, swiftness of apprehension, penetration of judgment, and facility of elocution, Bacon stated his aim was to "excite your princely cogitations to visit the excellent treasure of your own mind, and thence to extract particulars for this purpose agreeable to your magnanimity and wisdom" (Bacon, 2011a, vol. 3, p. 264). As was the case during Queen Elizabeth's reign, the King ignored his pleas and subsequent appeals for royal support.

Bacon sent the *Advancement of Learning* to several friends and patrons, including the Earl of Salisbury and Chancellor of Cambridge University, Lord Chancellor Ellesmere, Bishop Lancelot Andrewes, his friend Tobie Matthew, and Sir Thomas Bodley. In the cover letters, Bacon said the book was a product of his "vacant time," a child that he had "taught to go," and that he knew that he was "fitter to hold a book than to play a part," but that he had "led his life in civil causes; for which I was not very fit in nature, and more unfit by the preoccupation of his mind."[5] Constantly juggling the contemplative and active facets of his busy life, Bacon often mentioned that he wrote in his spare time: "to write at leisure that which is to be read at leisure matters little; but to bring about the better ordering of man's life and business, with all its troubles and difficulties, by the help of sound and true contemplations,—this is the thing I am at."[6] Yet, the recurrent mention of a preference for intellectual rather than legal or political tasks belied his earnest lifelong pursuit of the latter.

Bacon had proposed marriage to a wealthy widow in 1597 but was turned down and the following year she wed his long-standing adversary, Attorney General Sir Edward Coke. In May 1606, the 45-year-old Bacon married 14-year-old Alice Barnham, an alderman's daughter who he had identified as a suitable bride 3 years earlier. The marriage brought temporary financial relief, but Bacon was clearly aware that their age difference could create problems, as her dalliances with other men—possibly driven by his indifference to women—would do. Allegations of homosexuality were later leveled against Bacon, and his widow married his steward barely a month after Bacon's death.

---

[5] See letters upon sending the book of *Advancement of Learning* to Thomas Bodley, to the Earl of Salisbury, and to Tobie Matthew in Bacon (2011d, vol. 10, pp. 253, 256).

[6] Letter to Casaubon, 1609 (Bacon, 2011e, vol. 11, p. 147).

The marriage and attending celebrations did not distract Bacon from his Parliamentary and legal activities, nor from intellectual pursuits. At the end of 1606, he played a leading role in the debates on the naturalization of Scots resulting from the union between England and Scotland. Fulfilling one of his long-time aspirations, in June of the following year, he was named Solicitor General and had to write many legal opinions and Proclamations. At the same time, he was writing *Cogitata et Visa* (Thoughts and Conclusions), a short work that would be recast as a key component of *The Great Instauration* a dozen years later.

Following the death of the incumbent, in 1608, Bacon finally became Clerk of the Star Chamber, a position he had been named to almost two decades earlier. New duties and additional income prompted Bacon to review his situation and future prospects. He revised old notebooks (*Comentarious solutos*) containing annotations, journals, and schedules written over many years, and started a new one (*Comentarious novus*) to pen his thoughts and "remembrance of matter, form, business, studies, touching myself, service, others … without any matter of restraint."[7] Issues covered in this exercise included plans to ensure financial security and maintaining good standing with creditors, preparations for Parliamentary sessions and legal cases, ways of obtaining support for his experimental work, reminders to keep in contact with mathematicians, specimen collectors, and physicians, and tips to improve relations with the King and powerful patrons. Administrative and political issues outweighed intellectual ones in these notebooks, which contain several references to Bacon's use of flattery and deception to secure patronage and gain advantage.

In 1608, Bacon wrote a book defending Queen Elizabeth's reign, which was published only after his death and was well regarded by several commentators. He also wrote *Redargutio philosopharum* (The Refutation of Philosophers), criticizing arguments that conformed to preconceived ideas rather than to the empirical world, and advanced arguments he would develop in the *Great Instauration* a decade later. These activities were combined with his new position as treasurer of Gray's Inn, where Bacon had studied and practiced law.

While busy in his new position as Solicitor General and his legal work, Bacon continued to write and develop his views on how to reform knowledge. Aware that his views were thoroughly unfamiliar to contemporaries, he wrote *De Sapientia Veterum* (The Wisdom of the Ancients) recounting 31 well-known ancient myths that served "to instruct or illustrate." Bacon reinterpreted their meanings to pave the way for the reception of his novel ideas. He argued that "this method of instructing is grave, sober or exceedingly useful, and sometimes necessary in the sciences, as it opens an easy and familiar passage to the human understanding, in all new discoveries that are abstruse and out of the road of vulgar opinions."[8]

In 1610, Bacon found himself in the middle of a tussle between King James and the members of Parliament. It started as a dispute on Crown finances and taxes but

[7] See "Comentarius Solutus Sive Pandecta" (Bacon, 2011e, vol. 11, p. 62).

[8] See preface to Wisdom of the Ancients (Bacon, 1884, p. 321).

soon spilled over into debates on the nature of royal privilege and the rights of the House of Commons. Bacon tried to strike a middle ground between "the prerogative of the King … and the liberty of the subject,"[9] and while leaning toward the former, he was designated by his parliamentary colleagues to present James with a set of "Petitions and Grievances" on the question of impositions. After negotiating for a few months, there was no agreement and Bacon's efforts were wasted.

During 1611 and 1612, Bacon focused on his legal work, taking private cases, advising the King, acting as prosecutor, and intervening in administrative matters. In the latter year, he published an enlarged edition of his *Essays* with 38 entries, which he had originally planned to dedicate to Prince Henry. However, the 19-year-old prince died before the text was published, and Bacon had to scrap the dedication and write a brief one to his brother-in-law. Bacon also found time to write *Descriptio Globi Intellectualis* (Description of the Intellectual Globe), revising the classification of knowledge he had proposed in the *Advancement of Learning*, and *Thema Coeli*, in which he put forward his views on cosmology, distinguishing between dense or gross and rare entities, assigning the Earth to the former category and the rest of the universe to the latter. These texts would later be incorporated into *The Great Instauration*.

The death of the Lord Chief Justice in August 1613 set in motion a series of events that would see Francis Bacon appointed Attorney General, 20 years after he was first touted for the post by Lord Essex. He actively lobbied King James to promote the incumbent, Lord Coke, to Chief Justice and to appoint him in his place. Bacon argued that the position of Attorney General needed a man of "a quicker and more earnest temper," "of courage and speech and a grounded lawyer," that could "recover that strength to the King's prerogative which it hath in times past," offering himself as the most suitable candidate. After his appointment, Bacon wrote a letter thanking King James, in which he promised to "integrity and industry" in discharging his duties.[10]

His first task after appointment was to deal with the matter of duels, which had become a fashionable means of settling disputes among gentlemen. In his *Charge touching duels*, Bacon stated that they were an offense against the King because they "despiseth death, which is the utmost of punishments,"[11] and proposed severe penalties for those who engaged in duels. By that time, Bacon had been actively courting the King's new favorite, Robert Carr, Earl of Somerset, for whose marriage he wrote and financed a lavish masque in early 1614. According to contemporary accounts, additional displays of Bacon's newly found wealth included feasting the whole University of Cambridge at Christmas, dressing ostentatiously, and retaining a large number of servants.

---

[9] An argument of the King's solicitor in the Lower House of Parliament, proving the King's right of impositions (Bacon, 2011e, vol. 11, p. 191). About tussle between King James and the members of parliament, see (Jardine & Stewart, 1999, pp. 319–320).

[10] Letters to the King (Bacon, 2011e, vol. 11, pp. 381, 391).

[11] Charge touching duels (Bacon, 2011e, vol. 11, p. 403).

Parliament was convened in early 1614 and even though he was Attorney General, Bacon was elected member of the House of Commons. This sparked disputes about conflicts of interest, required searching for precedents of such dual roles and led to an appeal by the King to keep him in Parliament. Bacon soon became embroiled in convoluted negotiations regarding royal finances, which did not end well. Playing two parts in the long-running drama of Crown–Parliament relations became increasingly difficult for him.

Toward the end of 1614, Somerset was accused of poisoning a former associate imprisoned in the Tower of London, and his short-lived tenure as royal favorite came to a disastrous end. Bacon played a leading role in the prosecution of Somerset. As he had done in the case of an earlier favorite and benefactor, Lord Essex, Bacon assisted the Chief Justice, helping to convict Somerset and to obtain a confession from his wife. After the trial was over, he pleaded with the King to rehabilitate them, this time with success. Other judicial matters on behalf of the crown kept Bacon quite busy at this time, including an inquiry into Coke's performance as Chief Justice that would lead to his removal later in the year.

Following Somerset's fall, Bacon began, once again, the process of changing patrons. In August of that year, the King had met a charming young man, George Villiers, who quickly established himself as favorite and rose swiftly through the court ranks. By 1618, he had become Groom of the Bedchamber, Master of the Horse, Knight of the Garter, Baron Whaddon, Viscount Villiers, and Earl of Buckingham. In 1623, he became Duke of Buckingham and the highest-ranking non-member of the royal family. Bacon helped Villiers' advance and benefited from it; he provided advice to the new favorite and used his court and legal connections to assist him, while trying to secure his support to achieve even higher office.

A close working relation between King James, Buckingham, and Bacon was forged at this time. Partly as a reward for services and with Villiers' full support, in June 1616, Bacon was appointed to the Privy Council, and in March 1617, he became Lord Keeper of the Seal, the position once held by his father. Two months later, Bacon celebrated his accession to the Court of Chancery with a lavish procession of court notables and servants. Despite claiming that "this matter of pomp, which is heaven to some men, is hell to me, or purgatory at least,"[12] Bacon's luxurious lifestyle suggested a fondness for the privileges and material rewards of high royal office.

The marriage of Buckingham's brother to one of Edward Coke's daughters led to a first major disagreement between Bacon and his patron. Displeasing both King and favorite, he openly opposed the marriage, while his adversary, the former Chief Justice, recovered influence and standing. Royal support for the match made Bacon recant his opposition, but seeds of discontent that would bear bitter fruit had been planted in the minds of England's two most powerful men. Following reconciliation with Buckingham, Bacon began to receive frequent requests to assist and favor his

[12] Letter to the Earl of Buckingham, May 8, 1617 (Bacon, 2011f, vol. 13, p. 194).

followers in legal disputes, which made the Lord Keeper of the Seal appear subservient to the wishes of the favorite.

In January 1618, Bacon was appointed Lord Chancellor and, in addition to his work at the Star Chamber, devoted attention to clearing a backlog of cases in Chancery. At the same time, as a member of Privy Council, Bacon was heavily involved in a review to reduce royal household expenditures, which required carefully balancing his dedication to the task with his allegiance to a monarch well known for punishing those who crossed him. The heavy workload took a toll and Bacon began to fall behind in his multiple functions, while his health deteriorated.

Excepting the *Charge touching duels*, Bacon published no major work between 1613 and 1619, for he was extremely busy with his official duties and his quest for advancement and higher office. He was named Baron Verulam of Verulam in July 1618, and soon thereafter asked to lead a committee to investigate Sir Walter Raleigh. This confirmed a pattern in which Bacon played a leading role in the prosecution and conviction of disgraced former high officials, including Essex for rebellion, Somerset for poisoning, Raleigh for treason, and later that of Lord Treasurer Earl of Suffolk for misappropriating funds and of Attorney General Sir Henry Yelverton for legal transgressions. Apparently, Bacon was oblivious to the possibility that he could suffer a similar fate.

Rising High and Falling Hard: Bacon's Triumph and Disgrace

The October 1620 publication of the preface, plan of work, and second part of *Instauratio Magna* (*The Great Instauration*), the *Novum Organum*, testifies that Bacon continuously revised, updated, and developed his philosophical ideas in his scarce free time. In this work, Bacon aimed "to bring about a complete *Instauration* of the arts and sciences and all the learning of mankind, raised upon proper foundations." Although he was conscious that "while at the beginning this may appear infinite and beyond mortal capacity, once in train it will be found reasonable and sober," and argued he wanted to leave "some sign of his sincere concern for the good of mankind" (Bacon, 1994, pp. 3–4).

The Great Instauration was dedicated to King James. In a letter to the monarch, Bacon explained it was "no more than a new logic … to make philosophy and sciences both more true and more active … to enlarge the bounds of Reason and to endow man's estate with new value." He added:

> I have been about such work for near thirty years … and the reason why I have published it now, specially being unperfect, is … because I number my days and would have it saved. There is another reason of me doing so, which is to try whether I can get help in one intended part of this work, namely, the compiling of a natural and experimental history, which must be the main foundation of a true and active philosophy.[13]

[13] Letter to the King, 12th October 1620 (Bacon, 2011g, vol. 14, pp. 119–120).

The King responded with praise but warned that he had "as little spare time to read it as you had to write it,"[14] making it clear that Bacon's masterpiece was beyond his understanding or interest.

The Great Instauration consists of six parts, of which Bacon completed the first and second, leaving outlines and notes for the rest. The preface stated he had "established a true, lawful and lasting marriage between the empirical and rational faculties," and admonished that all men should "reflect on the true ends of knowledge, and that they seek it not from any intellectual satisfaction, nor for contention, nor to look down upon others, nor for reward, or fame, or power, or any of these baser things; but to direct and bring it to perfection in charity, for the benefit and use of life" (Bacon, 1994, pp. 14–15).

The second part, the *Novum Organum,* dealt with the "directions for the interpretation of nature," and presented Bacon's methodology for acquiring true and fruitful knowledge through "the better and most perfect use of reason in the investigation of nature." He proposed to derive "gradually, in a connected succession," progressively more general explanations, and to submit basic principles "to examination, until they are entirely established." The aim was to "overcome nature by action" and "command nature by obeying her." Along the way, he argued that systematic experimentation was essential, for "no amount of ingenuity or meditation or argument could ever replace or make up for hard work and investigation" (Bacon, 1994, pp. 19–21, 24, 43),[15] and criticized alchemists and magicians who slavishly followed recipes and blamed themselves for failing to achieve the desired results.

The *New Organum* made a crystal-clear plea for separating science from religion: "Natural philosophy in every age has met with a troublesome and difficult enemy … superstition and the blind, excessive zeal of religion." For Bacon, it was neither appropriate to use theological arguments in natural philosophy, nor to derive religious principles from scientific inquiry. In his view, progress in natural philosophy had been blocked "when religion, the most powerful influence over man's minds, has, through the ignorance and incautious zeal of some, been drawn to take sides against her." His arguments centered on avoiding the contamination of scientific inquiry with theological considerations, but he accepted a role for religion in deciding how its results should be used: "Let the human race only recover its God-given right over nature and be given the necessary power; then right reason and sound religion will govern the exercise of it" (Bacon, 1994, pp. 99, 101, 131).

Following the publication of *The Great Instauration*, Parliament was convened after a 7-year hiatus. Bacon spent the late part of 1620 figuring out how to defuse impending conflicts between the House of Commons and the King who, in poor health and afflicted with arthritis, was little inclined to compromise. In January 1621, Bacon celebrated his sixtieth birthday with a magnificent banquet, and soon after was created Viscount St. Albans in a ceremony with King James and Buckingham in attendance. By that time, Bacon's detractors and adversaries, who

---

[14] Reply from the King, 16th October 1620 (Bacon, 2011g, vol. 14, p. 122).

[15] About Alchemists, see Bacon (1994, pp. 94–95).

felt wronged by his judicial rulings and official actions, were spreading rumors about corruption and criticizing his ostentatious lifestyle. Persistent allegations of homosexuality, and particularly dalliances with young members of his household, led some of Bacon's enemies to focus on his "most abominable and darling sin" that "should have been tried at the Bar of Justice," and "satisfied the law most severe against that horrible villainy with the price of his blood" (D'Ewes, 1783, pp. 25–26).

Parliament sessions started at the end of January 1621. Two subsidies for the King were quickly agreed, but in return—as suggested by Privy Councilor Edward Coke, Bacon's lifelong foe—the House of Commons decided to hear grievances against government officials who had incorrectly awarded licenses, monopolies, and patents. During the proceedings, it came to light that Buckingham's relatives had benefited from such awards, and that Bacon had been involved in granting them. In addition, abuses that could be linked to Bacon were unearthed in the Court of Chancery, putting him in a rather vulnerable position. Advised he was under attack, the newly created Viscount shrugged warnings off, trusting—rather unwisely as it turned out—his closeness to the King and Buckingham.

Bacon's downfall was swift and devastating. Three months after becoming Viscount St. Albans, he was charged with bribery and two months later sentenced to pay a fine of 40,000 pounds, imprisoned in the Tower of London, barred from public office, and banished to the countryside. Two charges of bribery were brought against him in the mid-March 1621, but the number escalated to 28 in the following days. Some of the accusers were incensed, not because the Lord Chancellor accepted bribes, but because he did not rule in their favor. Alarmed and in deteriorating health, Bacon appealed immediately to Buckingham and the King for protection, but to no avail.

The House of Lords proceeded with the trial and heard numerous witnesses, while Bacon studied precedents and prepared a detailed rebuttal of the charges. He denied taking rewards to pervert justice and argued that gifts received from litigants had not changed his verdicts, that he had received them at times like New Year when it was customary to give presents, and that they had been made to his servants without his knowledge. However, after carefully preparing his defense and making repeated appeals to Buckingham and the King, by the end of April 1621, Bacon abruptly changed course and admitted guilt, asking for lenience from the Lords. Conflicting accounts of this reversal suggest that Bacon was either sacrificed to shield Buckingham, or that charges were so damning that, in failing health, he decided to "confess and acknowledge that I find matter sufficient and full, both to move me to desert the defence, and to move your Lordships to condemn and censure me."[16]

[16] Bacon's submission to the House of Lords (Bacon, 2011g, vol. 14, p. 243).

The Fruits of Exile: Profiting from Adversity and Courting Posterity

Bacon was imprisoned in the Tower of London at the end of May 1621 but remained there only a few days before being released by the King. Soon after, he retired to Gorhambury, his country estate. By the end of that year, Bacon's appeals to Buckingham and the King yielded a remission of his fine, but not a repeal of his banishment. His pensions remained unpaid and his pardon was postponed.

Defeated in his courtly endeavors, after decades of "honor without leisure" Bacon would have "leisure without honor" to fully engage in intellectual pursuits. He revised and expanded his scientific, historical, and philosophical texts, and set to project the image of a sage fallen from grace. According to Lisa Jardine and Alan Stewart, Bacon's outstanding biographers, "as he manufactured an impressive body of scientific and philosophical writings—worthy of a great man in retirement—Bacon tacitly erased all sighs that his 'thought' and his 'life' (in the political arena) had hitherto been intimately linked." Instead, he constructed a "before" and "after," before Francis Bacon was an "active politician … his outlook inevitably colored … by the times; after, he was a patrician thinker, selflessly pursuing his scientific endeavors for posterity" (Jardine & Stewart, 1999, p. 475). Nonetheless, hoping for a royal pardon, Bacon kept on asking friends and former patrons to intercede on his behalf, while taking time to deal with matters pending from his time at the Chancery.

The *History of King Henry VII*, published in March 1622, was the first product of forced retirement. Bacon appealed to King James for support to write a history of England and a digest of his laws, but his request fell on deaf ears. Without a steady source of income, frequently ill, and abandoned by many of his servants, Bacon kept on writing. During the second half of 1622, he completed several installments of his *Natural History*, two of which, *Historia ventorum* (History of winds) and *Historia vitae et mortis* (History of life and death), were published during his lifetime. In January 1623, with King James' authorization, Bacon was given access to the Paper Office Keeper's archives to write a history of King Henry VIII.

During most of 1623, Bacon kept on pressing his case to friends and former associates, trying to recover influence and return to the court, but without success. In October, he published an enlarged Latin translation of *The Advancement of Learning* with the explicit aim of reaching a wider audience in the Continent. Early in the following year, he wrote *Considerations Touching a War with Spain*, dedicated to Prince Charles but published after Bacon's death, and worked on *Sylva Sylvarum*, expanding his account of natural history. Two minor works, *Apophthegms, New and Old* and *Translation of Certain Psalms*, were published in December 1624. Despite intermittent illnesses, financial difficulties, and distractions derived from his former official functions, Bacon kept on working steadily.

King James died in March 1625, Prince Charles succeeded him, and, true to form, Bacon wrote to Buckingham asking to intercede with the new King; once again, without result. Plague, illness, and financial hardship kept Bacon in

Gorhambury preparing the third edition of the *Essays*, the last of his works he would see published. The latter part of the year was spent working on the *New Atlantis*, a fable about a utopian society ruled by scientists and virtuous statesmen, which would see the light of day after his death.

Weakened by sickness, in January 1626, Bacon traveled to London, probably to press his case in court, seek treatment for his illnesses, and conduct experiments. He set back in early April but became seriously ill along the way and had to stop in Highgate at the house of a longtime friend, the Earl of Arundel. Some accounts of his last days portray him as a martyr of empirical research, dying as a consequence of venturing outdoors in harsh winter to investigate the effects of cold in the preservation of bodies. Another version suggests that following long-standing habits, while in London Bacon inhaled nitrate and opiates, both considered medicinal in his natural history writings. These toxic substances took a heavy toll on his frail body, and the cold weather led to fits of coughing and vomiting during the return trip to Gorhambury, forcing him to interrupt the journey. A few days after stopping at Arundel's house, Sir Francis Bacon, Lord Verulam and Viscount St. Albans, died of suffocation on April 9, 1626.

References

Bacon, F. (1884). *Bacon's essays and wisdom of the ancients* (P. Shaw, Trans.). Little, Brown. Retrieved from http://archive.org/details/baconsessayswisd00baco

Bacon, F. (1994). In P. Urbach & J. Gibson (Eds.), *Novum Organum: With other parts of the great instauration*. Open Court.

Bacon, F. (2011a). The advancement of learning. In J. Spedding, R. L. Ellis, & D. D. Heath (Eds.), *The works of Francis Bacon: Vol. 3: Philosophical works 3* (pp. 321–491). Cambridge University Press.

Bacon, F. (2011b). In J. Spedding, R. Ellis, & D. D. Heath, (Eds.), *The works of Francis Bacon: Vol. 8: The letters and the life 1* (Digitally printed version). Cambridge University Press.

Bacon, F. (2011c). In J. Spedding, R. Ellis, & D. D. Heath, (Eds.), *The works of Francis Bacon: Vol. 9: The letters and the life 2* (Digitally printed version). Cambridge University Press.

Bacon, F. (2011d). In J. Spedding, R. Ellis, & D. D. Heath (Eds.), *The works of Francis Bacon: Vol. 10: The letters and the life 3* (Digitally printed version). Cambridge University Press.

Bacon, F. (2011e). In J. Spedding, R. Ellis, & D. D. Heath, (Eds.), *The Works of Francis Bacon: Vol. 11: The Letters and the Life 4* (Digitally printed version). Cambridge University Press.

Bacon, F. (2011f). In J. Spedding, R. Ellis, & D. D. Heath (Eds.), *The works of Francis Bacon: Vol. 13: The letters and the life 6* (Digitally printed version). Cambridge University Press.

Bacon, F. (2011g). In J. Spedding, R. Ellis, & D. D. Heath, (Eds.), *The works of Francis Bacon: Vol. 14: The letters and the life 7* (Digitally printed version). Cambridge University Press.

D'Ewes, S. S. (1783). *Extracts from the MS. Journal of Sir Simonds D'Ewes, with several letters to and from Sir Simonds and his friends. From the originals in the British Museum. MS. Notes.* J. Nichols.

Jardine, L., & Stewart, A. (1999). *Hostage to fortune: The troubled life of Francis Bacon*. Hill and Wang.

Rawley, W. (2011). The life of the right honourable Francis Bacon. In J. Spedding, R. L. Ellis, & D. D. Heath (Eds.), *The works of Francis Bacon: Vol. 1: Philosophical works 1* (pp. 3–18). Cambridge University Press.

Chapter 2
Bacon's Multifaceted and Controversial Legacy

Viewed either as a fraud or as the fountainhead of modern scientific rationality, the Baconian movement continues to inspire a great deal of interpretative effort.

Antonio Pérez-Ramos (1991)

Sir Francis Bacon's life and works have generated considerable controversy. His complex life encapsulated the concerns and pressures of his turbulent times. Bacon's works, life, and legacy provide material for a richly woven tapestry of interpretations. Perhaps no other figure of the early modern period has generated as much controversy regarding his intellectual contributions, public activities, and personal qualities. As his biographer Nieves Mathews put it, "it is not surprising that a man whose mental net was cast so wide should have aroused a considerable variety of responses" (Mathews, 1996, pp. 4, 442).

Close associates described Sir Francis Bacon as warm and amiable, but others reported him to be cold, unflappable, and incapable of showing emotion. He experienced the highs and lows of public life, and when obstacles emerged was always ready to search for alternative paths. Bouncing back and recovering after reversals of fortune required a capacity to tolerate humiliation, and to withstand slights by Queen, King, favorites, and powerful patrons while keeping ultimate objectives in sight.

Widely read, Bacon was familiar with ancient Greek texts (Parmenides, Heraclitus, Democritus, Empedocles, Plato, and Aristotle), classic Roman works (Tacitus, Livy, Pliny the Elder, and Virgil), the literary and philosophical contributions of Renaissance authors (Petrarca, Boccaccio, Dante, and Machiavelli), practical treatises on industry (Biringuccio, Agricola, and Palissy), and with the work of contemporary scholars (Telesio, Patrizi, Severinus, Campanella, della Porta, and Bodin). He collected and processed a vast amount of information, received and absorbed a variety of ideas, and remained in contact with continental thinkers through intermediaries, letters, and the occasional visitor.

As I waded through the 14 volumes of Bacon's complete works, compiled in the mid-nineteenth century by James Spedding, Robert Ellis, and Douglas Heath, I

F. Sagasti, *Knowledge is Power*, Innovation, Technology, and Knowledge Management, https://doi.org/10.1007/978-3-032-20668-8_2

wondered at his industriousness and wide-ranging interests (fortunately, the texts in Latin were followed by an English translation). I would find even more startling the widely divergent views and reactions his works would prompt in the centuries that followed.

Early Appraisals of Bacon's Work

British contemporaries responded with ambivalence and hostility to Bacon's philosophical and scientific writings, and occasionally with faint praise. Bacon's ideas were too radical and unfamiliar to be easily digested.

After reading *Cogitata et visa*, Sir Thomas Bodley acknowledged that Bacon was a "master workman" who had "worthy contemplations" on the means to procure knowledge, but wrote to him that "in case we should concur to do so as you advise, which is, to renounce or common notions, and cancel all our theorems, axioms, rules and tenets … there is nothing more certain that it would bring us instantly to barbarism." William Harvey, Bacon's and the King's physician, was fond of Bacon's wit but, either baffled or awed by Bacon's *Novum Organon*, said that "he writes philosophy like a Lord Chancellor" (Disraeli, 1859, p. 324). Greek scholar and Essex associate, Henry Cuffe, thought "a fool could not have written such a work, and a wise man would not" (Chamberlain, as cited in Disraeli, 1859, p. 325). King James, to whom Bacon dedicated the *Novum Organon*, said: "it is like the peace of God, that surpasseth all understanding" (Chamberlain, as cited in Disraeli, 1859, p. 326).

Reception to Bacon's ideas improved following his death. His personal secretary and chaplain, William Rawley, inherited most of his manuscripts and arranged their publication. As Bacon's public life faded from memory, his ideas on the organization of research were invoked by the Anglican reformers in the mid-seventeenth century. The creation of the world's first scientific society in 1662, the "Royal Society of London for the Improvement of Natural Knowledge," was inspired by Bacon's description of the "House of Solomon" in the *New Atlantis*. Henry Oldenburg, Robert Hooke, Robert Boyle, William Petty, Thomas Sprat, and John Wilkins, early members of the Royal Society, all gave credit to Bacon for inspiring observations and experiments.

During the late seventeenth and eighteenth centuries, Baconian ideas were widely disseminated. Czech educational reformer John Amos Comenius and German-British educator Samuel Hartlib organized a network of intellectuals inspired by Bacon's ideas. French intellectual François-María Arouet, known as Voltaire, had a high opinion of Bacon: "there was not a man who had any idea of experimental philosophy before Chancellor Bacon" (Voltaire, 1901, p. 22). He considered that Bacon's *Novum Organon* provided "the scaffold by means of which the edifice of the new philosophy has been reared" (Voltaire, 1901, p. 21). Voltaire praised Bacon for finding time to become "a great philosopher, a good historian and an elegant writer" (Voltaire, 1901, p. 20) amidst the "intrigues of the court and the affairs of his exalted employment" (Voltaire, 1901, p. 20).

Jean de Rond d'Alembert, one of the compilers of the French Encyclopedia, viewed Bacon "the greatest, most universal and most eloquent of philosopher, considering his sound and broad views, the multitude of subjects to which his mind turned itself, and the boldness of his style" (d'Alembert, 2009, "Part II," para. 23). Jean-Jacques Rousseau regarded Bacon as "perhaps the greatest of philosophers" (Rousseau, 1923, p. 44); Antoine-Nicolas de Condorcet wrote that Bacon was one of the "extraordinary personages" in the transition toward modernity, who "revealed the true method of studying nature, by employing the three instruments with he has furnished us for the discovery of her secrets, observation, experiment and calculations" (Condorcet, 1802, p. 147).

German philosopher Immanuel Kant started the second edition of his *Critique of Pure Reason* (1787) with a quotation from Bacon's *Great Instauration.* Considering him "the first and greatest student of nature in recent times" (Höffe, 2009, p. 55), Kant stated that it had taken one and a half centuries for natural philosophy to "find the highway of science," partly at "the suggestion of ingenious Francis Bacon" (Kant, 1787/1998, p. 108). He also thought that "gave a brilliant example of the method in his *Organon* of how the hidden constitution of natural things could be uncovered through experiments" (Kant, 2006, pp. 118–119).

Across the Atlantic Ocean, Thomas Jefferson and Benjamin Franklin, two of the Founding Fathers of the United States, were familiar with the Lord Chancellor's works. Jefferson considered Bacon, Locke, and Newton "the three greatest men that have ever lived, ... as having laid the foundations of those superstructures which have been raised in the physical and moral sciences."[1] Benjamin Franklin was familiar with Bacon's work and the April 1749 entry in his *Poor Richard's Almanack* reads: "On the 7th of this month, 1626, died that great little man, Sir Francis Bacon; *great* in his prodigious genius, parts and learning; and *little*, in his servile compliances with a little court, and submissive flattery of a little prince. ... He is justly esteem'd the father of the modern experimental philosophy" (his emphasis) (Franklin, 2004, p. 165).

Appraisals of Bacon's intellectual contributions and life continued to differ widely in the nineteenth century. Responding to contemporary concerns and influenced by personal biases, slight displacements in perspective configured, much like twists of a kaleidoscope, new patterns of interpretation. Bacon's injunction to dominate nature through understanding was ideally suited to support the Industrial Revolution, but Victorian morals demanded condemnation of his personal behavior, and advances in scientific research revealed limitations in his empirical approach.

Nineteenth-century British philosopher William Whewell considered Bacon as the "supreme legislator of the republic of science" (Whewell, 1847, p. 227) and literary scholar Isaac Disraeli thought him an inspiring visionary: "like the great prophet on the mount, Bacon was doomed to view the land afar, which he himself

[1] Letter to John Trumbull, Paris, Feb. 15, 1789 (Holmes, 2002, p. 107).

could never enter" (Disraeli, 1859, p. 324). John Herschel, one of the most influential scientist-activists at the time, stated in 1831, "previous to the publication of the *Novum Organum* of Bacon, natural philosophy, in any legitimate and extensive sense of the word, could hardly be said to exist" (Herschel, 1987, p. 105).

British historian Thomas Macaulay recognized his intellectual achievements but censured his personal qualities. For Macaulay, the Lord Chancellor combined a "singular union of audacity and sobriety ... with great minuteness of observation [and] amplitude of comprehension," which allowed him to stimulate the "discovery of *new* and *useful* truth" that gave "human mind a direction which it shall retain for ages" (his emphasis). But Macaulay also thought it was "painful to turn back from contemplating Bacon's philosophy to contemplate his life ... [because of] ... so many proofs of narrowness and selfishness, ... disingenuousness of the most devoted worshipper of speculative truth, [and] servility of the boldest champion of intellectual freedom" (Macaulay, 1837, pp. 93, 94, 95, 103, 104).

British biologist Thomas Henry Huxley argued he had "not the slightest desire to join the outcry against either the morals, the intellect or the great genius of Lord Chancellor Bacon," but dismissed the idea that "the methods of modern scientific inquiry originated with him" (Huxley, 1862, p. 57). After condemning Bacon for doubting Copernicus heliocentric theory, American chemist and historian John William Draper concluded: "the sacred name of philosophy should be severed from its long connection with that of one who was a pretender in science, a time-serving politician, an insidious lawyer, a corrupt judge, a treacherous friend, a bad man" (Draper, 1863, pp. 122, 517).

Sir Francis Bacon's works were paid attention to by Karl Marx and Friedrich Engels. For Marx, Bacon emancipated physics from theology and was "the real founder of English materialism and all modern experimental science. ... In Bacon, its first creator, materialism contained latent and still in a naive way the germs of all-round development. Matter smiled at man with poetical sensuous brightness" (Marx & Engels, 1956, p. 172). Engels saw Bacon as one of the greatest English philosophers but observed that his "method of investigation has also left us as a legacy the habit of observing natural objects and natural processes in their isolation, detached from the whole vast interconnection of things" (Engels, 1894, p. 27).

Rationalizing Contradictions

The inconsistencies between Bacon's intellectual, political, and personal lives challenged interpreters of his legacy in the second half of the nineteenth and first decades of the twentieth centuries. Some of them viewed these as complementary, others as parallel, and still others as reflecting the spirit of Bacon's times (Nichol, 1888, p. v). Firmly in the first group, German historian of philosophy Kuno Fischer wrote: "If we now compare Bacon's moral disposition with his scientific character, we shall find between the two not a puzzling contradiction, but, on the contrary, a natural analogy; only the very peculiarities that were injurious and perilous with respect to his practical life were advantageous to his scientific pursuits. ... *Bacon's character was as practical, as cool, as supple as the science which he desired and prescribed for his age*" (his emphasis) (Fischer, 1857, pp. 27, 32).

Richard William Church, Dean of St. Paul's Cathedral, was in the parallel lives camp: "there was the life of high thinking, of disinterested aims, of genuine enthusiasm, of genuine desire to delight and benefit mankind, ... And there was the ... worldly life, the life of supposed necessities for the provision of daily bread, the life of ambition and self-seeking" (Church, 1901, pp. 55, 187). American jurist Benjamin G. Lovejoy sought "to outline [Bacon] in his two roles of Truth-seeker and Place-hunter, in his courage and cowardice, strengths and weaknesses, glory and shame, ... he was at one and the same time the most selfish and the most philanthropic of men, the most timid and the most fearless" (Lovejoy, 1888, pp. 2, 184).

Among those who viewed Bacon's intellectual and political lives as influenced by his context, Scottish biographer and literary critic John Nicol argued "the truth between the excesses of adulation and iconoclastic zeal, is to be found in carefully considering the circumstances of the age in which Bacon lived—an age so wonderful because at once so magnificent and so mean. ... All the features bright and dark, of our Elizabethan age, its splendor, its daring, and the wearisomeness of its intrigue, are conspicuous in his career and character" (Nichol, 1888, pp. vii, 12).

Exeter professor Israel Levine offered three options to unravel the contradictions in Bacon's life and temperament: first, "we may conclude Bacon was a thorough hypocrite"; second, "his character, while not free from reproach, is on the whole an admirable one, and ... his faults are easily pardonable"; and third, Bacon possessed "a whole admirable nature but [was] ruined by his surroundings." Inclined toward the second and third options, Levine thought Bacon was not "capable of deliberate evil or malice" (Levine, 1925, pp. 53, 56, 58, 63, 62, 64).

Lisa Jardine and Alan Stewart wrote a meticulously researched biography of Sir Francis Bacon, in which they aimed "to present Bacon's life ... candidly, warts and all, without attempting to resolve its contradictions" (Jardine & Stewart, 1999, p. 9). They stressed Bacon "was careful to separate his life into a 'before' period of political intrigue, treacherous behavior of friends and social climbing, and an 'after' of austere scientific enquiry in a country retreat" (Jardine & Stewart, 1999, p. 19). In their view, this "has left posterity with two clearly incompatible versions of Francis Bacon. All subsequent biography has struggled to resolve them" (Jardine & Stewart, 1999, p. 19). Considering his "rich and crowded life," they find that "for a man actively engaged in public life throughout his adult years, Bacon's written legacy is impressive" (Jardine & Stewart, 1999, p. 8).

Faustian Visionary and Scientific Impresario

During the first half of the twentieth century, apologists and detractors continued to offer conflicting appraisals of Bacon's legacy. American pragmatist philosopher John Dewey viewed him as "the great forerunner of the spirit of modern life"

(Dewey, 1957, p. 28) and philosopher and mathematician Alfred North Whitehead considered Bacon "one of the great builders who constructed the mind of the modern world" (Whitehead, 1967, p. 54). For British philosopher and mathematician Bertrand Russell, Bacon "has permanent importance as ... the pioneer in the attempt al logical systematization of scientific procedure" (Russell, 2004, p. 583). However, French philosopher of science Alexander Koyré offered a radically different perspective: "'Bacon the founder of modern science' is a joke, and a bad one at that, ... In fact, Bacon understood nothing about science" (Koyré, 1978, p. 39).

Philosopher Karl Popper called Bacon "the spiritual father of modern science ... the founder and prophet of a rationalist church," but criticized Bacon's injunction to clear the mind of "anticipations, rash and premature" and of "prejudices," seeing it as "a kind of ritual" similar to that of the mystic that "purifies his soul to prepare it for the vision of God." In Popper's account, "bold ideas, unjustified anticipations, and speculative thought, are our only means for interpreting nature," but these must "carefully and soberly controlled by systematic tests" (Popper, 1968, pp. 278, 279, 280).

By the mid-twentieth century, many historians of science and philosophy continued to view Bacon as a key figure in the emergence of modern science. Historian of philosophy Frederick Copleston noted "there has been a strong tendency to depreciate Francis Bacon and to minimize his importance: but the influence of his writings was considerable, and the outlook which he represented has entered profoundly into the western mind" (Copleston, 1953, p. 308). Hermeneutic philosopher Hans Gadamer said Bacon's conception of experiment provided a "careful directing of our mind, preventing it from indulging in overhasty generalizations" (Gadamer, 2013, p. 357).

Bacon's emphasis on the importance of the crafts and practical skills as a key complement to speculative thought was recognized by numerous intellectuals. Classics scholar Benjamin Farrington emphasized that Bacon fought "for the idea that the philosopher, if he is to create a science fruitful in works, must overcome his contempt for the craftsman ... [and] bring learning into relation with industry and invention. ... New arts could be devised only by intelligence, by learning, by theory. Science must be applied to industry" (Farrington, 1949, p. 15). Australian science historian A. C. Crombie highlighted Bacon's "opinion that technics or, as he called it, the mechanical arts, had flourished just because they were firmly founded on fact and modified in the light of experience. Scientific thought, on the other hand, had failed to advance just because it was divorced from nature and kept remote from practical experiment" (Crombie, 1953, p. 276). Italian philosopher and historian Paolo Rossi emphasized Bacon "strove to rehabilitate the mechanical arts, denounced the sterility of Scholastic logic," and "saw the development of the mechanical arts as a new and exciting cultural event" (Rossi, 2013, p. 27).

"The Great Impresario of modern science ... not of modern scientific method, but of the modern scientific attitude" (Haydn, 1950, p. 274) was how American literary scholar Hiram Haydn characterized Bacon. American anthropologist and science historian Lorin Eiseley called him the "man who first fully visualized in all its splendor the 'invention of inventions'—the experimental method that would unlock the riches of the modern world, … a statesman and strategist of science rather than an individual discoverer." Eiseley cast Bacon as "the great synthesizer who alters the outlook of a generation," for which he "is apt to be the most envied, feared and hated man among his contemporaries" (Eiseley, 1973, p. 17).

Not all mid-twentieth century scholars praised Bacon and his legacy. Dutch mathematician Eduard Jan Dijksterhuis derided Bacon's failure to appreciate the importance of mathematics and said he "did not make a single positive contribution to science … consequently never produced any results" (Zagorin, 1998, p. 126). Medieval historian Lynn Thorndike thought "there is not much that one can say for Francis Bacon. He was a crooked chancellor in a moral sense and a crooked naturalist in an intellectual and scientific sense. He … could not think straight when he thought as a naturalist and tried to amass 'experiments' on the one hand and to grapple with magical tradition and superstition on the other" (Thorndike, 1958, p. 88).

Legal Reformer, Historian, Communicator, and Organizer

Bacon's legal and administrative reforms also drew the attention of his biographers. American writer Catherine Drinker Bowen pointed out that "Bacon's suggestions were eventually incorporated in the English legal system, thought the doing took centuries; Sir Francis's imagination far outrun his times" (Bowen, 1963, pp. 149, 155). British historian Hugh Trevor-Roper hailed Bacon's "serene, Olympian, disengaged intellect" that allowed him "to separate reason from ideology, from orthodoxy and heresy alike." Trevor-Roper also thought him "the greatest of social and legal reformers, the man who, had he been heard, might have forestalled revolution in England" (Trevor-Roper, 1962, pp. 74–76).

British philosopher Stephen Toulmin and British historian June Goodfield considered Bacon "one of the true modern historians. Instead of confining himself to sacred history, or to Greco-Roman times, he was prepared to treat the men and events of his own age as significant in their own right." In their view, Bacon had argued that "the men of modern times had built on the achievements of the ancients and so surpassed them" (Toulmin & Goodfield, 1965, p. 108), and his intellectual optimism differed completely from the outlook of the medieval tradition.

An emphasis on finding novel approaches to disseminate his ideas was a recurring feature of Bacon's work. Historian Lisa Jardine highlighted his "obsession with procedure and methods of presentation" and "how his theory of method as strategy led him to choose particular literary forms for particular didactic purposes, to render inaccessible ideas perspicuous for a popular audience" (Jardine, 2009, pp. 7–8, 15). Political philosopher Anthony Quinton mentioned that Bacon's "fondness for an aphoristic mode of expression is not just a bare idiosyncrasy of taste," because they were "particularly suitable for the presentation of tentative opinions" (Quinton, 1980, p. 76). British historian B. H. G. Wormald referred to Bacon's desire to reach as wide an audience as possible: "as in his natural science, so in his political science,

Bacon addressed himself to all times and to all places. ... [his] aim was to conquer all opinions" (Wormald, 2006, pp. 22–23).

From a different perspective, literary scholar Thomas H. Jameson quoted Percy Shelley's view that "Lord Bacon was a poet. His language has a sweet and majestic rhythm which satisfies the sense, no less than the almost superhuman wisdom of his philosophy satisfies the intellect" (Jameson, 1954, p. 1). Examining Bacon's theory of imagination, Jameson concluded: "Bacon will one day receive adequate credit for his foreshadowing of a new and scientific aesthetic" (Jameson, 1954, p. 26).

The "central place of organization in Bacon's work" was highlighted by American historian of science John Leary Jr. In his view, one of "Bacon's principal innovations' ... was his conception of the Great Instauration as a tightly organized and carefully governed enterprise of people working in concert. ... a new kind of social organization which would bind together, channel and integrate the labors of people involved in scientific inquiry" (Leary, 1994, pp. 8–9). Alluding to the secretive "House of Solomon" described in Bacon's *New Atlantis*, Leary concluded: "before dismissing Bacon [as] prophet ... we might consider twentieth-century science with its tightly organized and managed research institutions often operating in closely guarded secrecy ... [these] are perhaps the true descendants of Salomon's House. Here power in the service of profit or national advantage seeks the careful management of personnel and resources to establish that true Baconian 'empire' over nature" (Leary, 1994, p. 263).

Reappraising Bacon's Philosophy

The last several decades witnessed renewed interest in Bacon, his writings, and his legacy. Books, essays, papers, reeditions of his works, and newly available material for his biographers revived debates on his role in the emergence of modern science, the Industrial Revolution, and the Western mindset.

Finnish historian Markku Peltonen edited a book of original essays providing a broad and nuanced perspective on Bacon's scientific, philosophical, religious, political, rhetorical, historical, and moral writings. His introductory essay acknowledges that as a result of "tremendous strides ... in Bacon scholarship" (Peltonen, 1996, p. 1) and "new and important material ... his importance in early modern philosophy has been restored" (Peltonen, 1996, p. 2). Canadian philosopher Dennis Desroches distinguished between the various interpretations that fit under the label of "Baconianism" from what Bacon actually wrote (Desroches, 2006, pp. 1–2), and Spanish historian and Antonio Perez-Ramos urged "prudence when gauging the cavalier fashion in which most historians of philosophy ... understand and evaluate Bacon's heritage" (Pérez-Ramos, 1988, pp. 7, 31).

In a thorough analysis of Bacon's works, British philosopher Peter Urbach points out that Bacon expected "his scientific method to produce not infallible knowledge, but well-confirmed hypotheses of steadily increasing generality" (Bacon, 1994, p. 28). Scottish historian of science, John Henry, argued along the same lines:

"Before Bacon there was no such thing as science in our modern sense of the word. After Bacon, Western Europe was set on a course of discovery and invention that was to result in a civilization based on the power of science and technology" (Henry, 2002, p. 4).

For American political scientist Robert K. Faulkner, Bacon devised "an extraordinarily comprehensive plan ... that involves a total transformation of the human world that extends to all experiencing and reasoning." Reviewing numerous commentators before offering his own views, he provides a wide-ranging and balanced perspective of Bacon's extensive works and seminal contributions (Faulkner, 1993, pp. 4, 8).

British literary scholar Brian Vickers compiled a volume of essays on Bacon, indicating in the introduction there was agreement on "his integrity in the dedicated search of pilgrimage for truth; his flexible application of some central types of methods ... across several intellectual fields—science, law, history, psychology; his curiously anomalous position as a herald of the new scientific age who is also an incorrigible addict of modes of thinking which his expressed programme would replace: allegory, myth, iconographical symbolism, alchemy" (Vickers, 1968, pp. xvii–xviii). Vickers also edited Bacon's texts in English with extensive annotations and warned "many of Bacon's words have totally changed their meaning since he wrote, and not to be aware of their intended sense means that readers would receive at best a vague impression, if not a completely misleading one" (Bacon, 2002, p. vii).

The most visible Baconian debates of the early twenty-first century have their roots in contrasting views of the scientific revolution, the Enlightenment and their social and environmental impacts. These debates can be traced back to the mid-twentieth century views of Frankfurt School philosophers Max Horkheimer and Theodor Adorno, who thought "Bacon well understood the scientific temper which was to come after him," and viewed him as the herald of "instrumental reason" run amok. They laid the ground for critics of modernity and feminist scholars that would decry the consequences of the unfolding, deployment, and ambiguous success of Bacon's program (Horkheimer & Adorno, 2002, p. 2).

According to Carolyn Merchant, philosopher of ethics and environmental historian, "a deep divide exists between Bacon's supporters and detractors ... the deeper roots of this divide lie in perceptions of the Scientific Revolution as a grand narrative of progress and hope versus one of decline and disaster" (Merchant, 2008a, p. 148). In her view, "at one end of the spectrum is the view of the Frankfurt philosophers, who see Bacon as initiating a tradition of human power and dominion over nature ... [which] may be seen as complicit in some of humanity's current ecological, medical, and human survival problems. At the other end of the scale are those who view Bacon as the humble servant of nature who gave humanity new tools to uncover the truths of nature" (Merchant, 2008b, p. 734).

Reflecting on the contradictions associated with the unfolding of Bacon's program, Antonio Perez-Ramos pointed out that the idea of "scientific progress identified with a betterment of man's moral condition, has continued unabated, despite the glaring contradictions revealed by the war industry (technologically oriented science *effectively* kills) and by ecological perplexities (technologically oriented science *effectively* destroys man's environment and creates no other)" (Pérez-Ramos, 1996, p. 329).

The social and political implications of Bacon's views on knowledge generation and utilization were examined by Canadian political scientist Heidi Studer, who underscored their ambiguous character. She summarized the dilemmas that are inherent in the Baconian program: research pursuits may have good and bad uses, what can be good in one context may be bad in others, it is not possible to anticipate potential evil uses of what appear to be beneficial findings, and it is difficult to foresee long-term consequences of the use of scientific and technological knowledge. Studer concludes that:

> As we enter the twenty-first century—fearing terrorist bombs made with ordinary household materials, recognizing that several years have elapsed since the first public admission of successful human cloning, faced with the rise of the 'research culture,' surrounded by ecological disasters, threatened by nuclear proliferation, witnessing the demise of objectivity in academia—we could do worse than learn to reconsider Bacon's arguments and thoughts about the problems of science and technology (Studer, 1998, pp. 232–234).

Evelyn Fox Keller, gender scholar and physicist, has examined the ambiguous feminine/masculine character of Bacon's metaphors to depict the relations between God, man, and Nature: "to receive God's truth the mind must be pure and clean, submissive and open. Only then it can give birth to a masculine and virile science" (Keller, 1985, pp. 38–39). According to her: "Francis Bacon put forth a vision of a kind of knowledge, a veridical reading of the Book of Nature that would enable the translation of knowledge to power and thus restore man's proper dominion over nature" (Keller, 1992, p. 93).

Bacon's enduring capacity to motivate heated debate was evident in an exchange on essays written for the twenty-fifth anniversary of the publication of Carolyn Merchant's book, *The Death of Nature: Women, Ecology and the Scientific Revolution* (Cadden, 2006, p. 485). These essays aroused spirited criticism by Baconian scholar Brian Vickers, who charged that Merchant's book failed to draw "on a wide range of historical evidence, appropriately interpreted" and that "the feminists' indictment [of Bacon] was not based on a detailed and dispassionate analysis of is program for the reform of natural philosophy, but on a hostile interpretation of a few of his metaphors" (Vickers, 2008, 119, 141).

Merchant responded harshly to Vickers: "by using debasing words rather than historical events, metaphor rather than analysis, and pejorative terms rather than rational argument, Vickers attempts to sweep Bacon's critics from history." Nonetheless, Merchant offered a sober assessment of Bacon's legacy: "Were results of [Bacon's] experimental method useful? Unquestionably the answer is yes. Were there costs for peoples throughout the world, for the environment, and for the laboring classes? The answer, too, must be yes. Yet Bacon was a pivotal figure in a larger movement. He lived during a period of enormous expansion of knowledge, of social and intellectual upheaval, and of the widening and consolidation of political power. That he grasped and reflected those trends eloquently in his writings it to the benefit or, as some might suggest, the detriment of humankind. In either case, however,

Bacon stood for the revealing of the 'secrets of nature' for all to contemplate, admire, denounce, share, and put to use" (Vickers, 2008, p. 162).

Bacon's fable *The New Atlantis* has also generated renewed interest among scholars. American political philosopher Tobin Craig focuses on it to argue that in many of his works, Bacon "says very little about science or technology, even about the potential benefits of a new technological oriented science," but at the same time that "in his scientific writings and various manifestations on behalf of a new science, no thinker of the era shows a comparable vision for the untapped transformative potential of a funded, honored, organized, methodical, experimental science." Craig further states that, rather than describing a utopia, Bacon's "narrative of feigned cosmographical history" depicted a benign, just, science-based society that was "meant to be practically realizable" (Tobin, 2010, pp. 214, 218).

Along a similar but more nuanced vein, Louise Liebeskind, assistant editor of *The New Atlantis: A Journal on Technology and Society*, suggests that Bacon's *The New Atlantis* is not a premonition of the future but a thought experiment set in his own time, "revealing something great and terrible … an image of things that are not and can never be, not a model to be imitated" (Liebeskind, 2023, pp. 11, 31). For American political scientist Jerry Weinberger, "*the New Atlantis* suggests the problems, as much as the promise, of technology and the story raises questions about the ways and means of the scientific project, the ends and the limits of the conquest of nature, and the implications of science and technology for human life and values" (Weinberger, 2018, p. 110), while Faulkner considers that "the *New Atlantis* exhibits the most ominous of Bacon's political innovations: the relation between the promise of progress by control of nature and the management of people by control of human nature" (Faulkner, 1993, p. 230).

An overview of the changing perceptions on Bacon's legacy would not be complete without mentioning what some authors see as his occult and mystical leanings, and even his supposedly atheistic bent. Biographer and philologist Jean Overton Fuller explored his possible connections with Freemasonry and William Shakespeare.[2] Author Helene H. Armstrong portrayed Bacon as the illegitimate son of Queen Elizabeth and founder of secret societies.[3] Geomancer and specialist in sacred architecture Peter Dawkins attempted to "make known the more hidden life and work of this great man who, as head of the Rosicrucians c. 1580–1626, brought together the greatest talents of that time in order to create … the golden age of English Literature," and "completed writing [Shakespeare's] final plays" (Dawkins, 1997, pp. xiii, 77). Dave Patrick, writer and former business executive, edited a book of essays to celebrate Bacon's 450th birth anniversary, which focused on the mystical and esoteric aspects of his work and sought to recognize him "in his human and intellectual complexity, and not just the purified embodiment of so-called scientific reason" (Patrick, 2011, p. 7).

---

[2] See Fuller (1981).

[3] See Armstrong (1985).

Information and technology entrepreneur Peter Thiel and his associate, writer Sam Wolfe reinterpret Bacon's *New Atlantis*, arguing "we must approach it as theologian-detectives." They reach a somewhat startling conclusion that Bacon "dreamed of abolishing God" and that for this purpose he "deceives his readers with plot ambiguities, cryptic references, and an unreliable narrator. He wrote *New Atlantis* with the finesse of a criminal mastermind, afraid of being caught but determined to document his crimes."

Thiel and Wolfe added further that "Bacon enthroned the Antichrist in his utopia" and that he was "a closet atheist who invoked the Antichrist playfully." Mixing their analysis of Bacon's fable with references to the Bible and to Jonathan Swift's satirical account of Bacon's work in his *Gulliver's Travels*; to the superhero of the comic *Watchmen* in which, according to Thiel and Wolfe, its creator updated "Bacon's pro-science Antichrist for late modernity"; and to the characters of the long-running manga comic *One Piece*, they reach the surprising conclusion that, as a way to avoid either the Antichrist or Armageddon, Christians "pray for new miracles, new technologies, and strange new possibilities" (Thiel & Wolfe, 2025; Bhuiyan et al., 2025).

Bacon's Protean Legacy

Despite all that has been written about Bacon, he remains an elusive figure. Nagging questions on his motives persist: Was high position sought to support and advance his philosophical and scientific endeavors? Was his intellectual work aimed at achieving recognition to secure his place in court? Were his proposals to organize and support research as a means to imperial greatness? Perhaps the answers do not matter. Bacon's ideas mobilized energies and wills in ways that vastly exceed what he may have wished and succeeded to a degree that not even Bacon's active imagination could dream of.

Much as he described Proteus in *The Wisdom of the Ancients*—"a most extraordinary prophet, who understood things past and present, as well as future … [who] would change into all kinds of shapes" (Bacon, 1884, p. 360)—Bacon's image has often shifted shape in the eyes of his commentators. Moreover, just as for Bacon nature had to be put under duress to extract its secrets and truths, his life and work have been subject to intense scrutiny in search of overt and hidden meanings.

All things considered, we need to adopt a paradoxical mindset to assess Bacon's intellectual, legal, and political careers. They do not make sense if considered separately, either as parallel or as before and after his disgrace. Nor can his philosophical achievements be detached from his eager desire for recognition in his lifetime and in posterity. Bacon firmly believed his vast contemplative ends, desire to make all knowledge his province and "completely restart the whole operation of the mind" (Bacon, 1994, p. 38), would open up a new future for mankind. His advocacy of royal support for the advance of knowledge was closely intertwined with the pursuit of favors, influence, and wealth. Bacon's parliamentary, legal, administrative, and advisory activities required him to carefully structure arguments, integrate findings from a variety of sources, and persuade others. This helped shape his conception of scientific research as an organized, progressive, and cumulative endeavor, whose results had to be communicated and made intelligible.

In *The Advancement of Learning* and in the *New Organon*, as well as in other lesser texts on philosophical and scientific matters, Bacon proposed an approach to the generation and utilization of knowledge that soared high above those of contemporary scholars, philosophers, and sages. In contrast, his legal work, political advice, and historical texts, together with his correspondence, were firmly grounded on practical concerns: maintaining political stability, supporting the monarch, listening to the concerns of common people, and improving the conduct of state affairs. Literary works, such as his *Essays*, fables, and masques, struck middle ground and added to the confusion that bedeviled Bacon's decipherers for centuries.

As Bacon had intended, the aphoristic style of his texts encouraged multiple readings. Commentators have usually focused on a few aspects of his philosophical, scientific, political, and literary interests, which, leveraged by their interpretative zeal, led to the gradual emergence of various strands of Baconianism (Keller, 2018). Successive vintages of interpretation added layers of distortion, often colored by judgments on Bacon's personal life and behavior. His legacy acquired a life of its own and inspired many followers, who carried Bacon's torch and passed it to later generations. Yet, each handover blurred further what was, right from the beginning, a rather elusive set of concepts to grasp, often expressed in erudite, cryptic aphorisms. Bacon was a paradoxical and inscrutable character; no wonder that his life, works, and legacy have generated so much controversy.

References

Armstrong, H. H. (1985). *Francis Bacon—The Spear Shaker*. Golden Gate Press.

Bacon, F. (1884). *Bacon's essays and wisdom of the ancients* (P. Shaw, Trans.). Little, Brown. Retrieved from http://archive.org/details/baconsessayswisd00baco

Bacon, F. (1994). In P. Urbach & J. Gibson (Eds.), *Novum Organum: With other parts of the great instauration*. Open Court.

Bacon, F. (2002). In B. Vickers (Ed.), *Francis Bacon: The major works. [Including New Atlantis and the essays]*. Oxford University Press.

Bhuiyan, J., Kerr, D., & Robins-Early, N. (2025, October 10). Inside tech billionaire Peter Thiel's off-the-record lectures on the antichrist. *The Guardian*.

Bowen, C. D. (1963). *Francis Bacon: The temper of a man*. Little, Brown.

Cadden, J. (2006). Focus: Getting back to the death of nature: Rereading Carolyn Merchant—Introduction. *Isis, 97*(3), 485–486. https://doi.org/10.1086/508077

Church, R. W. (1901). In J. Morley (Ed.), *Bacon*. Harper & Brothers Publishers. Retrieved from http://archive.org/details/baconchu00churuoft

Condorcet, J.-A.-N. (1802). *Outlines of an historical view of the progress of the human mind*. J. Frank.

Copleston, F. C. (1953). *A history of philosophy* (Vol. 3). Newman Press. Retrieved from https://archive.org/details/historyofphiloso03copl/page/308/mode/2up.

Crombie, A. C. (1953). *Augustine to Galileo: The history of science*. Harvard University Press. Retrieved from http://archive.org/details/augustinetogalil006875mbp
d'Alembert, J. L. R. (2009). *Preliminary discourse* (R. N. Schwab & W. E. Rex, Trans.). The Encyclopedia of Diderot & d'Alembert Collaborative Translation Project. Retrieved from http://hdl.handle.net/2027/spo.did2222.0001.083
Dawkins, P. (1997). *Francis Bacon: Herald of the new age*. Francis Bacon Research Trust.
Desroches, D. (2006). *Francis Bacon and the limits of scientific knowledge*. Continuum.
Dewey, J. (1957). *Reconstruction in philosophy*. Beacon Press.
Disraeli, I. (1859). In B. Disraeli (Ed.), *Curiosities of Literature* (Vol. 3). Routledge, Warnes and Routledge.
Draper, J. W. (1863). *A history of the intellectual development of Europe*. Harper.
Eiseley, L. C. (1973). *The man who saw through time*. Scribner.
Engels, F. (1894). *Anti-Dühring: Herr Eugen Dühring's revolution in science*. International Publishers. Retrieved from http://archive.org/details/antidhringherr00enge
Farrington, B. (1949). *Francis Bacon: Philosopher of industrial science*. Henry Schuman.
Faulkner, R. (1993). *Francis Bacon and the project of progress*. Rowman & Littlefield.
Fischer, K. (1857). *Francis Bacon of Verulam. Realistic philosophy and its age* (J. Oxenford, Trans.). Longman, Brown, Green, Longmans, & Roberts. Retrieved from http://archive.org/details/cu31924029010219
Franklin, B. (2004). *Poor Richard's Almanack*. Barnes & Noble Publishing.
Fuller, J. O. (1981). *Francis Bacon, a biography*. East-West Publications.
Gadamer, H.-G. (Ed.). (2013). *Truth and method*. A&C Black.
Haydn, H. (1950). *The counter-renaissance*. Harbinger.
Henry, J. (2002). *Knowledge is power: How magic, the government and an apocalyptic vision inspired Francis Bacon to create modern science*. Icon.
Herschel, J. F. W. (1987). *A preliminary discourse on the study of natural philosophy*. University of Chicago Press.
Höffe, O. (2009). *Kant's critique of pure reason: The foundation of modern philosophy*. Springer Netherlands.
Holmes, J. (Ed.). (2002). *Thomas Jefferson: A chronology of his thoughts*. Rowman and Littlefield Publishers.
Horkheimer, M., & Adorno, T. W. (2002). In G. S. Noerr (Ed.), *Dialectic of enlightenment: philosophical fragments* (E. Jephcott, Trans.). Stanford University Press.
Huxley, T. H. (1862). The method by which the causes of the present and past conditions of organic nature are to be discovered: The origination of living beings. In *Professor Huxley's lectures to working men. On our knowledge of the causes of the phenomena of organic nature* (pp. 30–53). Robert Hardwicke. Retrieved from https://darwin-online.org.uk/converted/pdf/1862_Huxley_phenomena_CUL-DAR.LIB.315.pdf
Jameson, T. H. (1954). *Francis Bacon: Criticism and the modern world*. Frederick A. Praeger.
Jardine, L. (2009). *Francis Bacon: Discovery and the art of discourse*. Cambridge University Press.
Jardine, L., & Stewart, A. (1999). *Hostage to fortune: The troubled life of Francis Bacon*. Hill and Wang.
Kant, I. (1787/1998). *Critique of pure reason* (P. Guyer & A. W. Wood, Trans.). Cambridge University Press.
Kant, I. (2006). *Anthropology from a pragmatic point of view* (R. B. Louden, Trans.). Cambridge University Press.
Keller, E. F. (1985). *Reflections on gender and science*. Yale University Press.
Keller, E. F. (1992). *Secrets of life, secrets of death: Essays on language, gender and science*. Routledge.
Keller, V. (2018). Deprogramming Baconianism: The meaning of desiderata in the eighteenth century. *Royal Society of London, 72*(2), 119–137. JSTOR.
Koyré, A. (1978). *Galileo studies* (J. Mepham, Trans.). Humanities Press.
Leary, J. E., Jr. (1994). *Francis Bacon and the politics of science*. State University Press.

Levine, I. (1925). *Francis Bacon (1561–1626)*. Kennikat.
Liebeskind, L. (2023). If scientists were angels. *The New Atlantis: A Journal of Technology and Society*. Fall 2023. Retrieved from https://www.thenewatlantis.com/publications/if-scientists-were-angels.
Lovejoy, B. G. (1888). *Francis Bacon (Lord Verulam): A critical review of his life and character with selections from his writings*. T. Fisher Unwin. Retrieved from http://archive.org/details/franfrancisbaconlord00loveuoft
Macaulay, T. B. (1837). *The Life and Writings of Francis Bacon, Lord Chancellor of England: From the Edinburgh Review*. Harvard University.
Marx, K., & Engels, F. (1956). Absolute criticism's third campaign. In *The holy family or critique of critical critique*. Foreign languages Publishing House. Retrieved from http://archive.org/details/holyfamily00marx
Mathews, N. (1996). *Francis Bacon: The history of a character assassination*. Yale University Press.
Merchant, C. (2008a). Secrets of nature: The Bacon debates revisited. *Journal of the History of Ideas, 69*(1), 147–162.
Merchant, C. (2008b). The violence of impediments: Francis Bacon and the origins of experimentation. *Isis, 99*(4), 731–760.
Nichol, J. (1888). *Francis Bacon, his life and philosophy, Part I Bacon's life*. W. Blackwood and Sons.
Patrick, D. (Ed.). (2011). *The view beyond: Sir Francis Bacon: alchemy, science, mystery*. Polair.
Peltonen, M. (Ed.). (1996). *The Cambridge companion to Bacon*. Cambridge University Press.
Pérez-Ramos, A. (1988). *Francis Bacon's idea of science and the maker's knowledge tradition*. Clarendon Press, Oxford University Press.
Pérez-Ramos, A. (1991). Review article: Francis Bacon and the Disputations of the Learned. *The British Journal for the Philosophy of Science, 42*(4), 577–588. https://www.jstor.org/stable/687711
Pérez-Ramos, A. (1996). Bacon's Legacy. In M. Peltonen (Ed.), *The Cambridge companion to Bacon* (pp. 311–334). Cambridge University Press.
Popper, K. (1968). *The logic of scientific discovery*. Harper Torchbooks.
Quinton, A. (1980). In K. Thomas (Ed.), *Francis Bacon*. Hill and Wang.
Rossi, P. (2013). *Francis Bacon: From magic to science* (S. Rabinovitch, Trans.). Routledge and Kegan Paul.
Rousseau, J. (1923). A discourse on the moral effects of the arts and sciences. In *The social contract: And discourses* (G. D. H. Cole, Trans.). J.M. Dent and Sons. Retrieved from http://oll.libertyfund.org/title/638
Russell, B. (2004). *History of western philosophy*. Routledge.
Studer, H. (1998). Francis Bacon on the political dangers of scientific progress. *Canadian Journal of Political Science, 31*(2), 219–234.
Thiel, P. & Wofe, S. (October 1, 2025). Voyages to the End of the World, *First Things*. https://first-thisngs.com/voyages-to-the-end-of-the-world/
Thorndike, L. (1958). *A history of magic and experimental science. The seventeenth century* (Vol. 7). Columbia University Press.
Tobin, C. L. (2010). On the significance of the literary character of Francis Bacon's "New Atlantis for an understanding of his political thought". *The Review of Politics, 72*(2), 213–239.
Toulmin, S., & Goodfield, J. (1965). *The discovery of time*. University of Chicago Press.
Trevor-Roper, H. (1962). Men & ideas, Francis Bacon. *Encounter, 18*, 74–76.
Vickers, B. (Ed.). (1968). *Essential articles for the study of Francis Bacon*. Archon Books.
Vickers, B. (2008). Francis Bacon, feminist historiography, and the dominion of nature. *Journal of the History of Ideas, 69*(1), 117–141.
Voltaire. (1901). Letters concerning the English nation, letter 12, Chancellor Bacon. In *The works of Voltaire: A contemporary version* (W. F. Fleming, Trans.) (Vol. 19). E.R. DuMont. Retrieved from http://oll.libertyfund.org/title/666/81880.

Weinberger, J. (2018). In B. Price (Ed.), *Francis Bacon's New Atlantis: New interdisciplinary essays* (pp. 106–128). Manchester University Press. https://doi.org/10.7765/9781526137388
Whewell, W. (1847). *The philosophy of the inductive sciences: Founded upon their history*. J. W. Parker. Retrieved from http://archive.org/details/philosophyinduc02whewgoog
Whitehead, A. N. (1967). *Science and the modern world*. Free Press.
Wormald, B. H. G. (2006). *Francis Bacon: History, politics, and science, 1561–1626*. Cambridge University Press.
Zagorin, P. (1998). *Francis Bacon*. Princeton University.

Chapter 3
Sir Francis Bacon's Program

Despite all ... technical zigzags in the appreciation of methodological relevance, no serious questioning of the chief Baconian ideal has been articulated through the history of Western philosophy since the seventeenth century (Pérez-Ramos, 1996, p. 327).

Antonio Pérez-Ramos

"To aim knowledge at power over nature, and to utilize power over nature for the improvement of the human lot" is how German philosopher Hans Jonas defined in the late 1970s what is known as the "Baconian Program" (Jonas, 1984, p. 140). A decade and a half later, German philosopher of science Gernot Böhme indicated that Bacon's program "organizes science into an enterprise of inventions and institutionalizes it socially in such a way that its inventions are implemented for the benefit of man." In his view, Bacon's "invention of a method to make inventions" was an "epoch-making change for the system of human knowledge" that human conditions could be improved "primarily through the development of science and technology" (Böhme, 1992, pp. 2–3).

During the following decades, I sought to find out what was behind Jonas' and Böhme's accounts of the Baconian Program. Soon it became clear that Bacon himself had not put forward a set of propositions that may be considered a program, but that dispersed throughout his writings there were elements that could be retrospectively construed as such. As American Professor Vera Keller indicated, "neither Bacon nor those who followed him thought of his work in programmatic terms. ... A new term in the nineteenth century, the 'Baconian programme' achieved prominence in the middle of the twentieth century as a means to unite Bacon's epistemic interventions with his social aims, including notions of utility, the promotion of technological invention and economic growth" (Keller, 2018, p. 119).[1]

[1] Professor Keller refers to a book published by Wilhelm Windelband in 1892, translated into English as *A History of Philosophy with Especial Reference to the Formation and Development of Its Problems and Conceptions*, New York, Macmillan, 1893.

F. Sagasti, *Knowledge is Power*, Innovation, Technology, and Knowledge Management, https://doi.org/10.1007/978-3-032-20668-8_3

Reaching back through the fog of conflicting opinions to what Sir Francis Bacon did and wrote, and then fast-forwarding over the reactions they provoked over time, reveals both the initial freshness of his approach to knowledge generation and utilization, as well as the contemporary relevance of assessing and reinterpreting his ideas. Bacon lived at a time of major adjustments in our conceptions of the cosmos, the world and of humanity's place in them. The Copernican Revolution, humanistic philosophy, voyages of discovery, and the violent conflicts spawned by the reformation and counterreformation demanded new ways of thinking about the human condition. Bacon was aware of these historical shifts, viewing them largely a result of human ingenuity and of inventions such as gunpowder, the printing press, the telescope, and the compass.

Claiming that earlier attempts to explain natural phenomena had led to dead ends, Bacon asserted he had devised a better way to generate useful knowledge. Even though he made no major scientific discovery himself, he proposed a new conception of the scientific method, provided descriptions of nature and accounts of experiments, and made proposals for organizing and supporting scientific research. He sought to completely restart "the whole operation of the mind, so that from the very beginning it is not left to itself, but is subject to rule." This was primarily because "no force whatever can unfasten or break the chain of causes, and nature is only overcome by obeying her … knowledge and power, come in fact from the same thing; and failure of works derives mostly from ignorance of causes" (Bacon, 1994, pp. 38, 29).

Expanding Jonas' and Bohme's succinct summaries of Bacon's ideas, with the benefit of hindsight, his legacy—the Baconian Program—can be retrospectively reframed in terms of five distinct but partially overlapping components: method, purpose, direction, focus, and institutions.

The first of these refers to Bacon's methodological proposals for renewing natural philosophy and for restarting "whole operation of the mind"; the second, third, and fourth to the aims, orientation, and center of the quest for useful knowledge; and the last to how scientific inquiry should be organized and conducted. Other philosophers and students of nature dealt with some of these issues before Bacon, but he was the first to dwell on all of them, implicitly articulating a powerful and lasting set of proposals that gave rise to what may be called the "Baconian epoch." Each of these components will be briefly reviewed, quoting extensively from Bacon's works.

The preamble to *The Great Instauration*, written in the third person, provides a succinct description of Bacon's aims and motives (Box 3.1). The preface of the *Novum Organon* stated his wish to break with tradition: "I propose for my science the discovery not of arguments but of arts, not of things that are consistent with first principles, but of the principles themselves." This required: "a kind of logic, though the difference between it and ordinary logic is great, indeed immense. … in its end, in its method of demonstration, and in the starting point of inquiry" (Bacon, 1994, p. 19).

Box 3.1 Preamble to The Great Instauration

Francis of Verulam

Reasoning thus with himself came to
This conclusion that the knowledge of
His thoughts would be of advantage
To present and future generations

Believing that human understanding creates difficulties for itself and does not put to sober and sensible use the true means of help that are in man's power; from which manifold ignorance of things has come, and from that ignorance numberless ills; he thought that every effort should be made, by whatever means, to restore to its original condition, or at least to improve, that commerce between Mind and Things (to which almost nothing on earth, or at least nothing that is of the earth, can compare). … the primary notions of things, which the mind readily and passively drinks in, lays up, and accumulates (and from which all the rest flow) are defective and confused and carelessly abstracted from things; … As a result, that entire human reasoning that we apply in the investigation of Nature is poorly put together and constructed but is like some magnificent great pile without any foundation. … There was thus but one course left, namely, to try the whole matter afresh with better means of support, and to bring about a complete Instauration of the arts and sciences and all the learning of mankind, raised upon proper foundations. And while at the beginning, this might appear infinite and beyond mortal capacity, once in train it will be found reasonable and sober, more so in fact than those things that have been done hitherto. … Moreover, since he was unsure how soon these things would occur to anyone else, bearing in mind especially that he has so far found no one who has applied his mind to the same thoughts, he decided to publish at once as much as he has been able to complete. And this haste came not from ambition but from anxiety for his work; that in the event of his death there should yet survive some indication or design of what he conceived, and that there should at the same time survive some sign of his sincere concern for the good of mankind. He certainly held

any other ambition to be of less worth than that
which he had in hand, seeing that the matter
in question is either nothing, or is so
great as to be content with its
own merit, without
seeking any
further (Bacon, 1994, pp. 3–4).

Rather than completely discard knowledge received from Greek, Roman, and Medieval scholars, Bacon sought to sidestep controversy by placing his proposals on a different tack: "the honor and respect due to the ancients can be preserved intact and undiminished, … For if I were to declare that, while following the same roads as the ancients, I had produced better results than they, that would be certain to lead to comparison and argument over our respective talents and mental abilities such as no smooth words could avoid. … since my contention is that an entirely new way, untried and indeed unknown to them, lies open to the understanding, the case is altered. No more partisan strife; I merely appear as a guide, a position of quite modest authority, owing more to luck than to superior ability" (Bacon, 1994, p. 39).

With a call that still resonates with us four and a half centuries later, Bacon invited others to join him in the quest for fruitful knowledge: "… if there are many men who have the wish and the will not only to cling to and make use of knowledge already discovered, but to penetrate further; to conquer, not an opponent in argument, but Nature herself in action: to seek, in short, not elegant and probable conjectures, but certain and demonstrable knowledge: such men, true sons of learning. I invite to join me, if they will, so that we can pass by the outer halls of Nature, which any number of men have already trodden, to where at length the way into her inner chambers shall be revealed" (Bacon, 1994, p. 40).

Method: "The Perfect Use of Reason"

The first component of the Baconian Program deals with "the better use of reason in the investigation of Nature" (Bacon, 1994, p. 19). Bacon described a systematic and deliberate process to advance knowledge, which linked abstract concepts derived from intellectual work with empirical evidence obtained through careful observation. The proper way to proceed in science is "for experience first to kindle a light, then with that light to show the way, beginning with experience ordered and arranged, … and from that deriving axioms, and from the axioms thus established deriving again new experiments, just as the word of God operated in an orderly way on the unformed matter of creation. … a method rightly set up leads [men] through the forests of experience to the open country of axioms by an unbroken path" (Bacon, 1994, pp. 91–92).

For Bacon, nature could be understood and its secrets revealed, but only if proper procedures were employed. Before him, men "had chosen an entirely wrong and impassable road" in the quest for knowledge, leaving its pursuit "either to the fog of traditions or the giddy whirl of arguments or the fluctuations and meanderings of chance and rambling and disorderly experience" (Bacon, 1994, pp. 90–91).

Rejecting the sterile disputations ("giddy whirl of arguments") of scholastics, Bacon sought to make the products of scientific inquiry useful: "it cannot be that axioms established by argumentation should have any value for discovering new works; for the subtlety of Nature is far greater than that of argument. But axioms properly and methodically derived from particulars can well point to and indicate new particulars again, and so render the sciences active" (Bacon, 1994, pp. 49–50). His concept of induction—"that form of demonstration which upholds the sense, presses down upon Nature and is intent on and closely bound up with works"—involved collecting facts, avoiding premature theorizing, and building arguments step by step: "my method is to derive axioms gradually, in a connected succession, so as only a the end to arrive at the most general" (Bacon, 1994, p. 20).

Bacon derided the haphazard procedures ("rambling and disorderly experience") (Bacon, 1994, pp. 90–91) of alchemists, which he considered "more curious than rational" and made him "doubt whether to laugh or weep at them." The alchemist "nurses eternal hope and when the things does not succeed, he blames some error of his own, and in self-condemnation thinks he has no properly understood the words of his art or of its authors; … or else thinks that in his performance he has made some slip … whereupon he repeats his experiments endlessly; and if … he lights on some things that appear either novel or of commendable utility, he feeds his mind with good omens of this kind, magnifies and makes much of them, supporting the rest with hope" (Bacon, 1994, pp. 94–95).

Both ambitious and grandiose schemes to reform knowledge coexisted with restraint and patience in Bacon's mind; he thought "novelty, though it be not rejected, yet be held for a suspect," and had faith in gradual change "time is the greatest innovator, time … innovates greatly, but quietly, by degrees scarcely to be perceived" (Bacon, 2011c, vol. 6, pp. 434, 433). A metaphor about insects allowed Bacon to summarize his methodological approach:

> Those who have handled the sciences have been either Empiricists or Rationalists. Empiricists, like ants, merely collect things and use them. The Rationalists, like spiders, spin webs out of themselves. The middle way is that of the bee, which gathers its material from the flowers of the garden and the field but then transforms and digests it by a power of its own. And the true business of philosophy is much the same, for it does not rely only or chiefly on the powers of the mind, nor does it store the material supplied by natural history and practical experiment untouched in its memory but lays it up in the understanding changed and refined. Thus, from a closer and purer alliance of the two faculties—the experimental and the rational, such has never yet been made—we have good reason for hope (Bacon, 1994, p. 105).

In spite of ascribing nature's order to divine will, Bacon was adamant in cleansing scientific arguments from religious contamination. "The corruption of philosophy by a combination of superstition and theology is much more widespread and does the greatest harm both to whole philosophies and to their parts … Yet, some of the moderns have, with the greatest frivolity, indulged too far in this foolishness, as to try to found a natural philosophy on the first chapter of Genesis and the book of Job and other sacred writings … an unhealthy mixture of the divine and the human leads not only to fanciful philosophy but also to heretical religion. The healthy course therefore is to keep a sober mind and give to faith only that which is faith's" (Bacon, 1994, pp. 71–72).

Such arguments led Enlightenment philosophers to view Bacon as a champion of secularism, ignoring his view that religion should provide the ethical and moral criteria to guide the search for knowledge. Bacon did not reject religion but thought "a little natural philosophy and the first entrance into it inclines men's opinion to atheism; but on the other hand, much natural philosophy and deeper progress into it brings men's about again to religion" (Bacon, 2011d, vol. 7, p. 252).

Bacon also cautioned against assuming too much regularity in natural phenomena: "the human understanding on account of its own nature readily supposes a greater order and uniformity in things than it finds" (Bacon, 1994, p. 56). This led him to state that "mathematicians cannot satisfy themselves, except they reduce the motions of the celestial bodies to perfect circles, rejecting spiral lines and laboring to be discharged of eccentrics" (Bacon, 2011a, vol. 3, p. 395). Such caution led him to skepticism regarding Copernicus heliocentric scheme: "the same phenomena in astronomy are satisfied by the received astronomy of the diurnal motion and the proper motions of the planets with their eccentrics and epicycles, and likewise by the theory of Copernicus who supposed the earth to move; and the calculations are indifferently agreeable to both; so the ordinary face and view of experience is many times satisfied by several theories and philosophies; whereas to find the real truth requires another manner of severity and attention" (Bacon, 2011a, vol. 3, p. 365).

Even though mathematical knowledge was not necessary in Bacon's legal work, contrary to what critics have said, he had a clear appreciation of what mathematics could offer: "many parts of Nature can neither be invented with sufficient subtlety, nor demonstrated with sufficient perspicuity, nor accommodated into use with sufficient dexterity, without the aid and intervening of the Mathematics" (Bacon, 2011a, vol. 3, p. 360). He thought highly of the approach used in mathematics: "it is almost necessary in all controversies and disputations to imitate the wisdom of the Mathematicians, in setting down in the very beginning the definitions of our words and terms, that others may know how we accept and understand them, and whether they concur with us or not." In addition, Bacon considered mathematical exercises as aids to sharpen mental skills: "men do not sufficiently understand the excellent use of the Pure Mathematics, in that they do remedy and cure many defects in the wit and faculties intellectual" (Bacon, 2011a, vol. 3, pp. 360, 365, 396–397).[2] As Faulkner has highlighted, Bacon "ushers away 'pure mathematics' in favor of a 'mixed mathematics' that is useful for calculating motions of 'solids' or the relations of motions to effects" (Faulkner, 1993, p. 9).

Aversion to preconceived notions of natural phenomena and to premature generalizations derived from scanty evidence reflected Bacon's gradualist inclinations and cautious character. These were also evident in the conduct of his political, advisory, and administrative affairs. Bacon's logical style of argumentation and his emphasis on proper procedure were associated with his legal training and work, which required industrious fact gathering, careful assessment of evidence, and judicious concatenation of premises, qualifiers, and conclusions.

A set of precepts advanced by Bacon for the preparation of a natural history, which was to be the third part of *The Great Instauration*, gives an idea of how he thought scientific inquiry should be conducted:

> Firstly, questions should be introduced … which stimulate and encourage further investigation. … Secondly, in any new and delicate experiment, the procedure for performing it

[2]For an assessment of Bacon's proficiency and attitude to mathematics, see Bacon (2011a, pp. 509–512).

should be added, so that men be free to judge whether the information yielded by that experiment is reliable or not. ... Thirdly, if in any actual account there lurks any element of doubt or reservation, I would never have it suppressed or kept secret, but openly and clearly mentioned by way of a note or warning. ... Fourthly, it would not be out of place to intersperse observations now and then ... there should be added to those things that do occur those things that do not. ... Fifthly, a thing that completely undermines and destroys a believer may perhaps be of some help to an inquirer (Bacon, 1994, pp. 311–312).[3]

In addition, Bacon was well aware of the magnitude of the undertaking and thought it could only be done with support from the Crown, for it was "a royal task, and one involving much labor and expense" (Bacon, 1994, p. 111).

These injunctions could be paraphrased as: choose the right questions to ask, taking care they should lead to more interesting and fundamental questions; make public your assumptions and subject your results to peer review; clearly acknowledge and state the limitations of your approach and methodology; examine your findings and identify gaps and missing pieces of evidence; do not shy away from examining ideas and facts that question your basic premises; and make sure you have the support and means to carry out and complete your research.

Purpose, Direction, and Focus: The Promethean Centrality of Humanity

As previously stated, in Bacon's view, knowledge is to be acquired for producing useful works and improving the human condition. He ruled out contemplative ends and personal satisfaction, as well as entertainment, pleasure, and amusement, as worthy aims for natural philosophy. Never questioning that it is always better to have more knowledge, Bacon had an implicit faith in the inherent goodness of scientific inquiry and of the knowledge it generated. However, he was not oblivious to the possibility of misusing it for destructive purposes.

Bacon thought one of the greatest "diseases of learning" was:

... the mistaking or misplacing of the last or furthest end of knowledge. For men have entered into a desire of learning and knowledge, sometimes upon a natural curiosity and inquisitive appetite; sometimes to entertain their minds with variety and delight; sometimes for ornament and reputation; and sometimes to enable them to victory of wit and contradiction; and most times for lucre and profession; and seldom sincerely to give a true account of their gift of reason, to the benefit and use of men ... for the glory of the Creator and the relief of man's estate. But this is that which will indeed dignify and exalt knowledge (Bacon, 2011a, vol. 3, p. 294).

Directing and bringing knowledge "to perfection in charity, for the benefit and use of life" (Bacon, 1994, p. 15), required opening a path to "man's understanding entirely different from that known to men before us, ... so that the mind can exercise its rightful authority over the nature of things" (Bacon, 1994, p. 7). According to

[3] Aphorisms on the composition of the primary history, aph. 9.

Bacon, unraveling the mysteries and acquiring mastery over nature were divinely sanctioned tasks: "the beginning must come from God; … who is the author of goodness and the father of light. … Nor should we forget the prophecy of Daniel about the last days of the world: 'many shall pass through and knowledge shall be increased'. This clearly implies that it lies in destiny—that is, providence—that the passage through the world … and an increase in knowledge will come at the same period of time" (Bacon, 1994, p. 104). In Bacon's view, God and religion guide the quest for knowledge; scientific research and experimental philosophy provide the means for embarking on it.

In addition to advocating altruistic ends for the pursuit of knowledge, Bacon was interested in using knowledge in the conduct of human affairs. "There is a great affinity and consent between the rules of nature, and the true rules of policy: the one being nothing else but an order in the government of the world, and the other in the government of the estate." Thus, human actions and government policies are legitimate subjects of research and could be continuously improved through rigorous inquiry. As an example, he held "Persian magic, which was the secret literature of their kings, … an application of the contemplations and observations of nature unto a sense politic; taking the fundamental laws of nature, and the branches and passages of them, as an original or first model, whence to take and describe a copy and imitation for government" (Bacon, 2011f, vol. 10, p. 90).

A parallel between natural philosophy and the human and policy sciences was also drawn in Bacon's account of the myth of the Sphinx: "Sphinx has no more than two kinds of riddles, one relating to the nature of things, the other to the nature of man; and correspondent to these, the prizes of the solution are two kinds of empire, the empire over nature, and the empire over man." While "the true and ultimate end of natural philosophy is dominion over natural things," for Bacon, the riddle presented by the Sphinx and solved by Oedipus "regarded the nature of man; for he who has thoroughly looked into and examined human nature, may in a manner command his own fortune, and seems born to acquire dominion and rule" (Bacon, 1884, p. 412).

Notwithstanding his positive view of natural philosophy, Bacon was aware that knowledge could be used for negative purposes. His account of the myth of Daedalus and the Minotaur acknowledges the mechanical arts "have an ambiguous and double use and serve to produce as to prevent mischief and destruction; so that their virtue almost destroys or unwinds itself." While humanity is greatly indebted to the mechanical arts, they can also supply "instruments of lust, cruelty, and death," and it is possible to "plainly see how far the business of exquisite poisons, guns, engines of war, and such kind of destructive inventions exceeds the cruelty of the Minotaur himself" (Bacon, 1884, pp. 377, 376).

Bacon also had an eye toward posterity and sought to secure his reputation for future generations. In his dedication of the *Novum Organon* to King James, he expressed a wish that "after my death I may have the fortune to ensure by lighting this new torch in the dark shades of philosophy that this age will shine forth yet more gloriously to posterity" (Bacon, 1994, p. 5). He thought that the aspiration of immortality could be approached through the "dignity and excellence of knowledge and learning," and that "the monuments of wit and learning are more durable than the monuments of power or of the hands" (Bacon, 2011b, vol. 3, p. 318).

The direction and pace of progress in the sciences are the third component of the Baconian Program. The slow advance of natural philosophy was for Bacon the result of both neglect and an unfavorable environment: "for more or less twenty-five centuries over which the memory and learning of mankind extends, one can hardly pick out six that were fertile in sciences and favorable to their onward process." In his view, "the chief reason for the feeble progress of the science has been the shortness of those periods favorable to them" (Bacon, 1994, pp. 87–88). Still in times when "the genius and literature of mankind most flourished, only a very small share of men's effort was allotted to natural philosophy, even though it ought to be regarded as the great mother of the sciences"; therefore, "it is not surprising that men made little progress in it" (Bacon, 1994, pp. 88–89). At the same time, Bacon was concerned to keep a proper pace for the conduct of scientific inquiry: "the perfection of the sciences is to be looked for not from the swiftness of ability of any one inquirer, but from a succession. For the strongest and swiftest runners are perhaps not the best fitted to keep their torch alight; since it may be put out by going too fast or too slow" (Bacon, 2011c, vol. 6, p. 753).

As his appeals to King James showed, Bacon thought rulers should support and create a context favorable to scientific inquiry. "The glory of God is to conceal a thing; the glory of a king is to search it out" wrote Bacon quoting King Solomon, before distinguishing "three kinds or stages in human ambition":

> The first is shown by those who see to extend their own power in their own country, which is common and unworthy kind. The second by those who strive to extend their country's power and dominion among mankind, which sort has certainly more dignity but is no less covetous. But the man who labors to establish and extend the power and dominion of the human race itself over the whole universe displays an ambition (if ambition it can be called) that is without doubt healthier and nobler than the others. But the dominion of man over things rests solely in the arts and the sciences. For Nature is not ruled unless she is obeyed (Bacon, 1994, p. 131).

Material, political, and moral progress comes from the application of useful knowledge to understand and conquer nature. Bacon rebuffed pessimism and had faith in the progress of science: "by far the greatest obstacle to the progress of the sciences ... lies in man's despair, and in his supposition that such advances are impossible. ... We must look constantly for what hopeful gleam of light there is, and from what quarter it shows itself" (Bacon, 1994, pp. 102–103). In his view, "there are still many very useful things, which have not so far been discovered, hidden from us in the bosom of Nature ... No doubt they too will, at some future time, after many turnings and revolutions of the centuries, come forth, ... but the method I am now discussing they can be expected soon, all together and quickly" (Bacon, 1994, p. 114). For Bacon, there is no limit to human progress, barring that placed by the achievement of God's kingdom on Earth and the restoration of man's rightful place on Earth, lost after expulsion from Eden.

The fourth component of the Baconian Program is its sharp focus on humanity, which Bacon placed at the center of creation. Adhering to the humanistic perspective of the Renaissance, he believed God made everything in the world for the benefit of "Man," and his interpretation of the myth of Prometheus states this unequivocally:

> Prometheus clearly and expressly signifies Providence … the special and peculiar work of Providence was the creation and constitution of Man. … The chief aim of the parable seems to be, that Man, if we look to final causes, may be regarded as the centre of the world; insomuch that if man were taken away from the world, the rest would seem to be all astray, without aim or purpose … For the whole world works together in the service of Man, and there is nothing from which he does not derive use and fruit. The revolutions and courses of the stars serve him both for his distinction of the seasons and distribution of the quarters of the world. The appearances of the middle sky afford him his prognostications of weather. The winds sail his ships and work his mills and engines. Plants and animals of all kinds are made to furnish him with dwelling and shelter or clothing or food or medicine, or to lighten his labor, or to give him pleasure and comfort; insomuch that all things seem to be going about man's business and not their own (Bacon, 1884, p. 394).

Such a strong emphasis on the Promethean centrality of humanity is closely associated with the ethos of domination of nature pervading the Baconian Program. But, while Lord Verulam firmly anchored scientific inquiry and experimental philosophy to human concerns, he also thought its findings transcend earthly pursuits, helping to reveal divine designs and bringing man closer to God: "religion reveals the will of God … natural philosophy his power." For Bacon, "natural philosophy is, after the word of God, the surest antidote to superstition, and at the same time the most excellent nourishment for faith" (Bacon, 2011c, vol. 6, pp. 746–747).

Institutions: "A Fraternity of Learning and Illumination"

Institutional and organizational arrangements were a recurrent concern of Lord Verulam. He conceived scientific inquiry as a collaborative long-term undertaking that required a community of dedicated individuals. Working in concert, building on the work of their predecessors and passing the torch on to successive generations, they would vastly increase knowledge about natural and social phenomena. To make this conception a reality and reap the benefits of useful knowledge, Bacon envisaged institutional reforms, government policies, recognition schemes, and means of support to create favorable conditions for the advancement of learning.

A first task was "to consider what kind [of] acts … have been undertaken and performed by kings and others for the increase and advancement of learning." Bacon listed the construction of buildings and other physical facilities, the provision of endowments and financial resources, the establishment of libraries and publishing services, and the appointment and remuneration of lecturers and scientists. These works and acts of "many excellent princes and other worthy personages" were all good, but not sufficient for the advancement of learning. Rather than look back to "that which is already attained," Bacon proposed to "look unto that part of the race which is before us," to set an agenda for action (Bacon, 2011a, vol. 3, pp. 322–323).

Bacon found it strange that "so many great foundations and colleges in Europe ... are all dedicated to professions, and none left free to arts and sciences at large." This was "a great cause that has hindered the progression of learning, because these fundamental knowledges have been studied but in passage" (Bacon, 2011a, vol. 3, pp. 323–324). Bacon decried the excessive emphasis on professional teachings to the detriment of natural philosophy: "The great mother of the sciences has ... been demoted to the role of maidservant, ... However let no one expect much progress in the sciences—especially in their practical aspects—unless natural philosophy is extended to particular sciences, and particular sciences in turn lead back to natural philosophy" (Bacon, 1994, p. 89).

He also lamented "natural philosophy has hardly ever found a man able to give his whole and undivided attention" (Bacon, 1994, p. 89), and criticized "the smallness and meanness of the salary or reward which in most places is assigned to ... lectures of arts, or of the professions." The progress of science required that "lecturers be ... the most able and sufficient of men," but this would not be possible unless "their condition and endowment be such as may content the ablest man to appropriate his whole labor and continue his whole age in that function and attendance" (Bacon, 1994, p. 324).

The lack of equipment to study natural sciences and medicine was another problem identified by Bacon, for natural philosophers should not rely only on books, but also use "spheres, globes, astrolabes, maps, and the like, ... gardens and ... dead bodies for anatomies." He concluded that "there will be hardly any proficiency in the disclosing of nature, except there be some allowance for expenses about experiments" (Bacon, 1994, p. 325). In addition to a good library, among the things scientists needed, Bacon listed "a spacious, wonderful garden" in which diverse plants, rare beasts and birds, and a variety of fish would be kept; a "goodly huge cabinet" with engines, mechanical devices, and natural objects of all sorts; and "a still-house ... furnished with mills, instruments, furnaces and vessels."[4]

An additional concern of Bacon was the reluctance of university authorities to consult with "princes or superior persons of visitation" and consider "whether the readings, exercises, and other customs appertaining into learning, anciently begun and since continued, be well instituted or not; and thereupon to ground an amendment or reformation in that which shall be found inconvenient." In his view, "in as much as most of the usages and orders of the universities were derived from more obscure times, it is the more requisite they be re-examined" (Bacon, 2011a, vol. 3, p. 326).

Two other defects identified by Bacon were the relative isolation of universities and the need to define research priorities. In the first case, greater advances would come "if there were more intelligence mutual between the universities of Europe than now there is," and from "a fraternity of learning and illumination." To remedy the second, Bacon thought it necessary the "public designation of writers or

[4] "Letter to the second counsellor, advising the Study of Philosophy," 1594. See Bacon (2011e, p. 335).

inquirers concerning such parts of knowledge as may appear not to have been already sufficiently labored or undertaken" (Bacon, 2011a, vol. 3, p. 327).

Bacon was keen to widely disseminate knowledge acquired through systematic inquiry for the benefit of humanity, which meant to implicitly reject its private appropriation. His account of the House of Solomon puts in the words of one of its members: "We do publish such new profitable inventions as we think good. And we do also declare natural divinations of diseases, plagues, swarms of hurtful creatures, scarcity, tempests, earthquakes, great inundations, comets, temperature of the year, and divers other things: and we give counsel thereupon what the people shall do for the prevention and remedy of them" (Bacon, 2002, p. 488). However, Bacon argued that potentially dangerous findings should be secret. As Julian Martin put it in his account of the House of Solomon: "The fruits of the labors of the brethren are not automatically made public, and the issue of publication is important enough to require a full council. Why some knowledge is reserved is never discussed, but we may assume it is because Bacon believed knowledge can be socially and politically dangerous" (Martin, 2007, pp. 138–39).

The institutional and organizational component of the Baconian Program draws on Bacon's extensive use of assistants, correspondents, informants, commentators, and scribes both for his legal and philosophical activities. They helped shape his view of a hierarchical community of scholars, with central control and a well-defined division of labor. Bacon's parliamentary experience made him also realize the importance of persuasion, communication skills, and working in concert with others, while government work made him aware of the importance of fair rules and regulations, effective legal systems and incentives to align individual behavior with public objectives.

Bacon's agenda of institutional reforms can be summarized as: support fundamental and applied research, remunerate and reward scientists well, provide good laboratory and physical facilities, update university curricula periodically to make them relevant, promote international collaboration, define priorities to advance knowledge, disseminate findings widely, and create a favorable environment for science.

The House of Salomon

New Atlantis, a fable-cum-essay written by Bacon during the last years of his life, summarizes most of Bacon's proposals to mobilize scientific inquiry for the benefit of humanity. The narrator of the fable describes the mythical island of Bensalem, which he and his shipmates arrived at after sailing from Peru and being pushed off course by storms. Bensalem is a kingdom ruled by benevolent autocrats who, fully aware of the world outside, have chosen to remain isolated to keep their customs and way of life.

The main institution in Bensalem is the "society of Salomon's House; which house or college … is the very eye" of the kingdom. One of its members gives the narrator a description of the objectives of the House of Salomon: "The end of our

Foundation is the knowledge of Causes and secret motions of things; and the enlarging of the bounds of Human Empire, to the effecting of all things possible." He then gives a detailed account of the work done and the equipment used in different settings and laboratories—caves and towers, lakes and pools, streams and cataracts, artificial wells and fountains, special rooms and chambers—which are used for a great variety of physical, mechanical, chemical, biological, and medical experiments. The list includes a "mathematical house" with "exquisitely made" geometry and astronomy instruments (Bacon, 2011a, vol. 3, pp. 137, 156, 164).

The different types and numbers of fellows working in the House of Salomon portray a hierarchical and rigidly organized society, in which members have specific tasks. Bacon named the categories of fellows and briefly described their function. "Merchants of Light" traveled to foreign lands under the name of other nations to gather books, information, ideas, and equipment; "Depredators" selected and summarized experiments from books; "Mystery-men" collected and systematized experiments derived from the mechanical arts and liberal sciences; "Pioneers" devised and tried new experiments; and "Inoculators" carried experiments under the direction of other fellows.

"Compilers" were fellows in charge of organizing the information obtained by other types of members, putting them into categories, preparing tables, describing observations, and deriving axioms from them. "Benefactors" reviewed the experiments carried out at the House of Salomon to identify practical applications and theoretical implications. Two additional groups of fellows—the "Lamps" and "Interpreters of Nature"—were in charge of devising new experiments to delve deeper into nature, and of raising findings and discoveries to higher-level theories and laws of nature. Finally, the House of Salomon had many novices and apprentices to ensure continuity and the accumulation of knowledge, and a large number of servants and attendants to assist the fellows.

Bacon describes briefly the regulations and ceremonies observed in the House of Salomon, which publicize the benefits of knowledge and reward inventors. One of its "two very long and fair galleries" housed "samples of all manner of the more rare and excellent inventions," and the other contained statues of "all principal inventors" who were given a "liberal and honorable reward." Fellows toured the island of Bensalem publicizing the results of their work and announcing new useful inventions, disseminating information about anticipated weather and natural events, and providing advice on how to prevent disasters.

The final section of the *New Atlantis* provides a list of discoveries that would benefit mankind and could be construed as research priorities for the House of Salomon. Issues ranged from "the prolongation of life" and "mitigation of pain," to "making new species" and "transplanting of one species into another," and included "artificial minerals and cements" and "instruments of destruction, as of war and poison." Human needs, social demands, and a will to reveal nature's secrets drove the pursuit of knowledge at the House of Salomon.

Published after Bacon's death, the *New Atlantis* was reprinted many times during the second half of the seventeenth century. It became one of its most popular works, was translated into French and Latin shortly after publication, and was imitated and copied by other writers. The *New Atlantis* provides the first full description of a scientific society and a modern research laboratory, and in subsequent decades elicited the most varied responses.

A century after Bacon wrote *The New Atlantis*, Jonathan Swift lampooned the House of Solomon in *Gulliver's Travels*. He described Laputa, a flying island hovering over the land of Balnibarbi, where the king and prominent citizens were always engaged in theoretical disquisitions and distracted to a fault. Swift drew a caricature of scientists as aloof and oblivious, who required assistance to be aware of what goes on around them, and whose instructions to workmen were always misunderstood with disastrous results.

The Academy of Projectors at Lagado, the main city in Balnibarbi, was set up after some visitors to Laputa "came back with a very little smattering in mathematics, but full of volatile spirits acquired in that airy region." After returning they "began to dislike the management of everything below; and fell into schemes of putting all arts, sciences, languages, and mechanics upon a new foot." Once the Academy was established, the projectors invented all sorts of novel things, but "the only inconvenience is, that none of these projects are yet brought to perfection; and in the meantime, the whole country lies in miserable waste." Swift describes experiments to extract "sunbeams out of cucumbers," to "reduce human excrement to its original food," "building houses beginning by the roof," and employ the blind "to mix colors for the painters" (Swift, 1965, pp. 162–165).

Similar aims were pursued in speculative learning at the Academy of Lagado. One experiment consists of an array of movable squares with words written in them, which, when their handles are turned, present a new sequence of words at random. Assistants collect the "three or four words together that might make part of a sentence" and repeat the exercise to write whole books. Swift also describes a number of projects of the "school of political projectors" that seem outlandish precisely because they are obviously sensible and sound (Swift, 1965, pp. 169, 171).

Jonathan Swift's takeoff on the House of Solomon disparaged the work of scientific societies and laboratories, but other intellectuals took Bacon's ideas seriously and built on them. Writing nearly 200 years later, shortly before he died in prison, Antoine-Nicolas Condorcet's *Fragment on the New Atlantis, or the Combined Efforts of the Human Species for the Advancement of Science*, argued for an enhanced and democratic House of Solomon—a "universal republic of the sciences"—that "could only be fulfilled by the free and spontaneous will of those who cultivate the sciences" (Condorcet, 1976, p. 292).

Condorcet's *Fragment* began by stating, "Bacon conceived the idea of a society of men devoted solely to the search for truth. His plan embraced all the parts of human knowledge." Dwelling on the differences between Bacon's time and his own, and on the limitations that make the search for knowledge an arduous task, he proposed a detailed plan for the organization of a new type of scientific society. It would begin at the initiative of a few men drawing provisional conditions for its establishment, which would then be made public to invite others to join the society. Initial expenses would be covered by subscriptions from the associates, complemented with voluntary contributions. Members of committees would be renewed by thirds annually to avoid the "danger of personal opinions or sectarian prejudices." The first task of the society would be to publish "every tenth year a table of the truths with which the sciences had been enriched" (Condorcet, 1976, pp. 283, 299, 296).

Condorcet envisaged "two kinds of investigations" to be pursued by the society: those that required a very long time, and those that required a considerable initial investment. He proposed to establish two reserve funds, one to finance new research and the other to provide a fixed income to the society. Government could make contributions, but without any conditions. The society would zealously maintain its independence and decide on research projects according to "what it believes should be undertaken to accelerate the progress of the sciences." There would be various national associations, but also a "more general association … embracing all the peoples who have attained more or less degree of enlightenment and liberty, … [which] would assure among all the sciences and all the arts directed by their principles, as among all nations, an equilibrium of knowledge, industry, and reason necessary for the progress and the happiness of the human species" (Condorcet, 1976, p. 300).

Written 400 years ago, the House of Salomon is one of the first attempts to vividly describe the purposes, facilities, organization, and activities of a modern research institution. It provided a target for those, like Swift, who were skeptical of its aims, works, and results, but also a reference point for those, like Condorcet, who envisaged a bright future for humanity through science.

Assessing Bacon and His Legacy

Sir Francis Bacon was a self-conscious man. Even though he did not anticipate his sudden downfall in the court of King James, he was keenly aware of the vicissitudes of high officials. He had first-hand knowledge of the reversals of fortune they frequently experienced, and of how careers could arbitrarily be advanced or destroyed. As will be stressed later, he was fully cognizant of his position in court, of his reliance on more powerful patrons, and knew well how his political, legal, and administrative activities fitted into the affairs of the kingdom.

"Men in great place are thrice servants: servants of the sovereign or state; servants of fame; and servants of business," wrote Bacon in his essay *Of Great Place.* Seemingly puzzled by the desire "to seek power and to lose liberty: or to seek power over others and to lose power over a man's self," he reflected on the ups and downs of public service and courtly life: "the rising unto place is laborious; and by pains men come to greater pains; and it is sometimes base; and by indignities men come to dignities. The standing is slippery, and the regress is either a downfall, or at least an eclipse, which is a melancholy thing." Yet, positions of power gave "license to do good and evil." For Bacon, "the latter is a curse: for in evil the best condition is not to will; the second, not to can," and admonished: "power to do good is the true and lawful end of aspiring. … Merit and good works are the end of man's motion; and conscience of the same is the accomplishment of man's rest" (Bacon, 2011c, vol. 6, pp. 398–399). It is rather baffling to contemplate why he did not relate these reflections to his own case.

Bacon was also conscious of his place in the community of philosophers and scholars, and capable of reflecting on the strengths and weaknesses of his own intellectual work. He repeatedly emphasized the differences between his plans to renew natural philosophy and the prevailing scholarly and alchemic practices in his time. Aspiring to radically change the way in which the intellectual and material realms of human experience related to each other, Bacon was confident in the superiority and greater usefulness of his method. Nonetheless, though convinced his ideas and proposals would accelerate the advancement of learning, Bacon did not consider them the last word. He rather appraised them critically and thought they would improve over time, as his followers applied and perfected his methods of inquiry:

> I am not proposing any universal or comprehensive theory. I do not think the time has yet come for such a thing. Neither can I hope to live long enough to complete the sixth part of the Instauration (which is intended for the philosophy discovered by the legitimate interpretation of the Nature). I shall be content if it can work soberly and usefully in the intermediate stages, and meanwhile sow for men after me the seeds of a purer truth and play my part in the beginning of great things (Bacon, 1994, pp. 118–119).

Moreover, for Bacon, the process of generating knowledge and inventions to improve the human condition could itself be improved: "if the usefulness of just one particular invention has so impressed men that they deemed superhuman the man who could secure the devotion of the entire human race through some benefit he brought, how much loftier will it seem to discover something that will enable all other discoveries to be readily made?" In Bacon's approach, the scientific method can be applied to improve itself: "I, who consider the mind not only in its natural capacity but in its connection with things, cannot but believe the art of discovery may grow with the number of new discoveries" (Bacon, 1994, pp. 131–132). Thus, right from the beginning, the Baconian Program had a self-reflective character that allowed it to endure and maintain relevance.

Bacon had no illusions that the renewal of natural philosophy would be accomplished in his lifetime, and was rather restrained about the value of his own scientific findings, expecting his errors would be eventually corrected:

> And just as I am not the founder of a sect, so I do not make any lavish promises of particular works … but from works and experiments to extract causes and axioms, and again from those causes and axioms to extract new works and experiments, as a legitimate interpreter of Nature. … Nevertheless I frankly confess that my present knowledge of natural history, whether from books or from my own investigations, is neither full nor certain enough to satisfy the requirement of a legitimate interpretation. … men should realize that there may be many experiments in my natural history that are wrongly believed and accepted, which will soon, by the discovery of causes and axioms, be easily deleted and rejected (Bacon, 1994, pp. 119–120).

Finally, many of Bacon's writings, and especially his correspondence with patrons, friends, and commentators, stress that he had little time to devote to his intellectual work. He led a busy and complex life, in which intellectual and worldly affairs were inseparable, but saw himself as a lonely pioneer who made great strides under unfavorable conditions. No surprise he would argue that those fully dedicated to the task of reforming scientific inquiry could achieve much more:

> Anyone who is despondent should consider me a man of all men of my time the most occupied with affairs of state, not in very good health (which cost me much time), altogether a pioneer in this subject, following no man's footsteps, discussing this matter with no living soul, who has yet brought these matters some way, as I believe, by diligently forging ahead along the true road and submitting the mind to things. And then let him consider how much we can expect from men with abundance of leisure, collaborating with others, and over a period of years, after these directions of mine (Bacon, 1994, p. 116).

Providing a summary assessment of Sir Francis Bacon's character and legacy is a difficult task. All things considered, he could be defined as an imaginative, visionary, disciplined, royalist court official, who devoted his remarkable intellectual, political, and administrative skills and energies to transform natural philosophy, reform the English legal system and provide advice to Queen, King, and favorites. He was also a man of dubious reputation, who did not hesitate to employ underhanded practices when he thought higher ends demanded it.

His intellectual legacy, what was later called the Baconian Program, radically changed the way knowledge is generated and utilized; it would unfold and prevail, first in Europe and in the rest of the world, through four centuries. In the process, it would profoundly transform human actions and the biophysical systems that support life, alter the very conception of what is to be human, and open extraordinary possibilities for the future evolution of our species. Only a man as complex, inconsistent, and paradoxical as Bacon, who motivated such diverse reactions to his work and life, could have advanced a Program whose consequences would be as complex, inconsistent, and paradoxical as his creator.

References

Bacon, F. (1884). *Bacon's essays and wisdom of the ancients* (P. Shaw, Trans.). Little, Brown. Retrieved from http://archive.org/details/baconsessayswisd00baco

Bacon, F. (1994). In P. Urbach & J. Gibson (Eds.), *Novum Organum: With other parts of the great instauration*. Open Court.

Bacon, F. (2002). In B. Vickers (Ed.), *Francis Bacon: The major works. [Including new Atlantis and the essays]*. Oxford University Press.

Bacon, F. (2011a). New Atlantis. In J. Spedding, R. L. Ellis, & D. D. Heath (Eds.), *The works of Francis Bacon: Vol. 3: Philosophical Works 3* (pp. 119–166). Cambridge University Press.

Bacon, F. (2011b). The advancement of learning. In J. Spedding, R. L. Ellis, & D. D. Heath (Eds.), *The works of Francis Bacon: Vol. 3: Philosophical works 3* (pp. 321–491). Cambridge University Press.

Bacon, F. (2011c). In J. Spedding, R. Ellis, & D. D. Heath, (Eds.), *The works of Francis Bacon: Vol. 6: Literary and professional works 1* (Digitally printed version). Cambridge University Press.

Bacon, F. (2011d). In J. Spedding, R. Ellis, & D. D. Heath, (Eds.), *The works of Francis Bacon: Vol. 7: Literary and professional works 2* (Digitally printed version). Cambridge University Press.

Bacon, F. (2011e). In J. Spedding, R. Ellis, & D. D. Heath, (Eds.), *The works of Francis Bacon: Vol. 8: The letters and the life 1* (Digitally printed version). Cambridge University Press.

Bacon, F. (2011f). In J. Spedding, R. Ellis, & D. D. Heath, (Eds.), *The works of Francis Bacon: Vol. 10: The letters and the Life 3* (Digitally printed version). Cambridge University Press.
Böhme, G. (1992). *Coping with science*. Westview Press.
Condorcet, J.-A.-N. (1976). Fragment on the new Atlantis, or the combined efforts of the human species for the advancement of science. In K. M. Baker (Ed.), *Condorcet selected writings*. Bobbs-Merrill.
Faulkner, R. (1993). *Francis Bacon and the project of progress*. Rowman & Littlefield.
Jonas, H. (1984). *The imperative of responsibility: In search of an ethics for the technological age*. University of Chicago Press.
Keller, V. (2018). Deprogramming Baconianism: The meaning of desiderata in the eighteenth century. *Royal Society of London, 72*(2), 119–137. JSTOR.
Martin, J. (2007). *Francis Bacon, the state and the reform of natural philosophy*. Cambridge University Press.
Pérez-Ramos, A. (1996). Bacon's legacy. In M. Peltonen (Ed.), *The Cambridge companion to Bacon* (pp. 311–334). Cambridge University Press.
Swift, J. (1965). *Gulliver's travels*. The Folio Society.

Part II
The Baconian Epoch

Introduction to Part II

Sir Francis Bacon's program to dominate nature through understanding for the benefit of humanity was articulated in turbulent times. Medieval Europe's sluggish pace of change quickened in the late Middle Ages and the Renaissance. A rapid expansion of interactions between different cultures made it impossible to view their evolution independently after the fifteenth and sixteenth centuries. Improvements in the means of transport intensified trade and finance links, opened new markets, sped up the exchange of plant and animal species, and made available novel sources of raw materials and precious metals. The invention of the printing press accelerated the transmission of information and increased access to religious and secular texts. Worldwide networks of interaction emerged, putting in contact different ways of living and peoples far away from each other.

Bacon's ideas and proposals signaled a break with medieval scholasticism, magic, and alchemy. They championed systematic research and experimentation as methods to generate knowledge and recognized the contributions of artisans and craftsmen in advancing scientific inquiry. Their purpose, direction, and focus were informed by practical ends, aiming at mastery over nature and improvements in living standards. Their proposals on the organization and conduct of scientific inquiry set the stage for the creation of scientific societies and research laboratories, the first institutions of modern science.

By fits and starts, irreversible processes were set in motion as the Baconian Program began to unfold. The scientific and industrial revolutions, together with the Enlightenment and the worldwide spread of the capitalist system of production that emerged in Western Europe, aligned scientific research with technical and technological development, intertwining them with economic expansion. Knowledge of natural phenomena began to be acquired by methodically contrasting abstract theories with practical experiments. The discovery and mastery of laws that organize the physical world increased power over nature to a previously unthinkable extent. In parallel, the systematization of empirical results, obtained through trial and error, added to the improved understanding of natural phenomena and enlarged the set of technical and later technological responses. Enabled by this richer repertoire, production and service activities multiplied and diversified, productivity improved, and growing variety of goods reached distant places through trade.

Knowledge, Technology, and Production

Societies can be characterized by the state of their knowledge, technology, and production activities, and by the ways in which these interact with each other. Enabled by institutional arrangements and embedded in broader social, political, and cultural structures, the interconnected evolution of these three sets of activities set the pace for human development. In what can appropriately be designated as the "Baconian epoch," the various components of Sir Francis Bacon's program underlay the ways in which knowledge, technology, and production evolved and interacted.

Concepts, ideas, metaphors, theories, hypotheses, and other varieties of speculative thought are the means through which human beings apprehend and explain natural and social phenomena. Organized through mental constructs that include myth, magic, religion, and science, these abstractions also allow accounting for our inner lives and identities, thus giving meaning to human existence. Techniques and technologies comprise a great diversity of practices, processes, and procedures, often embedded in artifacts and devices, which provide a vast repertoire of responses to the challenges of the biophysical and social environments. Individuals and social groups engage in production and service activities that transform land, labor, natural resources, materials, energy, information, and other inputs into goods and services to satisfy their needs.

Myth, magic, and religion structured knowledge and speculative thought since time immemorial. They provided accounts of changes in the positions of celestial bodies, natural phenomena on earth, and human cycles of birth, growth, decay, and death. Creation myths and sacred narratives, transmitted orally from generation to generation, codified and communicated knowledge before the advent of writing. Archaic imagery and narratives helped register star and planet movements, made sense of changes in seasons and weather, provided guidance for agriculture, and organized social interactions.

Magic sought to achieve greater control over the circumstances that affect human beings. Incantations and rituals attempted to link the cosmic order with earthly endeavors, and to manipulate hidden forces. In less active form, magic led to mysticism to transcend the vicissitudes of human existence and directly access the sacred. Rising above powerful mythical and magical deities that capriciously decided fate and demanded appeasement, religion sought to provide an orderly way to account for natural phenomena and explain humanity's place in the cosmos. God's will rules the universe; interpreted by shamans and priests, it provided guidance for action, for worship, and for abiding His designs. None of the various forms of speculative thought disappeared as new ones emerged; while one or another predominated at certain times and places, they all coexisted and influenced each other.

Throughout history all human groups developed agricultural, irrigation, and animal husbandry practices; ways of cutting stones, working with wood and processing metals; and of making pottery, textiles, and other artifacts. They also devised construction methods, means of transport, and procedures to heal and take care of the sick. These responses to the challenges of the environment and society, a result of human ingenuity in action, increase continuously and create a richly endowed reservoir of techniques and technologies. Techniques are obtained and refined by trial and error that may be more or less systematic but are not informed by prior causal explanations of possible outcomes. Technologies are based on theories and hypotheses that anticipate outcomes and cause–effect relations, which are confirmed or rejected through experiments.

Initially, a social group has at its disposal a foundation of techniques that offer responses only to specific challenges and situations one by one; later it superimposes a layer of empirical knowledge that begins to detect and register variations in the efficacy of such responses by trial and error. At a subsequent stage, it actively develops a base of techniques arising from systematic experimentation, but without theoretical knowledge to guide the trials. As the Baconian Program unfolded and was consciously deployed, technology—which joined practice (*techné*) with reason (*logos*)—gradually superseded technique and became increasingly grounded on scientific research methods and results.

Products and services satisfy the needs and aspirations of the members of society, improve livelihoods, and expand the scope of human action. Over time, their growing variety, better quality, and lower cost make them more accessible and appealing to increasing numbers of consumers and users. Conditioned by cultural norms and values, needs and aspirations differ between social groups. They also change with the level of material wellbeing and the distribution of wealth and power, which shape the patterns of demand for products and services. Assisted by trade and information exchanges, inventions and efficiency improvements help in providing new and more valuable goods with fewer inputs.

Production and service activities make use of techniques and technologies selected from the accumulated set of potential responses to the challenges of the biophysical and social environments. Social values, expressed through customs and institutional arrangements, establish incentives and deterrents that condition the choice of specific techniques and technologies.

Before the Baconian epoch, the generation of knowledge was not primarily oriented toward technical improvements, while the variety and amounts of products and services grew together with the repertoire of techniques. Even as the Baconian Program unfolded, a large proportion of production and service activities continued to employ techniques, rather than science-based technologies. It would take nearly three centuries after Bacon implicitly articulated his program before the fusion of knowledge, technology, and production would be fully achieved to relentlessly drive economic growth and increase consumption.

As a result, the repertoire of responses to the challenges of the biophysical and social environments now comprises science-based and conventional technologies, as well as traditional techniques. The first emerge directly from advanced research, lead to radical innovations, and open up opportunities for new economic and social activities that could not be anticipated, or even imagined, without conducting scientific research. Conventional technologies cannot be directly traced to scientific knowledge acquired recently, but are science-infused, building on decades-old research results. They take advantage of the scientific approach to rigorous experimentation and are influenced by the intellectual climate that incorporates the methods and results of science. Traditional techniques rely almost exclusively on more or less rigorous trial and error but have proven effective at certain times and places. They evolve slowly by accretion, adding layer after layer of minor improvements and innovations. Advanced, conventional, and traditional technologies and techniques are used in different settings, sometimes coexist in certain locations, and can be combined to improve their responses to environmental and social challenges.

Societies generate and accumulate economic surpluses by expanding and modifying the range of products and services in such ways that their value to consumers and users is greater than the sum of the cost of the inputs utilized. Their evolution is conditioned by the manner in which economic surpluses are appropriated and allocated. Traditional uses of accumulation—characteristic of most civilizations and societies until the Baconian epoch—include securing food reserves; building roads and ports; constructing temples, palaces, and defense walls; waging war and maintaining armed forces; supporting religion and the priesthood; and providing patronage to the arts, crafts, and the pursuit of speculative knowledge.

New uses of accumulation began to spread during the late fourteenth and fifteenth centuries. Accompanying the expansion of European empires and the spread of capitalism, they began to predominate as the Baconian Program unfolded. Beyond traditional uses, accumulated surpluses were employed to open commercial routes, discover natural resources, increase labor productivity, facilitate economic transactions, and create or acquire technological knowledge. These, in turn, generated additional economic surpluses that were used, once more, to further the accumulation process.

A counterpoint between the range of products and services on the one hand, and of wants to be satisfied on the other, has been an intrinsic feature of the expansion and modification of production and service activities in all societies. Needs have spurred human ingenuity to devise new products and services, and to invent the means—techniques and technologies—of making them available. As the potential supply of goods and services increased, a corresponding growth in needs and aspirations turned into demand for new goods and services.

A wide variety of institutional arrangements were devised to organize and distribute goods and services. Over time, barter exchanges began to be structured through markets, which evolved from posts along main trade routes toward the convergence of sellers and buyers at specific places, such as bazaars and fairs, and toward the creation, centuries later, of self-regulating markets for exchanging goods, services and their symbolic representations. While self-regulating markets have come to be seen in modern times as the natural way of engaging in such activities, for most of history and in most of the world, reciprocity and redistribution arrangements, often mediated by hierarchical authorities, provided the institutional underpinnings for economic transactions (Polanyi, 1970).

The Unfolding, Deployment, and Success of the Baconian Program

A complex set of events converged in seventeenth-century Italy, France, England, and other parts of Europe for Bacon's ideas to begin taking hold, although they remained a visionary ideal for a long time. Barring favorable historical, political, social, and cultural circumstances, and without contributions from a few gifted thinkers, they might have remained a compelling but sterile vision. After slowly unfolding for two centuries, the Baconian Program would begin to be fully deployed in the second half of the nineteenth century, when science-based technologies became an engine of economic growth. It would then pervade an ever-widening range of economic and social activities in the twentieth century.

During the seventeenth century, Europe was part of an increasingly interconnected polycentric world. Raw materials, manufactures, gold, silver, money, foodstuffs, timber, people, slaves, ideas, artworks, pathogens, and other tangible and intangible goods were regularly traded over long distances, creating vast networks that drew the world together. From 1600 to 1820, Europe's share of world population and economic output were one sixth and one quarter, respectively, and Asia concentrated two thirds of population and economic activity. By the end of the nineteenth century, Europe's one fifth of world's population was responsible for nearly 40% of global production, while Asia's more than half of world's population accounted for less than 30% of world economic activity.

There were many reasons for this reversal of fortune. European State-backed military ventures and private profiteers employed violent force to acquire control of distant lands, enslave or exploit local populations, and impose unequal commercial exchanges. They used the proceeds to expand their own economic activities and to maintain their hold over colonies or trading outposts, often with the connivance of local rulers. These lopsided power relations were one of the sources of prosperity in the European imperial states for two and a half centuries.

But there were other forces at play that conferred Europe an advantage over other regions of the world. As the Baconian Program unfolded, the Scientific Revolution, the Enlightenment, and the Industrial Revolution created favorable conditions for productivity improvements and economic progress. Systematized empirical knowledge, complemented with inputs from science, was gradually put at the service of technical and, later, technological advance. Mindsets informed by new conceptions of the cosmos, nature, humanity, and society expanded the scope for initiatives to improve the human condition.[1]

The configuration of modern science in Europe during the seventeenth century took place amidst religious and political strife, in parallel with imperialist expansion. Persecution and power struggles led to instability in government and academic positions, which made leading intellectuals migrate to more tolerant places. Civil war during the 1640s, Cromwell's Protectorate in the 1650s, and monarchic restoration in the 1660s provided the background for the emergence of the world's first scientific society in England. In France, the absolutist reign of Louis XIV drove religious dissidents and leading natural philosophers abroad, while his key minister Jean Baptiste Colbert countered this by supporting science and enticing researchers to settle in France.

A weakened monarchy in rigidly hierarchical Catholic Spain, made rich by its American colonies, left little room for scientific pursuits. Fragmented Italy, largely under Spanish control during the seventeenth century and Austrian during the eighteenth century, lost its economic dynamism and intellectual leadership. Poland, Russia, and the Central European states of the Holy Roman Empire experienced bouts of instability that did not favor steady intellectual activity. National sovereignty, enshrined gradually after the 1648 Treaty of Westphalia that ended 30 years of religious wars, secured Dutch independence from Spain, reduced interstate conflicts, and strengthened European nation-states. The 1683 defeat of the Ottoman Empire army following the siege of Vienna removed the threat of invasion and left European countries free to focus on their own development and colonial ambitions.

During the seventeenth and eighteenth centuries, markets expanded their coverage in Europe and overseas. They were organized as large-scale, state-supported, mercantilist ventures, or as small-scale exchanges of goods, supervised by local authorities and guilds, and by their local counterparts in the rest of the world. Mercantilist policies levied duties on imported goods, required them to be transported in national ships, restricted trade with colonies, and sought to accumulate precious metals.

The English Poor Law of 1601, in which Francis Bacon was marginally involved as a parliamentarian, provided relief in the form of work, food, and shelter for various categories of poor people (Bacon, 2011, vol. 9, pp. 82–83). Administered at the parish level and complemented with regulations that prevented landowners from enclosing agricultural land for pasture and allowed peasant access to commons, it remained a barrier for the consolidation of a national labor market in England for two and a half centuries.

Merchants and industrialists became progressively more sophisticated in their dealings with financers, and novel forms of bankrolling commercial and industrial ventures emerged as technical advances opened new business possibilities. Luxury and exotic goods, demanded by wealthy minorities and mostly imported from

[1] See, for example Quinn (2024), Darwin (2008), Frankopan (2023), Sharman (2019), Jay (2000), Mokyr (1990), and Mendelssohn (1976).

faraway lands, stimulated trade and encouraged local industry to imitate or replace them. As economic conditions improved and productivity gains lowered prices, once-exclusive products—sugar, tobacco, brandy, and cotton cloth among them—became accessible to larger segments of society, spurring innovation and prompting further differentiation efforts by the rich.

The emergence of self-regulating markets and the treatment of labor and land as commodities would wait till the mid-nineteenth century. By that time, the Industrial Revolution had taken hold in England and was spreading to Europe, North America, and other parts of the world. Competition demanded productivity improvements that increasingly relied on technical innovations and would eventually incorporate science-based technologies.

Joseph Needham's comparisons between Chinese and European progress in knowledge and techniques posed the question of why modern science did not emerge in China, India, or other relatively advanced societies of the sixteenth and seventeenth centuries. A combination of long-drawn historical processes, contacts with other civilizations, unusual circumstances, and powerful intellectual personalities set the stage for the rise of modern science in Europe rather than elsewhere (Needham, 1975, 1978). While alternative paths to mobilize knowledge for improving the human condition may have been possible, the unfolding, deployment, and success of the Baconian Program, together with the expansion of markets and capitalism, successfully framed European and North American efforts to dominate nature through understanding, and the rest of the world through technical and technological prowess.

Like a piece of tightly crumpled paper suddenly released, the Baconian Program unfolded by fits and starts for two and a half centuries. Irregularities, folds, and creases prevented a full appreciation of the program's contours and dimensions but, with the benefit of hindsight, it is possible to grasp how it mobilized knowledge to improve the human condition. Closely intertwining science, technology, and production, by the late nineteenth century it had fully unfolded; all was in place for its conscious deployment in the twentieth century and for reaping its heralded benefits. Yet, cracks and blemishes, faint at first but more visible with the passage of time, prefigured the undesirable consequences that the unfolding, deployment, and success of the Baconian Program would eventually bestow on humanity.

Historical processes fade, merge, and metamorphose into each other, making it difficult to define precise dates and single events to mark beginnings and ends. Aiming at narrative coherence, part II of this book organizes the swirl of events associated with the Baconian Program describing its background and articulation till the beginning of the seventeenth century, its unfolding from the seventeenth through the nineteenth centuries, and its deployment and success in the twentieth century. Please notice that it has been difficult to organize these chapters by both chronological and thematic criteria, which has led to some repetitions and some displacements in the sequence of events.

References

Bacon, F. (2011). In J. Spedding, R. Ellis, & D. D. Heath (Eds.), *The works of Francis Bacon: Vol. 9: The letters and the life 2* (Digitally printed version). Cambridge University Press.

Darwin, J. (2008). *After Tamerlane: The rise and fall of global empires, 1400–2000*. Bloomsbury Press.

Frankopan, P. (2023). *The Earth transformed: An untold history*. Alfred A. Knopf.

Jay, P. (2000). *The wealth of man*. Public Affairs.

Mendelssohn, K. (1976). *The secret of western domination*. Praeger Publishers.

Mokyr, J. (1990). *The lever of riches: Technological creativity and economic progress*. Oxford University Press.

Needham, J. (1975). *Dentro de los cuatro mares: El diálogo entre oriente y occidente*. Siglo XXI.

Needham, J. (1978). *De la ciencia y la tecnología chinas*. Siglo XXI.

Polanyi, K. (1970). *The great transformation: The political and economic origins of our time*. Beacon Press.

Quinn, J. C. (2024). *How the world made the West: A 4,000-year history*. Random House.

Sharman, J. C. (2019). *Empires of the weak: The real story of European expansion and the creation of the new world order*. Princeton University Press.

Chapter 4
Toward the Baconian Epoch

Bacon was a great genius who helped to shape the modern world,
but geniuses do not spring from nowhere.

John Henry (2002, p. 11)

Bacon's reading habits convey the impression of a voracious, but unsystematic reader.

Lisa Jardine (2009, p. 9)

Sir Francis Bacon did not develop his proposals to "restart the whole operation of the mind" (Bacon, 1994, p. 38) in a void. Bacon knew the works of Classical, Medieval, and Renaissance authors, read accounts of travelers to distant lands, followed the technical developments of his time, had an interest in commerce and the practical arts, was familiar with the practice of magic, remained deeply imbued with religious ideas, and was also familiar with the ins and outs of exercising power in the English court.

In addition to his direct acquaintance with numerous texts of European authors, he also indirectly absorbed the contributions of intellectuals in other parts of the world who influenced the Roman, Greek, Persian, Arabic, and Turkish scholars with whom Bacon was familiar. As Josephine Quinn has indicated, Western or European culture, of which Bacon was a shining example in his time, was "in large part a product of long-standing links with a much larger network of societies, to south and north as well as east" (Quinn, 2024, p. 13).

A historical overview of the evolution of knowledge, techniques, and production until the end of the sixteenth century provides a backdrop to the emergence of Bacon's ideas and the components of what we now know as the Baconian Program.

F. Sagasti, *Knowledge is Power*, Innovation, Technology, and Knowledge Management, https://doi.org/10.1007/978-3-032-20668-8_4

Knowledge

Mythical and magical thought viewed nature as inextricably linked with the realms of the divine and the human. In contrast, Greek philosophers advanced the idea that natural phenomena were distinct entities that could be made intelligible and examined on their own, and that life experiences, perceptions, and observations could be generalized and extracted from their concrete settings while preserving their essential features. Abstract thinking gradually led to the development of symbolic logic, geometry, algebra, and various branches of mathematics, usually linked to astronomy and astrology. Unevenly developed throughout the world, these advances provided a set of rules for the manipulation of concepts and ideas, making possible the development of theories to account for apparently diverse phenomena and to establish causal relations between them.

Astronomical observations challenged ancient thinkers to offer explanations for the movement of celestial bodies and the regularities of natural events. During the second and third centuries BC, the combination of Babylonian numerical procedures and Greek geometric conceptions of the cosmos led to significant advances in planetary astronomy. Aristarchus of Samos proposed that the Earth moves around the Sun, Hipparchus of Nicaea provided estimates of the distance between the two, and Eratosthenes of Alexandria calculated the Earth's circumference rather accurately for his time.

Working in Alexandria, Claudius Ptolemy developed an astronomical scheme that matched observation records, placed Earth at the center of the universe, and retained the circular motion of celestial bodies. His conceptual advances were successful in predicting the movements of the planets, including their apparent retrograde motion, and endured until the fifteenth and sixteenth centuries when Copernicus's heliocentric scheme replaced them.

The rise of Islam in the late seventh century and its expansion over a wide geographical area coincided with the translation of texts from Greek and Syriac into Arabic and the Hellenization of Islamic culture. A loosely unified Islamic state enabled the circulation of people, books, and ideas; coupled with patronage from powerful rulers and merchants, intellectual activity revived, and Greek learning was recovered. Highly skilled translators made available in Arabic the whole corpus of classical natural philosophy, medicine, mathematics, astronomy, and astrology.

Observatories, libraries, and translation centers were established in Cordoba, at the Western end of the Islamic empire; Cairo and Damascus at the center; and Baghdad and Maragha at the Eastern end. The Baghdad House of Wisdom, founded by Harun al-Rashid in the late eight century, functioned as research institute for several 100 years. Muhammad ibn Musa al-Khwarizmi worked there during the ninth century; integrating Greek, Indian, Persian, and Babylonian contributions; he established the basis for algebra and trigonometry, revised astronomical tables, and corrected Ptolemy's geographical calculations.

At the beginning of the eleventh century, Abu Ali al-Husayin ibn Abdallah ibn Sina (Avicenna) wrote a medical text that circulated widely in Europe for centuries and numerous works on mathematics, astronomy, philosophy, and physics, among other subjects. With centuries of uneasy coexistence of Christian and Islamic populations and culture, and with large libraries and a sizable number of scholars in Cordoba, Toledo, Seville, and other cities, Spain became a leading center for translating Arab treatises into Latin. The presence of Jewish scholars enriched the Spanish intellectual climate, as testified by the work of philosopher, physician, and rabbi Moses Maimonides, who reconciled Aristotle's teachings with those of the Bible. The leading figure in the twelfth century was Ibn Rushd (Averroes), a prolific Islamic polymath based in Cordoba, who wrote on philosophy, medicine, logic, law, astronomy, mathematics, physics, geography, and cosmology.

Economic growth, increasing trade and commerce, and the rise of urban centers in Europe during the late Middle Ages created a demand for education and led to the creation of new secular and church schools. The establishment of universities throughout Europe provided a home for educational and scholarly endeavors. Powerful secular and religious patrons supported the rise of universities in Bologna, Paris, Oxford, Cambridge, Salamanca, Valladolid, Padua, and Salerno in the thirteenth century, and later in other European cities. Aristotle's works on logic, philosophy, physics, cosmology, and natural history were widely used in these academic circles. Islamic medical texts and, to a lesser extent, works on Greek and Islamic mathematics, were also part of the curricula.

The exercise of human reason to study natural phenomena, advocated by the followers of Aristotelian methods, clashed with the dominant role awarded to faith and revelation by the guardians of religious tradition. Some aspects of Aristotle's philosophy were inconsistent with Christian doctrine: an eternal instead of God-created cosmos, a deterministic bent that threatened free will, and a treatment of the soul as the "form" of the body that did not allow for physical immortality.

Attempts to overcome these inconsistencies and align classical with religious teachings characterized the rise of Scholasticism. Following a path traced centuries earlier by St. Augustine, Robert Grosseteste, and Roger Bacon, leading Scholastic thinkers argued that truth emerged when reason was kept subsidiary to faith. Grosseteste put forward the idea that mathematics and geometry were necessary to understand the physical world. He reinterpreted the biblical Genesis as starting with the creation of light, reasoned about how the Sun generates heat and how the Moon influences tides, and also suggested the use of lenses to increase the size of objects under observation.

Franciscan friar Roger Bacon, a disciple of Grosseteste, advocated the deliberate use of both reason and experience to acquire knowledge. He referred to mathematics as the "gate and key" to science, made discoveries in optics, proposed reforms to the calendar, and described various possible mechanical devices, including flying machines and automobiles.

Siger of Brabant and Boethius of Dacia, who taught at the University of Paris, followed a more radical path adhering closely to the teachings of Aristotle and Averroes. They attempted to separate philosophy from theology, arguing that rational arguments should be followed wherever they led, irrespective of their theological implications.

Although Siger and Boethius remained in the church and accepted its ultimate authority, Etienne Tempier, the Bishop of Paris, condemned their views and barred them from teaching at the university. Tempier issued a broad condemnation in 1277, with 219 detailed propositions that forbade teaching the views of Aristotle, Averroes, and even several of St. Thomas Aquinas. They also denounced astrology, denied that cosmic events affected earthly and human pursuits; condemnation number 92 rejected the idea derived from ancient Greek sources: "that with all the heavenly bodies coming back to the same point after a period of thirty-six thousand years, the same effects as now exist will reappear" (Tempier, 2010, p. 545).

As the Middle Ages gave way to the Renaissance and the hold of Scholasticism weakened, advances in the humanities, literature, and fine arts, as well as in political philosophy, matched progress in natural sciences. These developments changed how Europeans perceived themselves, society, nature, and religion. Humanist writers, artists, and philosophers—Dante, Erasmus, Petrarch, Boccaccio, Paracelsus, and Machiavelli, among others—exalted the self-creating possibilities and perfectibility of human beings, sought inspiration and approaches to art in nature, and aimed at describing the workings of society. In addition to opening up new avenues for the exercise of creativity in the arts and sciences, Renaissance humanists promoted tolerance and diversity. Dante's *Divine Comedy* placed Islamic philosophers Averroes and Avicenna in limbo, and controversial scholar Siger of Brabant in heaven.

Leading Renaissance artists, architects, and inventors—including Paolo del Pozo Toscanelli, Albrecht Durer, Leon Battista Alberti, Filippo Brunelleschi, Piero della Francesca, Michelangelo Buonarroti, and Leonardo da Vinci—improved on ways of registering nature, focused attention on the human body, and stressed the importance of careful observation and attention to detail. Advances in perspective theory and practice, largely based on geometric and numerical methods transmitted through the work of Islamic scholars, were widely employed in painting and architectural design.

The invention and perfecting of the telescope, together with developments in algebra and geometry, helped to reinterpret existing astronomical records. Superseding Ptolemy's geocentric circles and profusion of epicycles with Earth at the center, Nicholas Copernicus developed an alternative explanation of the movements of planets that placed the Sun at the center. In addition to Copernicus, Tycho Brahe, Johannes Kepler, and Galileo Galilei linked observations with mathematical models that simplified accounts of the movements of celestial bodies and improved astronomical predictions.

William Gilbert, natural scientist, astronomer, and physician to Queen Elizabeth and King James, recounted his experiments with magnetism and electricity in *De Magnete*, an influential book published in 1600. He proposed the Earth functioned as a giant magnet, which allowed determining cardinal points with a compass. Bacon acknowledged Gilbert's discoveries but criticized that he applied his efforts "to working out some single experiment" and "after the most painstaking studies of the lodestone, immediately erected a philosophy that suited his own favorite subject" (Bacon, 1994, pp. 79, 62).

By the time Francis Bacon began his natural philosophy endeavors in the late sixteenth century, the intellectual climate in Europe had shifted toward accommodation between religious beliefs and natural philosophy. God's inscrutable designs and capacity to perform miracles had to be accepted on faith, but Christian conceptions of divine omnipotence reached a compromise that viewed God as prime mover, establishing at the moment of creation, once for all, laws for nature to follow and for humans to discover. The assumption that there exists in nature a hidden order, established by divine fiat, became a motivating force for unveiling the mysteries of the universe. As Bacon stressed in his writings, the unpredictability of natural phenomena was due to human ignorance to be dispelled by rigorous inquiry.

Techniques

The repertoire of technical responses available during Bacon's time evolved gradually in Europe from Greek and Roman sources, with significant inputs from Northern Africa, the Middle East, India, and China. Trade, travel, migration, colonization, and military expansion, considerably helped by the role played by Islam during the Middle Ages, exposed European artisans and workers to foreign ways of producing goods, building infrastructure, and providing services.

Greek craftsmen were able to build sophisticated mechanical devices, such as the first-century BC Antikythera machine that performed astronomical computations. Exact measurements and conceptual abstractions were required to construct and anticipate the functioning of complex mechanical devices, such as the water clocks, pumps, pneumatic machines, and the rudimentary steam engines of Ctesibius and Heron, Alexandrian inventors in the third and first centuries BC. Waterwheels, pumps, and aqueducts were widely used in Roman times; bridges, temples, and forts were built and maintained; carts and roads, as well as ports and ships were the main means of transport; and weaving, pottery, metalworking, and other manufacturing activities occupied many workers.

Agriculture was the mainstay of the economy throughout the medieval period. New plow designs and better harness for horses and oxen improved agricultural productivity. Crop rotation and diversification, together with the introduction of new cultivation methods, were responsible for increases in food production. A thirteenth-century text on agricultural management by Walter of Henley suggests these practices were well established in England, and his methodical and practical approach led historian Jean Gimpel to suggest he was "one of the first men known to have applied experimental methods to agriculture" (Gimpel, 1976, p. 39). As cities grew, urban industry began to complement agricultural activities; by the mid-fourteenth century, a survey in Nuremberg registered 50 different categories of artisans.

Advances in building techniques allowed the construction of large Gothic cathedrals. Both religious symbols and expressions of craftsmen's skill, these constructions incorporated innovations such as pointed arches, ribbed vaults, flying buttresses, and stained-glass windows. Mechanical devices for lifting heavy loads were also improved to assist in construction. Existing practices were codified as architects and master builders left designs and notebooks describing calculations and construction procedures for roads, canals, dams, bridges, locks, aqueducts, drains, sewers, fortifications, and other public works. Techniques to exploit forests, quarries, and mines provided construction materials and were improved to supply a growing demand.

Toward the end of the first Christian millennium, inanimate energy supply replaced animal and human sources of power. Used for a variety of tasks, watermills became ubiquitous all over Europe. A survey in England during the late eleventh century recorded more than 4500 watermills, providing an affordable source of power for grinding, milling, tanning, and other manufacturing activities. As timber became scarce, the use of coal increased significantly, primarily as fuel but also for iron furnaces, glassmaking, and other industrial activities. Widespread coal burning in London in the late thirteenth century led to the first recorded incident of atmospheric pollution.

Innovations in shipbuilding, sail design, and the use of the compass, together with new charts and information on sea and coastal conditions, made navigation more reliable and long-distance trade common. Sailing ships replaced man-powered galleys and cannons replaced warriors, allowing maritime powers to embark on exploration and conquest expeditions. These technical advances helped establish vast networks of commercial routes linking distant ports, connected in turn to feeder roads that enabled exchanges with the hinterlands. The extensive movement of goods and people, and the rise of economic activity associated with it, brought forth what some scholars consider the first wave of "globalization" in the sixteenth century.

Spreading westward from Central Asia, the European adoption of the stirrup, cavalry, crossbow, and catapults during the eighth to tenth centuries altered how war was waged. The use of gunpowder and firearms further changed conditions on the battlefield. Recurrent and protracted armed conflicts between European states demanded advances in military equipment and tactics. Improvements in forging techniques and cannon manufacture raised the stakes for warring parties and prompted the design of fortresses capable of withstanding artillery barrages. Niccolo Fontana Tartaglia's studies of projectile motion in the first half of the sixteenth century improved cannon accuracy.

A century later, Galileo devised mathematical theorems and conducted experiments to describe projectile trajectories, develop the laws of motion, and study the strength of materials. His *Dialogues Concerning Two New Sciences* was set in the Venice arsenal, the leading factory at its time, because Galileo thought its activity "suggests to the studious mind a large field for investigation, especially … mechanics; all types of instruments and machines are constantly being constructed by many artisans, among whom there must be some who … have become highly expert and clever in explanation" (Galilei, 2004, p. 183).

Mechanical clocks had been devised in China in the eleventh century but were vastly improved and widely adopted in Europe starting in the thirteenth century. A variety of devices of all sizes were devised to keep time, mark the seasons, register the dates of religious festivities, and keep track of astronomical events. Church clocks and bells marked the passage of time, allowed the coordination of human activities, and established the rhythm of life in towns and villages. As mechanical devices to measure the passage of time became more complex and sophisticated, time was sliced into smaller intervals and recorded with increasing accuracy. The standard division of a day into 24 h, an hour into 60 min, and a minute into 60 s, derived from Babylonian and Egyptian conceptions, was widely adopted in the fourteenth century.

Clocks delinked the experiencing of time from the natural cycles of day and night, transforming it from something imposed by nature into an abstract dimension. Time became a variable in mathematical equations to describe the movement of heavenly bodies and the trajectories of terrestrial objects. Bishop Nicholas Oresme thought the universe was gigantic clockwork and God a perfect clockmaker who "made a clock and let it run and continue its own motion by itself" (Oresme, as cited in Grant, 2005, p. 46).

Toward the first half of the sixteenth century, medicine made great strides with Andreas Vesalius' work on human anatomy. His extensively illustrated *De humani corporis fabrica* (On the Fabric of the Human Body) provided the first comprehensive description of the skeletal, muscular, circulatory, and nervous systems, and corrected widely accepted mistakes made by Galen centuries earlier. Although astrological and alchemical considerations still managed to appear in the diagnosis and cure of many diseases, improved knowledge of the human body led to better treatment of illnesses and surgical interventions. Bacon's own inquiries into the prolongation of life and the improvement of health made use of disparate sources of knowledge and evidence about the human body.

Four different techniques were combined in the mid-fifteenth century to create what Bacon considered one of the most important technical achievements of humanity: the printing press. First, paper, which superseded parchment, came to Europe from China through the Islamic empire. Printing mills were established in Baghdad and Damascus during the ninth century, in Spain a century later, and reached Italy and England in the late thirteenth century. Second, movable types in ceramic and wooden versions appeared in China in the eleventh century and shortly thereafter in Korea. Johann Gutenberg, a skilled German metalworking artisan, devised metallic movable types representing individual letters of the Roman alphabet, which became widely used in Europe. Third, Gutenberg also developed charcoal and oil-based printing inks that were more permanent than water-based ones. Fourth, the screw printing press, derived from existing wine and linen presses, allowed exerting uniform pressure to print a page and increase the productivity of bookmaking.

Printed books replaced manuscript copies at much lower cost, improved the accuracy and permanence of texts, standardized and codified knowledge, and allowed the large-scale dissemination of religious, political, technical, scientific, and literary writings beyond the confines of universities and monasteries. By 1500, there were more than 1000 public printing presses in Europe producing tens of thousands of books. Illustrated treatises on agriculture, mechanics, metallurgy, medicine, and alchemy circulated extensively, making once jealously guarded information available to a larger number of practitioners.

Technical knowledge, which by the fourteenth century had been accumulating mostly as a result of trial and error and of systematic but nontheoretical experimentation, began to grow and diffuse rapidly. The shortage of labor due to epidemics and increases in living standards spurred innovations to improve productivity. As the economic value of techniques became evident, intellectual property rights emerged in the form of cash payments for inventions and patents conferring a temporary monopoly on the inventor. Filippo Brunelleschi, builder of the cupola of Florence's cathedral, was awarded in 1421 a patent for the design of a special ship to carry construction materials (which nevertheless sank with marble during its maiden voyage), and the Republic of Venice established a patent system in 1474. In 1601, Sir Francis Bacon wrote an argument in favor of granting patent rights:

> If any man out of his own wit, industry or endeavor, find out anything beneficial to the Commonwealth, or bring any new invention which every subject of this kingdom may use; yet in regard of his pains and trave therein, her Majesty perhaps is pleased to grant him a privilege to use the same only by himself or his deputies for a certain time.

The improvement of techniques by trial and error required engaging in production to assess the results of different methods, and the capacity to withstand losses from failed attempts. Benedictine and Cistercian monasteries were effective institutions for this purpose. They combined scholarly pursuits and learning with production and experimentation. The economic surplus generated by monks and laymen working in monastic fields and factories allowed risk-taking and time for reflection. The movement of people between monasteries disseminated technical knowledge.

A vast network of autonomous Benedictine monasteries spanned Europe in the latter half of the first Christian millennium. The *Rule of St. Benedict* established a common set of norms for all of these, covering governance, daily activities, monk behavior, admission requirements, and administrative procedures. Benedictine monasteries emphasized manual labor, cultivated fields, produced energy, had artisan shops, and regularly exchanged information on technical matters. Cistercian monasteries ran factories, employed water mills, used iron ore, produced wine, exploited forests for timber and fuel, cultivated fields and raised sheep, and disseminated metalworking techniques.

Medieval guilds played a major role in the development and diffusion of techniques. Created primarily to defend their interests and improve their fortunes, these associations of artisans, craftsmen, or merchants supervised teaching and certification processes for members, who advanced from apprentice to master craftsmen.

Formal technical training, quite distinct from the traditional universities, emerged during Francis Bacon's time. Sir Thomas Gresham, founder of the Royal Exchange, left a considerable inheritance in 1575 to the City of London and the Mercers Company to establish a technical college. His intention was to provide experienced men without formal academic qualifications access to higher learning. Gresham's will stipulated that three of the seven professorships should be on scientific matters, and that the astronomy professor should also teach navigation. Gresham College opened in 1597, but struggles between the trustees and the professors prevented it from achieving its founder's objective. It became instead a respected academic research institution that hosted the first meetings of the Royal Society.

Francis Bacon recognized the importance of the work of artisans, craftsmen, and practitioners, whose skill and dexterity helped to translate ingenuity and resourcefulness into practical devices. A vastly enlarged and improved repertoire of technical responses began to interact with developments in natural philosophy and the sciences, creating an intellectual climate favorable to the emergence of Bacon's ideas on how to use knowledge to improve the human condition.

Production

Production activities evolved slowly during the first Christian millennium, hand in hand with improvements in the repertoire of techniques. Geared primarily to self-consumption, agriculture was the main economic activity. Food surpluses were traded in towns and cities for manufactured goods. They sustained imperial, feudal, and local authorities that provided security and governance; paid for building cathedrals, palaces, fortresses, roads, and ports; financed wars, crusades, and armies; helped to maintain churches, abbeys, and religious hierarchies; and allowed speculative thought and the arts to develop.

As economies diversified and technical innovations spread, a broader base of production activities provided additional resources to support social undertakings. Infant mortality, short life expectancy, war, famine, and disease kept demographic pressures in check, and population grew slowly during the first millennium AD. Population in Europe doubled from 1000 to 1300 and reached about 70 million, which, together with urbanization, generated pressures to improve agriculture and increase food production.

The bubonic plague (1348–1353) killed about a third of the population in the Eurasian landmass. By the end of the fourteenth century, Europe had lost about forty percent of its population. The plague broke out first in China around 1346, and moved westward through Central Asia, India, Persia, and Egypt, arriving in France through Marseille in 1348. In a few months, it had reached all of France, a year later the rest of Europe, and Russia in 1351. Aided by warmer climate conditions, rats and fleas multiplied and carried the pathogen; crowded towns, palaces, and other closed environments allowed for quick and lethal contagion. Infected people were quarantined to halt the spread of the plague, and with so many workers succumbing to disease, food and other necessities became scarce, leading to price increases, revolts, and repression.

A commercial and financial bourgeoisie of merchants and bankers, different from aristocracy and feudal lords, from functionaries and courtiers, and from peasants and laborers, emerged in European cities starting in the fourteenth and fifteenth centuries. As guilds of merchants and craftsmen gained importance, city authorities awarded them charters and patents that conferred trading monopolies. While this often led to abuses, they helped to ensure the quality of goods and services provided by guild members.

According to historian Ferdinand Braudel, during the fifteenth century, the "exchange economy was an imperfect one … it certainly had not succeeded in joining the total production to the total consumption, for an enormous share of the production was absorbed by the self-sufficient family or village and did not enter the market circuit." A majority of peasants "lived in their villages in an almost autonomous way, virtually in an autarchy," alongside an active and powerful minority engaged with "a market-oriented economy and expanding capitalism began to spread out." Peasant and market economies were not totally isolated from each other but interacted through barter and the transfer of agricultural surpluses. Market-mediated exchanges were still far from fully connecting rural areas, towns, and cities, but they began to organize production, distribution, and consumption in wider geographical areas (Braudel, 1977, pp. 5, 16–17, 23; Wallerstein, 1974, p. 18).

While slow and fraught with peril, long-distance land trade routes and travel had become well established by the thirteenth and fourteenth centuries. Accounts of Marco Polo's travels to China inspired explorers and travelers, and a Southern sea route to the Indian Ocean and Asia helped gain access to lucrative trade that enriched European cities. Christopher Columbus's trips across the Atlantic Ocean and the discovery of America opened up a new continent for Europeans to conquer, providing access to hitherto unimagined riches. Geographic discoveries, contacts with new peoples, and unknown varieties of plants and animals required efforts to interpret what was found in the new lands and stimulated speculative thought.

Improved means of transport led to greater specialization and division of labor between economies in Europe and in other parts of the world. By the end of the fifteenth century, the accelerated circulation of products, services, and ideas configured extensive trade and exchange networks controlled from Europe. Starting in the early 1500s, large amounts of silver flowed to Spain from its American colonies, and then found its way to English, Dutch, and Italian financiers and merchants. In turn, they used it to engage in trade with China, where there was a large demand for silver coinage.

A variety of institutions, some related to incipient state organizations and others to private associations, emerged over time to structure production and service activities. As the geographical scope of trade in goods and services expanded, market transactions encompassed agents outside the community of personal contacts embodying trust relations. Impersonal exchange with strangers demanded new ways of curtailing opportunistic behavior, making market dealings reliable and reducing transaction costs. The proper functioning of markets required well-established property rights, agreement on trading rules, means to validate and enforce contracts, weights and measures standards, and information on the behavior of economic agents. The widespread use of money to facilitate market exchanges demanded stable currencies and institutions to issue metal coins and paper notes. Financial and insurance organizations were created to ease transactions that spanned long distances or occurred over extended periods of time.

Regulation of commerce and finance gave courts a growing role in resolving disputes and required lawyers to argue cases, clerks to keep records and places to train them. During the reign of Elizabeth I, Gray's Inn, where Sir Francis Bacon learned and taught law, was one of the four influential associations of lawyers and judges that instructed aspiring members of the legal profession. Legal and judicial activities often focused on resolving commercial and property disputes, which gave Bacon a close view of the functioning of the English economy.

A fragmented Europe of competing kingdoms, regions, and city-states, each with their respective merchant classes, spurred invention and innovation. As the Baconian Program began to unfold, Europe was poised for an extraordinary expansion and diversification of production and service activities. Over time, these would rely less on techniques obtained by trial and error and more on technologies influenced by or derived from scientific research. No other region of the world was ready to begin linking knowledge, technology, and production in a sustained and systematic manner.

Beyond Europe

Before Sir Francis Bacon's time, several civilizations had reached levels of intellectual, technical, and economic development rivaling and surpassing that of Europe. Many of these had established contact with each other through trade, migration, invasions, and information exchanges, although voyages to America and a sea route to the Indian Ocean would begin only at the end of the fifteenth century. In addition to its own heritage, Europe received and absorbed multiple influences that helped shape the distinct outlook of the Baconian epoch.

Starting in the eighth century, the Muslim Empire put in contact Greek, Roman, Indian, and Persian sources of knowledge with Europe. Islam spread widely through North, East and West Africa, Northern India, Southern China, and the Indonesian archipelago, and Arabic became a lingua franca for merchants and scholars. During the fourteenth and fifteenth centuries, when the importance of the Indian Ocean rivaled that of the Mediterranean, the Islamic Empire controlled trade routes that linked Europe and Asia. Islamic dominance in the Middle East cut Europe off from direct contact with Asia and the Indian Ocean, prompting efforts to find alternative routes that came to fruition when Bartolomeu Dias went around the Cape of Good Hope in 1488.

With a cultural continuity that extended over thousands of years through periods of stability and turmoil, China was an advanced civilization in Bacon's time. Its population doubled from 50 million in 800 AD to 115 million in 1200 AD, when it was about twice that of Europe. In the late thirteenth century, Marco Polo reported China had several cities with one million inhabitants. An ideographic language was developed more than a 1000-years BC, and centuries later it had more than 5000 characters.

From mid-first millennium BC, Confucianism, Taoism, and Buddhism became the dominant schools of speculative thought in China. The philosophy of Confucius valued harmony, justice, humility, and obedience to authority. Focusing on ethical, social, and political issues, it paid scant attention to natural phenomena. Confucianism became the ideology of a powerful centralized bureaucracy selected through rigorous exams, isolated from artisans, and those engaged in practical arts. Incorporating ideas from Taoism and other sources, twelfth-century scholar Zhu Xi proposed a neo-Confucian approach that shed its mystical connotations and favored the study of nature.

Chinese achievements in mathematics included the use of negative numbers, fractions, permutations, and combinations, as well as the development of simultaneous equations and geometrical coordinates that can be expressed algebraically. Deciphering astrological omens was important for Chinese rulers and led to the development of observation instruments, the compilation of astronomical records, and the preparation of elaborate calendars. Not encumbered by Christian conceptions of the immutability of the heavens, Chinese astronomers were able to register and identify the appearance of supernovas.

During the Song dynasty (960–1279 AD), China was the world's technical leader. Food production increased with the introduction of new rice varieties and cultivation methods, and with the extensive use of large-scale irrigation systems comprising reservoirs, canals, and drainage built over centuries. Although not underpinned by theoretical advances, numerous developments in mineralogy, metallurgy, pottery, and chemistry demonstrated the ingenuity of Chinese artisans and workers. Magnetic devices, initially used in the third century BC for divination, geomancy, and for deciding the location of buildings, evolved into the compass and by the twelfth century were used in navigation. Advances in clockmaking included sophisticated water clocks, escape mechanisms, and gears. A seismograph was built in the second century AD, and weather records were maintained over long times. Movable type for printing was widely used in the twelfth century, and an encyclopedia that had more than 900 volumes was compiled in 1403. Chinese advances in preventive and curative medicine included the technique of acupuncture, still used today.

India has a tradition of speculative thought and technical developments stretching back well into the first millennium BC, with Hinduism, Buddhism and, later, Islam, becoming the dominant creeds. Myth, magic, and religion interacted over centuries to configure a complex landscape of beliefs and practices, which included struggles between numerous gods of different types, deities intermingling with humans and demanding sacrifice, elaborate rituals to appease divine anger, cyclic conceptions of the universe, a belief in reincarnation, and four self-contained castes in a rigidly stratified society.

Buddhism emerged in the sixth century BC, when Siddhartha Gautama had a revelation that made him abandon earthly pursuits and devote his life to the search for absolute spiritual liberation. Focusing on individual salvation and following a middle way of moderation, renunciation, and personal sacrifice, Buddhism aimed to break the fateful cycle of reincarnations to attain eternal bliss in the Nirvana. Islam was introduced in the eighth century by trading colonies in the Malabar Coast, reaching Punjab in the eleventh century and establishing the Delhi Sultanate at the beginning of the thirteenth century.

Notwithstanding religious traditions that would not appear to favor rigorous study of natural phenomena, Indian science historian A. Rahman has pointed, "there is evidence of considerable scientific activities during the medieval period. … However, the methods and techniques of acquiring knowledge remained limited to observation and analysis, and the next logical step—to carry out experimentation and develop it as an explicitly recognized technique—never took place" (Rahman, 1972, p. 223). In addition to a rich tradition of medical practice, by the second half of the first Christian millennium, Indian scholars had made advances in astronomy, with detailed records of observations and calendarmaking, and in mathematics, with the proper use of zero, the use of fractions and equations, and geometrical calculations.

Technical advances in alchemy and chemistry included the manufacture of dyes, perfumes, and various mineral salts; the production of herbal compounds and medicines; and the development of accurate weights, balances, and measures. Metallurgical techniques allowed working with copper, iron, tin, gold, silver, lead, and several alloys to produce utilitarian and decorative objects. Agricultural techniques included mixing and rotating crops, tree grafting, the use of astronomical data to guide planting, and elaborate irrigation schemes. Technical improvements were also evident in textile, brick, wine, liquor, and pottery manufacturing.

Maintaining 3000 years of dynastic continuity, Egypt was one of the most advanced ancient civilizations of its time. Speculative thought, techniques, and the organization of production reached high levels of sophistication. Dominated by a pantheistic religion that emphasized the afterlife, Egyptian achievements included the use of a complex hieroglyphic language, well-kept astronomical and hydrological records, elaborate medical practices, the use of mineral and vegetal substances in preserving bodies, and the construction of large temples, pyramids, and cities. Conquered by the Romans in the first century BC, Egypt became part of the Byzantine Empire in the fourth century, before Islamic rule took over three centuries later. The Library of Alexandria, established in the third century BC, became one of the most important ancient centers of learning, where many scholars had access to classic Greek texts and operated through the third century, before it was destroyed by fire.

Southern Africa was the cradle of human civilization thousands of years ago. African societies had to respond to the challenges of a varied and often-hostile environment. Complex divination systems explained natural and social phenomena in terms of causal relations made effective by magic or mythical interventions. Ancestors and the unborn were included in elaborate kinship structures that organized social relations and identities, and endowed rulers with quasi-divine power.

Stimulated by demand for products such as ivory, salt, gold, and slaves, starting in the ninth century, trading routes were established in Northern and Western Africa, and between the East African coast and the mineral-rich Southern Central region. Occupying a large extension in West Africa, the Ghanaian Empire flourished between the ninth and thirteenth centuries. It was followed by the Malian Empire, which lasted about 400 years. Mansa Musa, its most celebrated emperor, reigned from 1312 to his death in 1337 and made Timbuktu one of the leading centers of Islamic learning of the time, where scholars practiced astronomy, poetry, theology, and architecture. A devout Muslim, Mansa Musa made an ostentatious pilgrimage to Mecca in 1324, carrying gold in abundance and with an entourage of thousands.

Searching for a sea route to the Indian Ocean, Portuguese sailors explored the West Coast of Africa in the early fifteenth century, often abducting knowledgeable locals to obtain navigational intelligence. They founded trading posts in Sierra Leone and further south to exchange gold and slaves for textiles and guns. Sailing around the Cape of Good Hope in 1497, Vasco da Gama reached India a year later, allowing Portugal to establish a significant naval and trading presence in the Indian Ocean, where Chinese vessels had dominated decades earlier.

Before the arrival of the Spaniards in America, the Aztec, Maya, and Inca civilizations had achieved high levels of material, social, and intellectual development. The Mayas made progress in astronomy, conceived a heliocentric system by 1000 AD, were able to predict eclipses, and their mathematical skills included the use of zero. As in other cultures, myths codified knowledge regarding agricultural practices, astronomy, and other production activities. They also provided narratives that legitimized rigid hierarchical social and political organizations, with religion playing a major role.

Pre-Hispanic achievements in agriculture and irrigation, architecture and town planning, medicine and public health, metallurgy, textiles, and ceramics suggest high levels of technical development. The sophisticated use of ecosystems at different altitudes, which allowed cultivating a variety of products, testifies to the technical ingenuity of ancient Andean civilizations. Agriculture produced enough food for consumption and storing reserves, making famines infrequent until the arrival of the Spanish conquerors. A rigid theocracy centralized and distributed food surpluses over a large territory, which allowed maintaining priests and warriors, supporting arts and crafts, building irrigation and road systems, and constructing temples, palaces, and cities.

The European conquest of the Americas brought a demographic catastrophe of even greater proportions than the bubonic plague in Europe and Asia. Local populations were overwhelmed by a combination of new diseases and lethal weapons wreaking havoc throughout the Americas. Estimates of survival rates in the Aztec and Inca empires a few decades after the arrival of the Spaniards range from one in four to one in nine inhabitants, while in the Caribbean entire populations were wiped out by smallpox and other diseases. Production and social activities collapsed and were reorganized to serve the interests of the conquerors, and most survivors were forced into servitude in mining, agriculture, and household chores.

Ideas from Other Lands

The unique combination of cultural, political, economic, and social circumstances in Europe during the sixteenth and seventeenth centuries did not emerge in other world regions. Despite significant achievements, non-European civilizations were far from articulating what we now consider as the Baconian Program.

Developments in faraway lands were mentioned in Bacon's books, essays, plays, and correspondence. He referred often to Egypt and Persia, highlighted the development of gunpowder and the manufacture of porcelain in China, and also the fondness of the Chinese for silver instead of gold. He quoted Jose de Acosta's *Natural and Moral History of the Indies* on the movement of tides and winds and mentioned the works of Garcilaso de la Vega on the customs of the Incas. Bacon thought greed was a key motive for the Spanish conquest of Mexico and Peru: "it cannot be affirmed … that it was the propagation of the Christian faith that was the adamant of that discovery, entry and plantation; but gold and silver and temporal profit and glory." He also considered the Incas "had magnificent temples … they had strict and regular justice," and that they "proceeded in a kind of martial justice with their enemies, offering them their law, as better for their own good, before they drew their sword" (Bacon, 2011, vol. 7, pp. 20–23).

Nonetheless, Bacon considered the period between Classical civilizations and his own times as barren of contributions: "only three revolutions and eras of learning can rightly be so called: those of the Greeks, of the Romans, and lastly of us, that is the nations of Western Europe, to each of which barely two centuries can fairly be assigned. The intervening ages of the world were miserable, as far as any bounteous or happy harvest of scientific knowledge is concerned." He was dismissive of the "Arabs or the schoolmen, who in the intervening periods did more to crush science with their numerous treatises than increase the sum of knowledge."

Bacon made extensive use of the ideas and findings of medieval Christian and Islamic scholars, and indirectly of those they had relied on. Was he fully aware and cognizant of these developments? Did he think they were important or not? Regardless of the answer, it is clear that Bacon built his implicit program, directly or indirectly, on foundations laid during the ages he disparaged (Bacon, 1994). Widely read, intellectually restless, and fully immersed in the affairs of the English court, Sir Francis Bacon was well placed to absorb and transcend what was available to the contemporary educated elite of his time. He integrated a large, dispersed, and disjointed body of knowledge and practice into a coherent set of ideas that would, centuries later, be viewed as a long-term program for humanity.

Referring to Isaac Newton in ways that could equally apply to Francis Bacon, British cultural philosopher Stephen Toulmin wondered about the role of the individual in history: "Do the men of any generation take those steps which, in the intellectual climate of their time, are 'ready to be taken'? Or can they leap far ahead of their time, forcing thought along genuinely new and creative paths? … Whether he is a politician or scientist, a man can do in his own time only a job which is there to be done; but there may be many different *ways* in which he can do it" (Toulmin &

Goodfield, 1961, pp. 229–230). There is no doubt that Bacon was the right man, in the right place at the right time to articulate his unique views and implicit program, but this in no way diminishes his genius, industriousness, foresight, and achievements.

References

Bacon, F. (1994). In P. Urbach & J. Gibson (Eds.), *Novum Organum: With other parts of the great instauration*. Open Court.

Bacon, F. (2011). In J. Spedding, R. Ellis, & D. D. Heath (Eds.), *The works of Francis Bacon: Vol. 7: Literary and professional works 2* (Digitally printed version). Cambridge University Press.

Braudel, F. (1977). *Afterthoughts on material civilization and capitalism*. Johns Hopkins University Press.

Galilei, G. (2004). Dialogues concerning two new sciences (1638). In L. Lefaivre & A. Tzonis (Eds.), *The emergence of modern architecture: A documentary history from 1000 to 1810*. Psychology Press.

Gimpel, J. (1976). *The medieval machine: The industrial revolution of the middle ages*. Penguin Books.

Grant, E. (2005). Reason and authority in the middle ages: The Latin West and Islam. In N. Koertge (Ed.), *Scientific values and civic virtues*. Oxford University.

Henry, J. (2002). *Knowledge is power: How magic, the government and an apocalyptic vision inspired Francis Bacon to create modern science*. Icon.

Jardine, L. (2009). *Francis Bacon: Discovery and the art of discourse*. Cambridge University Press.

Quinn, J. C. (2024). *How the world made the West: A 4,000-year history*. Random House.

Rahman, A. (1972). *Trimurti: Science, technology & society. A collection of essays*. People's Publishing House.

Tempier, É. (2010). Condemnation of 219 proposals (T. Williams, Trans.). In A. Hyman & J. J. Walsh (Eds.), *Philosophy in the middle ages: The Christian, Islamic, and Jewish traditions* (3a ed.). Hackett Publishing.

Toulmin, S., & Goodfield, J. (1961). *The fabric of the heavens, The development of astronomy and dynamics*. Harper Torchbooks.

Wallerstein, I. (1974). *The modern world-System I, Capitalist agriculture and the origins of European world-economy in the sixteenth century*. Academic Press.

Chapter 5
Configuring Modern Science

*Knowing '**how**' was starting to become as important as knowing '**why**.' In the course of time, these two ambitions would become ever more similar, as Europe learned more about nature, including its human habitants, the better to command it. The modern world is, in this sense, much like the world envisaged by Francis Bacon.*

Peter Dear (his emphasis) (2009, p. 166)

As Bacon's program began to unfold, scientific research, technological development, and production activities in Europe accelerated their evolution and became more closely intertwined. Against the backdrop of the Scientific Revolution, the Enlightenment, and the Industrial Revolution, advances in any one of these fields fed into the others by providing conceptual tools, experimental devices, and practical challenges, thus creating multiple reciprocal stimuli that spurred further progress in all.

Modern science began to be configured during the seventeenth century, a time of uneasy coexistence of religious and rationalistic approaches to the study and explanation of natural phenomena. Advances in mathematics, improvements in scientific instruments, and systematic experimentation, together with a favorable sociopolitical context, helped to ground and disseminate Bacon's ideas and provided a setting for the gradual unfolding of his implicit program. A brief review indicates how scientific advances during the unfolding of Bacon's program paved the way for the subsequent emergence of science-based technologies.

Mind, Matter, and God

Starting from the awareness of one's own existence ("I think, therefore I am"), French philosopher René Descartes' *Discourse on Method* (1637) laid out rules for rigorous deductive reasoning. Rejecting any role for spiritual forces in natural

F. Sagasti, *Knowledge is Power*, Innovation, Technology, and Knowledge Management, https://doi.org/10.1007/978-3-032-20668-8_5

phenomena, Cartesian dualistic philosophy kept mind and matter apart, and "tried to find in general the principles of first causes of everything which is, or which may be in the world, without considering to the end anything but God alone" (Descartes, 1968, pp. 80–81).

Both Descartes and Bacon saw science as a hierarchically organized cooperative effort to generate "knowledge which is most useful in life, … by which … make ourselves, as it were, masters and possessors of nature" (Descartes, 1968, p. 78). Like Bacon, Descartes also claimed "I have no excessive love of fame," although he probably meant it more (Descartes, 1968, p. 88).

Thomas Hobbes, one-time secretary to Bacon, proposed a materialistic philosophy to explain natural phenomena and human behavior that privileged deductive reason to derive conclusions starting from first principles but left little room for experimental induction in the search for knowledge. For Hobbes "*science* is the knowledge of consequences, and dependence of one fact upon another; … when the like causes come into our power, we see how to make it produce the like effects" (Hobbes, 1963, pp. 85–86).

Robert Boyle, a wealthy natural philosopher, businessman, and theologian with mystical and alchemical leanings, thought the physical world was organized by the "two grand and most catholic principles of bodies, matter and motion" (Cohen, 1985, p. 154). "God gave motion to matter; … and established those rules of motion, and that order amongst things corporeal, which we call the laws of nature" (Boyle, 1725, p. 187).

Seventeenth-century natural philosophers struggled in different ways to provide explanations of the relations between matter and mind. Descartes' dualism, Hobbes' radical materialism, and Boyle's materialistic-theistic conceptions were among the options provided to understand mind–body interactions, as were those provided later by Leibniz, Huygens, and Newton. All of these sought, in distinct ways, to reconcile the material world with mental states and God's existence.

Mathematics, Instruments, and Experiments

Advances in mathematics, together with better instruments that improved observation, measurement, and experimentation, played a major role in the configuration of modern science. They allowed expressing physical laws in the form of equations, facilitated calculations, and led to predictions that could be empirically tested. Experiments and observations, described, communicated, and replicated, established facts and findings on which to build and corroborate theories. Scientific instruments made it possible to conduct new experiments and provided precise measurements for use in mathematical calculations.

Logarithms, probability theory, and calculus were among the key mathematical advances during this time. Logarithms eased arithmetical and algebraic calculations. Probability theory was applied to games of chance, the estimation of life expectancy and, after incorporating objective and subjective components, to personal, judicial, and financial decisions. English statistician and Presbyterian minister Thomas Bayes developed in the mid-seventeenth-century a method to estimate the probability of an event when it was known that in similar circumstances it has "happened a certain number of times and failed a certain other number of times," laying the ground for what is known as conditional probability.[1]

Calculus was independently developed by German polymath Gottfried Leibniz and English physicist Isaac Newton. It provided a powerful tool for the study of natural phenomena by allowing quantitative representations of continuous changes in physical variables. Leibniz devised procedures for determining the maxima and minima of mathematical functions and for working with infinitesimal quantities. Newton developed the method of fluxions, his term for differential calculus, and used it for computations included in his 1687 *Principia Mathematica*.

Systematic experimental science began with the work of a small group of intellectuals who gathered in Oxford in the 1640s and continued their work in London. In addition to Robert Boyle, these included Robert Hooke, inventor, experimenter, and Boyle's assistant; Christopher Wren, architect and astronomer; William Petty, economist and naval reformer; John Wilkins, clergyman, master of Trinity College at Cambridge; and Samuel Hartlib, natural philosopher and Bacon enthusiast. This variegated group of intellectuals credited Bacon with inspiring the creation of the "Royal Society of London for the Improvement of Natural Knowledge."

Robert Boyle and Robert Hooke, two of the most active members of the Society's early days, exemplify how modern science began to take shape. "Since the late happy conjunction of mathematics and philosophy, and the application of them both to matter and the bodies about us, many noble discoveries have been made, all tending to enlarge the understanding and to give us a command of nature," wrote Boyle. He wanted "only to render the expectations of advantages to be received [from a future progress in the knowledge of nature] probable; to do which, is taking a good step towards the attainment of the things themselves, as Sir Francis Bacon well observes" (Boyle, 1725, pp. 1, 117).

Boyle also thought "experimental philosophy may as well advance trades, as an inspection of them promotes their interests … the happy influence they may have on each other is an excellent means to enlarge the empire of mankind" (Boyle, 1725, p. 131). His will endowed a series of lectures that would play a key role in disseminating Newtonian ideas in the following decades (Boyle, 1772, pp. cxxxviii–cxxxix).

Robert Hooke was a gifted experimentalist, astronomer, physicist, surveyor, inventor of mechanical devices, and professor of geometry at Gresham College. Using a microscope he devised and built, Hooke made numerous observations of natural and man-made objects; the drawings in his 1665 *Micrographia* showed, for the first time, details unavailable to the naked eye. A tireless worker despite a frail constitution and a quarrelsome disposition, Hooke built vacuum spheres,

[1] Letter of Richard Price to John Canton (Bayes & Price, 1763, p. 371).

barometers, chronometers, microscopes, telescopes, lenses and prisms, micrometers and surveying equipment for himself and other natural scientists.

Italian experimenter Evangelista Torricelli devised in 1644 an instrument to measure atmospheric pressure. French natural philosopher Blaise Pascal used this device for meteorological observations in the 1650s, and in subsequent decades portable versions of the barometer, as Boyle named it, were used in France for surveying. In the Netherlands, experimenter, merchant, and lens maker Anton van Leeuwenhoek designed, built, and used microscopes to describe protozoa and bacteria, taking the initial steps in the field of microbiology.

Working mostly in France, in 1665–1666, Dutch natural philosopher Christiaan Huygens studied centrifugal forces, gravity, and elasticity, developed a wave theory of light, and published *Horologium oscillatorium sive de motu pendularium* (1673), a treatise reporting on his invention of the pendulum clock. Echoing Bacon, Huygens thought difficulties in the study of physics could not be overcome "except by starting from experience … and then by conceiving certain hypotheses … But even so very much hard work remains to be done, and one needs not only great perspicacity but often a degree of fortune."[2]

The biological sciences advanced mainly through systematic observation. The study of plants and animals progressed from *in situ* traveler descriptions, to collecting dead samples in herbariums and museums, and to the gathering of live specimens in botanical gardens and zoos. English naturalist John Ray established the foundations for modern botany and zoology, developed classification schemes for plants and animals, and was the first to put forward the concept of species based on the capacity to produce offspring.

As the potential rewards of rigorous experimental inquiry became visible, tensions arose between disseminating results to claim priority and keeping them confidential to register patents. Publication became the means of claiming scientific precedence, but secrecy and communication delays made it difficult to unambiguously determine who came first. The budding scientific communities in England and Europe became embroiled in disputes about scientific priority and accusations of plagiarism at an early stage. Research on timekeeping to determine longitude was considered strategic, received military support, and was often shrouded in secrecy; Boyle required his experiment assistants to sign confidentiality agreements; and rival claims by Hooke and Huygens to have invented the pocket watch spring regulator caused lengthy disputes.

Seamlessly integrating observations, experiments, and mathematical formulations of physical phenomena, English polymath Isaac Newton decisively shaped the modern scientific outlook during the second half of the seventeenth century. He formulated the laws of motion and universal gravity, developed theories of light and colors, made astronomical discoveries, and invented differential calculus in parallel with Leibniz. Newton was also interested in alchemy, chronology, and the interpretation of Scripture, to which he devoted substantive time over decades.

[2] Letter to Tschirnhaus, May 18, 1687 (Huygens, 1901, p. 153). See also Bell (1950, p. 210).

Newton showed the same physical laws apply to terrestrial and celestial bodies, with gravity acting at a distance with a force inversely proportional to the square of the distance between their centers. He contrasted mathematical models with empirical evidence, progressively adjusting abstract representations to approach the real world. As he put it in *Principia*, "we offer this work as mathematical principles of philosophy; for all the difficulty of philosophy seems to consist in this—from the phenomena of motions to investigate the forces of nature, and then from these forces to demonstrate the other phenomena" (Newton, 1730, p. lxviii).

Developments in gravity theory, calculus, and the nature of light generated conflicts between Newton, Hooke, Leibniz, and Huygens, and heated debates between their followers. Robert Hooke advanced some thoughts on gravitation in his 1669 "System of the World" lecture at the Royal Society, and in a pamphlet on *An Attempt to Prove the Motion of the Earth from Observations* (1674). He postulated that bodies attract each other through gravitation, a force that diminishes with distance, and that they tend to move in a straight line "till they are by some other effectual powers deflected and bent" (Hooke, 1674). However, he did not provide rigorous mathematical or empirical proof of his assertions. Newton came up with similar but more advanced ideas and backed them with mathematical calculations and data.

Irascible Newton and quarrelsome Hooke maintained tense and conflicting relations for a long time, with disputes on the inverse square law of gravitational attraction, the design of telescopes, and the nature of light. Newton used the phrase "System of the World" in *Principia Mathematica* without referring to Hooke (Newton, 1846; Gribbin, 2003, pp. 158–159). "If I have seen farther, it is by standing on the shoulder of Giants," stated Newton in a February 1676 letter to Hooke. It has been interpreted as recognition of the predecessors to his towering achievements, but also as a reference to Hooke's frail constitution and denial that Newton owed him any intellectual debt (Gribbin, 2006, pp. 222–223; Dolnick, 2011, p. 291).

Leibniz praised *Principia* in a letter to Newton but prompted him to provide a causal explanation of gravity. For Leibniz, the lack of a mechanical explanation of gravity amounted to requiring continuous divine intervention—"a perpetual miracle"—to keep celestial order and the universe running smoothly. The Leibniz–Newton controversy on gravity soured their relation, which broke completely over claims to priority in the development of calculus (Janiak, 2014, pp. xxxiv, 111, 115–116).

Toward Useful Science

The later decades of the seventeenth century saw the beginning of collaboration between science and technical endeavors, for natural philosophers were not averse to engaging in practical matters. Newton was appointed Warden of the British Mint in 1696 and focused on preventing counterfeiting and establishing a proper monetary system. In the late 1760s, Leibniz devised a variable-gear windmill to raise water from mineshafts, which demonstrated its usefulness but broke down too frequently for commercial use, primarily because of the inadequacy of the materials it was built with.

Links between astronomy and navigation exemplified the convergence between scientific inquiry and practical concerns. Naval supremacy required the accurate determination of longitude at sea, which depended on precise celestial observations. The Paris (1671) and Greenwich (1676) observatories were established for this purpose; both of them received public support, the first directly from the French Royal Treasury and the second through the Ordnance Department of the British Crown. However, efforts to develop practical methods of determining longitude at sea would take several decades more, and bear fruit with the development of the marine chronometer in the mid-eighteenth century.

The reconstruction of London after the 1666 fire provided another example of the incipient convergence of natural philosophy and practical pursuits. Christopher Wren, Robert Hooke, Robert Boyle, and other members of the Royal Society were directly involved in redesigning the physical infrastructure of England's capital and many of its buildings. Applying mathematical concepts, Hooke and Wren used an inverted catenary curve as a guide to build the masonry dome of St. Paul's Cathedral. Throughout Europe, mathematical calculations were increasingly used to assist in the construction of water-supply and drainage systems, canals, locks and bridges, as well as fortifications, palaces, and houses.

A lesser-known example was the use of scientific principles in the conservation of forests; according to Kenneth Pomeranz: "Europeans began to … understand the importance for the ecosystem as a whole of protecting trees … this advance owed much to the application of European science—Newtonian mechanics played an important role in understanding how trees recycled water and affected local climates" (Pomeranz, 2000, p. 58).

Mechanical philosophy encouraged breaking down problems and studying their parts, an intellectual attitude that expanded to other activities. William Petty, a founder of the Royal Society and proponent of "political arithmetic," used this approach in his 1654–1656 survey of Ireland. Invoking Bacon's inspiration to preserve "the body politic … both in health and strength" by "knowing the symmetry, fabric and proportion of it," he designed and built surveying instruments, divided tasks, organized teams, carried out fieldwork, registered and verified measures, and methodically reported on the findings, anticipating the division of labor that would become widespread practice a century later (Pacey, 1974, pp. 138–140; Gay, 1995, pp. 344–345).

The Social and Political Context of Rigorous Inquiry

The liberal Anglican political-religious context prevailing in England during the second half of the seventeenth century provided a propitious setting for the configuration of modern science. Devout scientists like Robert Boyle advocated a form of liberal Anglicanism that, according to Margaret Jacobs, "designated science as a unifying force among all moderate Protestants," while assisting "in the integration of the new science into the mainstream of English and eventually European thought" (Jacob, 1998, pp. 7, 60–62). The Glorious Revolution of 1689 that brought William of Orange to the throne consolidated Liberal Anglicanism and helped the Royal Society in establishing a space for independent scientific inquiry into natural and social phenomena. The practical philosophy of the Royal Society helped to develop linkages between scientific inquiry and the expanding commercial and industrial interests of English merchants.

In contrast, Galileo's condemnation by the Inquisition made Catholic Italy and Spain inhospitable to science in the seventeenth century, displacing it Northwards and Westwards to Protestant regions. In places like absolutist France and commerce-dominated Netherlands, incipient scientific communities carved spaces for independent inquiry by stressing the social, economic, and political utility of science. The long and tortuous process of separating science from religion reached an accommodation, more or less on terms that Sir Francis Bacon had anticipated when condemning the "the corruption of philosophy by a combination of superstition and theology" (Bacon, 1994, p. 71).

Occult and spiritual forces were rejected as explanations for natural phenomena. Vitalist and animist notions of a cosmos infused with purpose and intention, inherited from Aristotelian philosophy, were discarded in favor of mechanistic views. The centuries-old and pervasive analogy of the universe as clockwork fostered mechanical explanations of celestial and terrestrial events, and even considering animal and human bodies as complex machines. Ultimate causes receded into theistic disquisitions, and teleological explanations of natural phenomena gave way to purposeless, inanimate matter obeying inflexible natural laws. Asking "why?" became much less important than knowing "how?"

Results of scientific inquiry led to an expansion of the cosmos into the vastly large and the minutely small. The telescope magnified the scale of the observable universe, and the microscope focused attention on the tiny features of the natural world. The discovery of fossils, speculations about the cooling and age of the Earth, and expectations of distant events to come broadened time horizons into the past and into the future, placing humanity in a temporary sliver of cosmic time expanse. The bounds of phenomena subject to human understanding were considerably enlarged and challenged religious traditions. Exploration, trade, colonization, and exchanges with peoples in faraway lands challenged beliefs and enriched the mental landscape of Europeans, prompting accommodations with non-Western cultural ways and practices.

European authors were conscious of the unique circumstances that led to the emergence of modern science and the Baconian Program. Bernard de Fontenelle, a long-lived author and secretary of the French Academy of Sciences, was fully aware of the uniqueness of Europe. His *Conversation on the plurality of worlds* (1686) ended stating "Europe is in possession of a degree of genius which has never extended to any other part of the globe, at least not to any distant part. It is not perhaps able to diffuse itself over a great proportion of the earth at once, and some invincible fatality prescribes to it very narrow bounds. Let us then make use of it while it is in our possession" (de Fontenelle, 1803, p. 150).

Yet, the conceptual changes brought about by modern science remained the province of highly educated scholars and were not commonly accepted among the majority of people. Magic, alchemy, and the occult were pervasive and coexisted with more sophisticated religious and scientific outlooks; even Boyle, Locke, and Newton shared a long-standing interest in alchemy, and Leibniz had mystical leanings. Late seventeenth-century natural philosophers were a minority group in English society. As the *Philosophical Transactions* show, they combined rigorous and worthy experiments with mundane inquiries and outlandish attempts to manipulate natural phenomena. As Simon Shaffer has pointed out, this made the Royal Society "a focus of debate and a target of satire" (Shaffer, as cited in Bryson, 2010, p. 137), and its members were tolerated in a bemused way by the uninitiated.

Utopias, Religion, and Science

The emergence of modern science would be incomplete without an account of the European writers of the sixteenth and early seventeenth centuries who developed a distinct literary form to convey their views on how rigorous knowledge should be used to organize society. Fictional accounts of travelers visiting remote islands described virtuous, well-governed, and prosperous communities, guided by Christian values and informed by philosophical inquiries.

Sir Francis Bacon's *New Atlantis* was not the first utopian work in which science improved the human condition. More than a century earlier, Thomas More's *Utopia* (1516) described an ideal society where natural philosophy, which would later become scientific inquiry, was held in high esteem. *City of the Sun* (1614), written by Italian friar Tommaso Campanella, and *Christianopolis* (1619) authored by Lutheran pastor Johann Valentin Andreae, were published before the *New Atlantis* appeared in 1627, shortly after Bacon's death.

More's Utopians found "great pleasure" in exploring the "secrets of nature" and, in doing so, they also managed to "win the highest approbation of the Author and Maker of nature. ... He has set forth the visible mechanism of the world as a spectacle for man, whom alone He has made capable of appreciating such a wonderful thing." They "think that the investigation of nature, with the praise arising from it, is an act of worship acceptable to God," but are also mindful of the practical aspects of knowledge: "trained in all learning, the minds of the Utopians are exceedingly apt in the invention of the arts which promote the advantage and convenience of life" (More, 1964, pp. 106, 137).

City of the Sun dwellers learned natural philosophy from an early age. One of the three leaders of the city, called Wisdom, was "the ruler of the liberal arts, of mechanics, of all sciences with their magistrates and doctors, and of the discipline of the schools." Among doctors under his purview were experts in astrology, cosmology, arithmetic, geometry, grammar, rhetoric, logic, medicine, politics, and ethics.

Paintings in the walls of this city were used for educational purposes and depicted mathematical figures, metals and minerals, plants, animals, mechanical devices, and instruments. Furthermore, *City of the Sun* people were "certain … a very learned man has the knowledge of governing. … for one cannot know so many arts and sciences thoroughly, who is not esteemed for skilled ingenuity, very apt at all things, and therefore at ruling especially" (Campanella, 2013, para. 39).

Christianopolis has been considered the "culmination of Christian humanist scientism" (Olson, 1982, p. 275). It describes a city and its inhabitants devoted to learning and Christian worship. As in Campanella's *City of the Sun*, one of the ruling triumvirs is in charge of the "sphere of human learning" and supervises a school with departments for grammar, rhetoric, and languages; logic, metaphysics, and theosophy; arithmetic, geometry, and "mystic numbers"; astronomy and astrology; and also, natural science, medicine, history, and ethics. In addition to learning, people of this city dedicated to Christ value highly the work of "clockmakers, organ makers, cabinetmakers, sculptors and masons" and "their artisans are almost entirely educated men" (Andreä, 1916, pp. 186, 221, 157).

"Here in truth you see a testing of nature herself; everything that the earth contains in her bowels is subjected to the laws and instruments of science," states the narrator of *Christianopolis*, adding that "men are not driven to work with which they are unfamiliar, like pack-animals to their task, but they have been trained long before in an accurate knowledge of scientific matters, and find their delight in the inner parts of nature. … Unless you analyze matter by experiment, unless you improve the deficiency of knowledge by more capable instruments, you are worthless." The city has a laboratory "dedicated to chemical science and fitted out with most ingenious ovens and with contrivances for uniting and dissolving substances," and another for physics and biology; a pharmacy that contains "the most carefully selected collection in the world"; and "a place given over to anatomy, that is, the dissecting of animals." There is also a hall dedicated to "mathematical instruments," a "mathematics laboratory," and a large library (Andreä, 1916, pp. 196–200).

The publication of *Christianopolis* was preceded in 1614 by that of *Fama Fraternitatis*, attributed to Andreae and one of the founding texts of the Rosicrucian movement. It describes a secret society devoted to generating, acquiring, and preserving knowledge. There has been speculation that *Fama* may have influenced Sir Francis Bacon's *New Atlantis*, which gave rise to the idea that Bacon could have been a mastermind behind the Rosicrucian movement.

Unfolding on Course

First in England and later in other parts of Europe, by the end of the seventeenth century, modern science had acquired many of its characteristic features: rationally derived hypotheses and mathematical formulations, rigorous observation and experimentation, communication and replication of results, cumulative advance and expectations of continuous progress.

Going well beyond what Bacon had sketched as the scientific method, the contrast between hypotheses, increasingly expressed in mathematical terms, and careful observations and experiments became common practice among natural philosophers. Time, distance, weight, and size began to be precisely measured, treated as variables amenable to mathematical formalization, and inserted into equations that could predict future states to be confirmed empirically. As metalworking techniques improved, the accuracy and usefulness of scientific instruments improved, allowing more exact observations and valuable experiments.

It was accepted that few and simple laws could explain the workings of nature, partly because of the assumption that God operated in the most efficient way. Analytical approaches that divided problems into smaller components were adopted, and simplicity was preferred when alternative theories explained facts equally well. Newton stated this clearly: "as in mathematics, so in natural philosophy, the investigation of difficult things by the method of analysis, ought ever to precede the method of composition. This analysis consists in making experiments and observations, and in drawing general conclusions from them by induction, and admitting of no objections against the conclusions but such as are taken from experiments, or other certain truths" (Newton, 1730, Query 31; Pacey, 1974, pp. 137–140; Galileo, Newton, Leibniz, as cited in Dolnick, 2011, pp. 124–125, 138, 273).

Seventeenth-century techniques advanced rather slowly, primarily through increasingly systematic trial and error. Although there were no significant inventions deriving directly from scientific advances, scientific attitudes began to influence the evolution of technical responses to the challenges of the biophysical and social environments. There was halting convergence between rigorous science and practical endeavors, leading to what British historian of science J. D. Bernal called a "marriage between the craftsman and the scholar" (Bernal, 1971, vol. 2, pp. 384–385).

The idea of progress encapsulated the purpose, direction, and focus of the Baconian Program, gradually lost its religious undertones, and became a secular concept focusing on human improvements. Separating the realms of the divine, where faith ruled, and of the human, where reason reigned supreme, opened a path for humanity to advance by its own efforts.

A variety of formal and informal organizations—scientific academies, observatories, technical colleges, gentlemen's clubs, salons, coffee houses, and public lectures—emerged in the second half of the seventeenth century to complement universities as gathering places for natural philosophers, and to disseminate the results of scientific inquiry. Financed by member subscriptions, the sale of publications, and the occasional gift from wealthy patrons, the Royal Society in England became the leading scientific institution of its time. The *Academie des Sciences* in France, created in 1666, was fully funded by the Royal Treasury; academy members were paid a salary and government priorities guided their work. Both academies published their own scientific journals, the main vehicle to place discoveries and findings on record, and itinerant lecturers gave conferences and performed experiments at public gatherings to spread scientific ideas.

Sir Francis Bacon inspired the creation of the Royal Society and also influenced the orientation of the French Academy. Exchanges of scientific and technical information between leading European scholars became the norm, even when countries were at war. A network of correspondents was set up between academies, universities, associations, and individual researchers, with some key persons acting as hubs. German-born diplomat and natural philosopher Henry Oldenburg, the first secretary of the Royal Society, was a tireless organizer who published many of the letters he received in the academic journal he founded, *Philosophical Transactions*. Right from the beginning, there were tensions between the open dissemination of scientific findings and the control of information for economic and strategic purposes. During the 1667 Dutch and English war, Oldenburg was accused of espionage and was briefly imprisoned in the Tower of London.

In a 1666 letter to Colbert, founding member Christiaan Huygens wrote: "The principal occupation of the Assembly [Academy] and the most useful must be, in my opinion, to work in natural history somewhat in the manner suggested by Verulam" (Dear, 2009, p. 113; Huygens, 1895, p. 95). Even if Bacon's vision of scientific inquiry leading to major improvements in the human condition remained as yet unfulfilled, by the beginning of the eighteenth century, the unfolding of the Baconian Program was clearly on track.

References

Andreä, J. V. (with University of California Libraries). (1916). *Christianopolis: An ideal state of the seventeenth century* (F. E. Held, Trans.). Internet Archive. Retrieved from http://archive.org/details/johannvalentinan00andrrich

Bacon, F. (1994). In P. Urbach & J. Gibson (Eds.), *Novum Organum: With other parts of the great instauration*. Open Court.

Bayes, M., & Price, M. (1763). *An essay towards solving a problem in the doctrine of chances. By the Late Rev. Mr. Bayes, F. R. S. communicated by Mr. Price, in a letter to John Canton, A. M. F. R. S.* Royal Society of London. Retrieved from https://archive.org/details/philtrans09948070

Bell, A. E. (1950). *Christian Huygens and the development of science in the seventeenth century*. Edward Arnold and Company. Retrieved from https://archive.org/details/christianhuygens029504mbp/page/n7/mode/2up

Bernal, J. D. (1971). *Science in history: Vol. 2: The scientific and industrial revolutions*. MIT Press.

Boyle, R. (1725). *The philosophical works of the Honourable Robert Boyle esq.: Abridged, methodized, and disposed under the general heads of physics, statics, pneumatics, natural history, chymistry, and medicine* (Vol. 1). W. and J. Innys. Retrieved from https://archive.org/details/philosophicalwor01boyl/page/186/mode/2up

Boyle, R. (1772). In T. Birch (Ed.), *The works of the honourable Robert Boyle: In six volumes, to which is prefixed the life of the author* (Vol. 1). J. and F. Rivington. Retrieved from https://books.google.com.pe/books?id=LqYrAQAAMAAJ&hl=es&pg=PP11#v=onepage&q&f=false

Bryson, B. (Ed.). (2010). *Seeing further: The story of science, discovery, and the genius of the Royal Society*. Harper Perennial.

Campanella, T. (2013). *The city of the Sun*. Project Gutenberg. Retrieved from https://www.gutenberg.org/files/2816/2816-h/2816-h.htm

Cohen, J. B. (1985). *Revolution in science*. Harvard University Press.

de Fontenelle, B. (1803). *Conversations on the plurality of worlds* (E. Gunning, Trans.). J. Cundee, Ivy-Lane. Retrieved from https://www.gutenberg.org/ebooks/66559

Dear, P. (2009). *Revolutionizing the sciences: European knowledge and its ambitions, 1500–1700*. Princeton University Press.

Descartes, R. (1968). *Discourse on method and the meditations* (F. E. Sutcliffe, Trans.). Penguin Books.

Dolnick, E. (2011). *The clockwork universe: Isaac Newton, the Royal Society, and the birth of the modern world*. Harper Perennial.

Gay, P. (1995). *The enlightenment: An interpretation. The science of freedom* (Vol. 2). Norton & Company.

Gribbin, J. (2003). *Science a history*. Penguin Books.

Gribbin, J. (2006). *The fellowship: The story of a revolution*. Penguin Books.

Hobbes, T. (1963). In J. Plamenatz (Ed.), *Leviathan*. Meridian Books.

Hooke, R. (1674). *An attempt to prove the motion of the earth from observations*. Royal Society of London. Retrieved from https://archive.org/details/bim_early-english-books-1641-1700_an-attempt-to-prove-the-_hooke-robert_1674

Huygens, C. (1895). *Correspondence* (Vol. 6). M. Nijhoff. Retrieved from https://archive.org/details/oeuvrescompltesd06huyg/page/n12/mode/1up

Huygens, C. (1901). *Oeuvres Complètes de Christiaan Huygens* (Vol. 9). M. Nijhoff. Retrieved from https://archive.org/details/oeuvrescompltes01huyggoog/page/n13/mode/2up

Jacob, M. C. (1998). *Scientific culture and the making of the making of the industrial west*. Oxford University Press.

Janiak, A. (Ed.). (2014). *Isaac Newton: Philosophical writings*. Cambridge University Press. Retrieved from https://vdoc.pub/documents/philosophical-writings-shsrfq1u9540

More, T. (1964). In E. L. Surtz (Ed.), *Utopia*. Yale University Press.

Newton, I. (1730). *Opticks: Or A treatise of the reflections, refractions, inflections and colours of light* (4th ed.). William Innys at the West-End of St. Paul's. Retrieved from https://books.google.com.pe/books/about/Opticks.html?id=GnAFAAAAQAAJ&redir_esc=y

Newton, I. (1846). *Newton's Principia: The mathematical principles of natural philosophy* (A. Motte, Trans.). Daniel Adee. Retrieved from https://archive.org/details/newtonspmathema00newtrich/page/n7/mode/2up

Olson, R. (1982). *Science deified & science defied: The historical significance of science in western culture*. University of California Press.

Pacey, A. (1974). *The maze of ingenuity: Ideas and idealism in the development of technology*. MIT Press.

Pomeranz, K. (2000). *The great divergence, China, Europe and the making of the modern world economy*. Princeton University Press.

Chapter 6
Enlightenment, Industry, and Engineering

Francis Bacon, indeed, is a pivotal figure in understanding the Industrial Enlightenment and its impact.

Joel Mokyr

Bacon's implicit program continued to gradually unfold in the eighteenth century, fostering new ways of appreciating natural phenomena, human behavior, social interactions, and the roles of religion, faith and God. As reason expanded its reach and began to inform a broader range of human actions, Bacon's vision of dominating nature through understanding became sharper and more approachable. It influenced the work of intellectuals and inventors who advanced modern science, improved techniques, changed production and transformed society.

The Enlightenment was a loose but coherent movement that championed a materialistic, secular, and rationalistic outlook. It dispensed with divine intervention, viewed human progress as indefinite, and applied the scientific method to an expanding range of natural and social phenomena. Enlightenment ideas influenced politics, religion, ethics, and philosophy; inspired human rights and freedom-of-speech legislation, gave rise to a renewed appreciation of art and literature, and stirred revolutionary movements.

The Industrial Revolution began in England and spread to Continental Europe in the late eighteenth century. Both driving and driven by mechanization and technical innovation, it transformed agricultural into industrial economies, changed the structure of manufacturing and boosted capital accumulation. Improvements in agriculture preceded the Industrial Revolution as higher crop yields, a shift toward market-oriented production, greater investments by farmers and landlords, and a more effective use of labor increased agricultural output and food production, which sustained population growth and released workers for manufacture and industry.

The world economy remained polycentric during the eighteenth century, with Europe accounting for about one sixth of world population and one quarter of global production but slowly increasing its share of world economic activity and wealth. Various parts of the world—England, Scotland, Holland, Flanders, Northern France,

F. Sagasti, *Knowledge is Power*, Innovation, Technology, and Knowledge Management, https://doi.org/10.1007/978-3-032-20668-8_6

Northeast America, Central Japan, and the Yangtze Delta in Central East China—displayed significant economic dynamism at the beginning of the eighteenth century, but only in Britain propitious conditions would lead to sustained industrial growth by the end of the century.

According to American historian Kenneth Pomeranz, the unequal relation that emerged between European powers and their colonial lands "anticipated, even before industrialization, the self-perpetuating division of labor between primary product exporters and manufacturing regions in the modern world" (Pomeranz, 2000, p. 25). As the Baconian Program began to unfold, following Spain's incursion in the Americas (Crosby, 1969) and Portugal's ventures in Asia through the Indian Ocean, Europe benefited from the ecological and natural resources bounty of colonial exploitation:

> In tropical islands ... Europeans were able to observe the relationships among changing land use, climate ... colonial botanists, surgeons, and officials who worked out these relationships learned an enormous amount about how to manage ecosystems from south Chinese and especially south Indian practices, which were in many ways more advanced than their own. ... empire helped Europe erase its technological disadvantage in agroforestry ... providing crucial imports of knowledge along with the import of resources (Pomeranz, 2000, p. 58).

In contrast to what happened in its colonies, the convergence of the Enlightenment and the Industrial Revolution in England led to fruitful problem-solving approaches, and eventually to the widespread adoption of technical innovations. What Nobel Prize economic historian Joel Mokyr called the "Industrial Enlightenment" was characterized by "a belief in the possibility and desirability of economic progress and growth through knowledge. ... a pervasive belief in the Baconian notion that we can attain material progress through controlling nature" (Mokyr, 2005, p. 291).

As a consequence, "the elites of the eighteenth-century West created the attitudes, the institutions and the mechanisms by which new useful knowledge was created, diffused, and put to good use" (Mokyr, 2005, p. 291). The closer links between scientific research and practical pursuits would lead to the emergence of science-based technologies that superseded trial-and-error techniques.

Mathematics and Natural Sciences

The intellectual landscape in Europe during the first decades of the eighteenth century was dominated by the dissemination of Newtonian ideas. John Teophilus Desaguliers, natural philosopher and Royal Society experimenter during Newton's presidency, and Dutch natural philosopher Willem Jacob van Gravesande lectured, wrote books and organized public experiments to disseminate Newton's work. After spending 3 years in London in the late 1720s, Jean Marie Arouet, better known as Voltaire, wrote *English Letters*, a book that made Newton's ideas on the System of the World, gravity, the laws of motion, optics, calculus and chronology available to French and European readers (Voltaire, 1999, p. 67).

Mathematics made significant advances throughout Europe in the early 1700s and would provide the tools for advances in physics and other fields. Working in the academies of St. Petersburg and Berlin, Leonhard Euler made fundamental contributions to differential and integral calculus, number and graph theories, and applied them to astronomy, physics, logic, music and the design of lenses and ships. Italian and French mathematician Jean-Louis Lagrange worked on algebra, analytic geometry, differential equations, calculus of variations, and number theory at the Prussian Academy of Sciences, the French Academy of Sciences, and the École Polytechnique. He helped establish the metric system of units in the 1790s. His "Lagrange points" indicated where to place, 200 years later, artificial satellites in geostationary orbit around the Earth.

New scientific instruments and rigorous data gathering furthered scientific discoveries that would soon find practical applications. Incremental improvements on Hooke's and van Leuwenhoek's microscopes allowed German chemist Andreas Marggraf to verify the identity of various chemical compounds.

Advances in geology, botany and zoology relied on systematic observation and data recording. Mining required information about the location of mineral deposits and detailed geological maps, which led to the development of stratigraphy to identify layers of different rock formations. In the late eighteenth century, Abraham Gottlob Werner, a professor at the Mining Academy of Freiburg, Germany, and English canal builder William Smith, were among the first to provide detailed explanations of geological formations.

Swedish botanist Georges Linnaeus and French naturalist George-Louis Leclerc, Count de Buffon, devised schemes to identify and classify "the three grand kingdoms of nature ...animals, ... vegetables ... and minerals," organized them according to "classes, orders, general, species and varieties" (Linnaeus, 1806, p. 3) and proposed a nomenclature for plants and animals that is still in use.

German-born astronomer William Herschel, who settled in England in the mid-eighteenth century, built large reflecting mirrors that increased the range of telescopes and made visible binary stars and nebulae. Herschel's observations of nebulae linked time and distance: "a telescope with a power of penetrating into space ... has also, as it may be called, a power of penetrating into time past. ... when we see an object of the calculated distance at which one of these very remote nebulae may still be perceived, the rays of light which convey its image to the eye, must have been ... almost to millions of years on their way" (Herschel, 1802, pp. 498–499). His experiments on prisms to decompose light led him to discover what later would be called infrared light, which became an invaluable modern cosmology tool and would later find many practical applications.

Although electrical phenomena had been known for a long time, the first practical device to store static electricity, the Leyden jar, was devised independently in 1745–1746 by Dutch physicist Pieter van Musschenbroek and German jurist and physicist Ewald Georg von Kleist. It became a staple item in most laboratories and was used in public demonstrations and experiments to show the power of electricity. American scientist and statesman Benjamin Franklin described electricity as a fluid, distinguished between positive and negative electricity, demonstrated it can magnetize and demagnetize iron needles, and showed a pointed conductor can draw off an electric charge. Franklin invented the lightning rod, which allowed for safely conducting electric discharges to Earth, and improved the safety of houses and ships during thunderstorms.

During the 1750s and 1760s John Mitchell, Daniel Bernoulli, Johann Lambert and Joseph Priestley suggested electric forces follow an inverse square law, similar to Newton's gravity. Henry Cavendish, English chemist and physicist, provided a mathematical treatment of electricity as a fluid in 1771 and hypothesized that electrically charged particles attracted and repulsed each other "with a force inversely as some less power of the distance than the cube" (Cavendish, 1771, p. 585). Building on experiments by physician Luigi Galvani in Pavia, Alessandro Volta, professor of experimental physics at Bologna, invented the battery in 1799. It produced a continuous current and superseded the Leyden jar, which could only store static electricity, thus opening up new ways of using electricity in chemical experiments, such as separating hydrogen and oxygen in water through electrolysis.

Chemistry made significant advances largely due to more accurate instruments to measure temperature and weight, which allowed a better control of chemical reactions. In 1723 German chemist George Stahl defined chemistry as "the art of resolving mixed, compound or aggregate Bodies into their Principles; and of composing such Bodies from those Principles" (Stahl, 1730, pp. 1, 393–424). French chemist Antoine Lavoisier began experiments that led him to discover phosphorus and sulfur, determine that oxygen fueled combustion, and that air was a mixture of gases. His *Traité Elementaire de Chimie* (1789) gave accounts of his experiments and observations and described "all the instruments and manipulations relative to elementary chemistry" (Lavoisier, 1789, p. 292).

English natural philosopher Joseph Priestley identified alkaline air (ammonia), nitrous air (nitric oxide), marine acid air (hydrochloric acid), and dephlogisticated air (oxygen) during the 1770s and 1780s. His *Observations on a Different Kinds of Air* (1775) began with an epigraph from Bacon's *Instauration Magna*, admonishing to discard ancient "volatile and preposterous philosophies" and approach God's creation "with minds washed clean from opinions to study it in purity and integrity" (Bacon, 2011, p. 132).

English clergyman and botanist Stephen Hales established clear links between chemistry and botany in his book *Vegetable Staticks* (1727). In 1771, Joseph Priestley found that irrespirable air could be restored by the presence of plants. Working in the same laboratory as Priestley, a few years later Dutch physician Jan Ingenhousz discovered photosynthesis, establishing that plants absorb carbon dioxide and produce oxygen.

Medicine found a firmer footing during the eighteenth century, as systematic observation and analysis improved anatomical studies, the description of diseases, and the effectiveness of treatments. American physician David Ramsay described how the medical profession had been "raised from an uncertain conjectural art to the high peak of credit and usefulness," and credited Lord Bacon, whom he called "the father of all modern science," with having "directed physicians to the proper mode of advancing their own profession" (Ramsay, 1801, p. 6).

Many lives were saved as the practice of vaccination against smallpox was brought to Europe and America from Constantinople in the early eighteenth century. Its use spread after Lady Mary Wortley Montagu, the wife of the British ambassador to the Ottoman Empire, had her son vaccinated against smallpox in 1718 and took vaccination to England. Cotton Mather and Zabdiel Boylston used vaccination to reduce the effects of the 1721–1722 smallpox epidemics in Boston, although the practice generated a fierce controversy at the time. Voltaire and the contributors to the Encyclopedia actively campaigned for inoculation; Dutch botanist Jan Ingenhousz was a proponent of vaccination to prevent smallpox, and took to Vienna at the request of Empress Maria Theresa in the 1770s. Ramsay mentioned in his review "the practice of inoculation, is of late so much improved, and simplified, that ... the dangers are now comparatively slight" (Ramsay, 1801, p. 27), and also referred to Edward Jenner, an English physician and member of the Royal Society, who in 1796 inoculated a child with cowpox, a less virulent form of smallpox, and succeeded in preventing his catching the infectious disease.

Theories, experiments, and observations increased the stock of knowledge, making it necessary to collect and organize the rapidly growing amount of information. Using Bacon's scheme to classify knowledge as a start, philosopher Denis Diderot and mathematician Jean Rond d'Alembert published the French Encyclopedia, a monumental work that attempted to codify and disseminate widely the accumulated stock of scientific, technical, historic, and literary knowledge. The first volume appeared in 1751, but the project became mired in controversy, faced religious opposition, and was halted by the courts; the publication of the seventeenth and final volume took place 20 years later. Buffon began his 44-volume encyclopedia *Histoire Naturelle, Generale et Particuliere* in 1742, and worked half a century on it. The Encyclopedia Britannica, modeled on his French counterpart, published its first bound edition in Edinburgh in 1771, after first appearing as a pamphlet in weekly installments.

Human and Social Sciences

As modern physical and, to a lesser extent, biological sciences began to consolidate, the study of man and society began its long, elusive, and still ongoing quest to emulate the precision and predictive power of the natural sciences. Attempts to find some common features of human nature while allowing for distinctions, and a growing interest in how institutions shaped and were shaped by individual behavior, led to early attempts to establish the fields of psychology, sociology, political science, and economics.

Appealing to "the great Lord Verulam's authority ... who, not servilely thinking learning could not be advanced," English philosopher John Locke laid the ground in the last decades of the seventeenth century with his works on human understanding, language, education, religious toleration and government. Interested not in the mind's essence but in how it functioned, he focused on the "discerning faculties of a man, as they are employed about the objects they have to do with" (Locke, 1999, p. 23), and thought "ideas and images in men's minds are the invisible powers that constantly govern them" (Locke, 1881, pp. 6–7).

Neapolitan historian and philosopher Giambattista Vico and French lawyer and political philosopher Charles Louis de Secondat, Baron de Montesquieu, among others, championed the study of social and political issues in the first decades of the eighteenth century. Vico's *New Science* (1725) attempted to make human affairs intelligible, grounding them on experience and history. He contended his *New Science* "will give us the basis of certitude … following the method of philosophizing made most certain by Francis Bacon, Lord of Verulam, but carrying it over from the things of nature … to the civil affairs of mankind" (Vico, 1948, pp. 60–61, 92).

Montesquieu applied ideas derived from natural philosophy to the study of social and political systems. Echoing the work of Newton, in 1748, he compared honor to gravity: "it is with this kind of government [monarchy] as with the system of the universe, in which there is a power that constantly repels all bodies from the center, and a power of gravitation, that attracts them to it. Honor sets all the parts of the body politic in motion, and, by its very action, connects them" (Montesquieu, 1777, pp. 32, 8). His arguments for the separation of legislative, executive, and judicial powers have been highly influential. The statement that "all men are created equal" in the US Declaration of Independence followed Montesquieu's view that "in the state of nature, indeed, all men are born equal; but they cannot continue in this equality: society makes them lose it, and they recover it only by the protection of the laws" (Montesquieu, 1777, pp. 155).

The study of history, practiced since ancient times, acquired its modern form with English historian Edward Gibbon. During the more than a dozen years, he worked on his masterpiece, *History of the Decline and Fall of the Roman Empire* (1776–1789), Gibbon "carefully examined all the original materials that could illustrate the subject," and "always endeavored to draw from the fountainhead; … curiosity, as well as a sense of duty, has always urged me to study the originals" (Gibbon, 1845, pp. 16–17).

François Quesnay, Robert Anne Turgot, and other Physiocrat political economists offered an integrated perspective on how economies function. They viewed land and agriculture as the mainspring of wealth and economic growth, advocated free trade, and sought to remove all restrictions on economic activity. Quesnay's 1750s *Tableau Economique* detailed the flows of goods and money exchanged through national and foreign trade.

David Hume's *Political Discourses,* published in the second half of the eighteenth century, recognized the importance of competition among merchants to reduce prices and expand commerce, considered foreign trade beneficial, and described how the stock of money affected wages and interest rates. Hume also saw a clear link between progress and the political system: "it is impossible for the arts and sciences to arise … among any people, unless that people enjoy the blessing of a free government" (Hume, 1826b, p. 128).

According to Scottish political economist and moral philosopher Adam Smith's treatise *An Inquiry into the Nature and Causes of the Wealth of Nations*, advances in human wellbeing were the result of pursuing individual aims subject to the discipline of impersonal market forces but regulated by moral sentiments and institutions that aligned individual with collective interests (Smith, 1776/2007, pp. 435–436, 438). Attributing to the division of labor "the greatest improvement in the productive powers," he was also aware of the negative consequences of excessive specialization: "the man whose life is spent in performing a few simple operations, … has no occasion to exert his understanding, … and generally becomes as stupid and ignorant as it is possible for a human creature to become" (Smith, 1776/2007, pp. 9–10, 52, 506).

Smith was also fully persuaded of the limitations of rulers: "civil government, … is, in reality, instituted for the defense of the rich against the poor," and wary of the power of businessmen: "the mean rapacity, the monopolizing spirit, of merchants and manufacturers, who neither are, nor ought to be, the rulers of mankind, though it cannot, perhaps, be corrected, may very easily be prevented from disturbing the tranquility of anybody but themselves" (Smith, 1776/2007, pp. 465, 318). His prescient warnings help to understand some features of the current state of affairs.

Philosopher and social reformer Jeremy Bentham sought to apply the inductive method to legislation and moral science, proceeding "from particulars to generals" as "Bacon, … Locke and Newton learnt what they have taught us"(Bentham, 1952, pp. 99). Bentham founded the utilitarian school of political economy, and defined utility as "that property in any object, whereby it tends to produce benefit, advantage, pleasure, good, or happiness, … or … to prevent the happening of mischief, pain, evil, or unhappiness to the party whose interest is considered" (Bentham, 1907, p. 12; Bentham, 1952, pp. 101–102).

Attempts to draw parallels between natural philosophy and human sciences led to comparisons between the achievements of Bacon and Newton to those of leading social philosophers. Scottish philosopher John Millar, a student of Adam Smith, thought "the great Montesquieu pointed out the road. He was the Lord Bacon in this branch of philosophy. Dr. Smith is the Newton" (Millar, 2006, p. 648). Possibly prompted by such comparison, British philosopher Jeremy Bentham aspired to establish solid foundations for the social sciences: "The present work as well as any other work of mine that has been or will be published on the subject of legislation or any other branch of moral science is an attempt to extend the experimental method of reasoning from the physical branch to the moral. What Bacon was to the physical work, [French philosopher Claude-Adrien] Helvetius was to the moral. The moral world has therefore had its Bacon, but its Newton is yet to come" (Bentham, 1952, pp. 100–101).

Technical Progress and the Economy

Science-based technologies were still a few decades into the future, but by the end of the eighteenth century the scientific method was widely accepted and began to inform technical improvements. Rigorous experimentation, with incremental and systematic alterations of one variable after another to observe results, improved the workings of physical devices and the performance of chemical reactions, and identified regularities that led to scientific laws.

Advances in navigation and clockmaking, construction and hydraulics, power generation and transport, iron and steel, and ceramics owed much to systematic trial-and-error experiments. As the eighteenth century advanced, progress in these fields became increasingly dependent on the use of sophisticated instruments, complex machinery associated with mathematics, physics, and to a lesser extent, chemistry.

Sailors had long used astronomical tables to determine longitude, but in the eighteenth century they began to employ timekeeping devices. Prizes established in England and France in the mid-1700s encouraged the design, manufacture, and testing of clocks to establish longitude at sea. English clockmaker John Harrison devised his first marine chronometer in 1735 and received the prize established by the British Parliament in 1772. However, Harrison's chronometer was quite expensive, and it took a decade and a half before Thomas Earnshaw simplified its design, cutting production costs and making it affordable. In 1756 French clockmaker Pierre le Roy invented a chronometer with a new type of escapement and in 1769 he won the prize established by the French Academy.

The development of the chronometer relied primarily on clockmaker skills accumulated over centuries. Nonetheless, in the first half of the eighteenth century, Huygens, Harrison, and other researchers and clockmakers experimented with the thermal expansion of solids and measured the dilation rates of various metals. This led to the construction of pendulums and springs with two metals that expanded at different rates, thus compensating the effect of temperature variations and improving clock accuracy.

Construction provided a fertile ground for linking mathematics and physics to practical endeavors. Building canals, harbors, bridges, roads, locks, water supply, fortresses, palaces, churches, and houses depended primarily on the accumulated experience of skilled craftsmen. Physical science concepts developed by Galileo, Descartes, Hooke, Wren, Newton, and Leibniz, among others, gradually found their place in construction and architectural design, laying the ground for civil engineering to emerge as a distinct profession.

Theoretical and practical advances in mechanics and hydraulics improved the design of buildings and waterworks. Swiss mathematician Daniel Bernoulli established the relations between pressure, density, and velocity in the flow of fluids, and developed the basic principles of hydrodynamics in the late 1730s. Military engineer and scientist Bernard Forest de Bélidor's *La Science des Ingenieurs* (1729) provided detailed instructions to design and construct fortifications and civil works, and his four-volume *Architecture Hydraulique* (1737–1739) subtitled "the art of conducting, elevating and managing waters for the different needs of life," did the same for waterworks.

Water mills remained the main source of industrial power in Europe in the first half of the eighteenth century, and improvements derived from rigorous experiments increased their efficiency significantly. John Smeaton, inventor, civil engineer, and member of the Royal Society, conducted many tests to redesign waterwheels. In addition, Smeaton's experiments with building materials led to the widespread use of hydraulic cement.

The contribution of scientific research methods to the development of the steam engine was one of the first instances of laboratory experiments leading to improved industrial machinery. Following earlier trials done by Christiaan Huygens in the 1670s, French physicist Denis Papin experimented with gunpowder explosions to expel the air out of a cylinder with a piston, allowing atmospheric pressure to drive the piston back. His experiments suggested it was possible to construct a steam-powered machine.

The availability of coal, its low cost and the proximity of coal deposits to manufacturing and consumer demand centers made it an obvious source of energy in England, particularly at a time when forests were dwindling. However, frequent flooding reduced the efficiency of mining operations. English military engineer and inventor Thomas Savery designed the "Miner's Friend," a steam-powered machine to pump water out of deep mines. Thomas Newcomen, a Baptist preacher and iron-worker, improved on Savery's design and his engine was first installed in a mine in 1712.

In 1763, James Watt, an instrument maker at the University of Glasgow, was given the task of examining why Newcomen engines used large quantities of steam. Systematic experimentation allowed him to increase power sixfold, to use a quarter of the fuel of a similar atmospheric steam engine, and to reduce operational costs substantially (Robinson & McKie, 1970, pp. 229–231). In 1775, after obtaining an extension of the patent for his steam engine from Parliament, Watt entered into partnership with businessman Mathew Boulton. They spread risk and took advantage of the technical skills of other manufacturers by subcontracting the production of engine parts. John Wilkinson, a key Boulton and Watt supplier, improved the accuracy of cylinder boring machines, which made engines function more efficiently. In 1781, Watt designed a way to transform the linear movement of pistons into rotary motion and in 1789, invented the "governor," a pioneering speed-regulation device and precursor of all types of feedback devices to control mechanical equipment.

The Watt engine became widely used not only because of its superior technical characteristics, but also due to the business model adopted by the partners. They enticed customers by collecting royalties on the actual use of their engines as measured by the number of piston strokes, for which Watt devised a tamper-free counting machine. To further promote their business, in some cases, Boulton and Watt invested in the mining operations of their clients.

The first steam engines were large and stationary, and worked primarily in mines and factories. As they became smaller, they began to be used in transport. French inventor Joseph Cugnot devised a steam carriage in 1769, Marquis de Jouffroy d'Abbans succeeded in powering a paddle-wheel vessel upstream in the Saone River in 1783, and William Murdoch, a Boulton and Watt employee, built a working model of a steam-powered carriage a year later.

Cloth making was an ancient and well-known craft, in which incremental innovations were made all over the world during centuries. Skilled artisans and craftsmen were responsible for trial-and-error improvements in spinning, weaving, and finishing fabrics. A 1798 petition from the town of Carlisle watch and clockmakers against taxes argued "...the cotton and woolen manufactories are entirely indebted for the state of perfection [of their] machinery ... to the clock and watch makers, great numbers of whom have, for several years past ... been employed in inventing and constructing as well as superintending such machinery" (Thompson, 1967, p. 60).

The machines devised by James Hargreaves, Richard Arkwright, and Samuel Crompton, three English inventors lacking formal education, transformed the textile industry. Hargreaves' spinning jenny mechanized the production of cotton weft, Arkwright's water-frame spinner used rollers to speed and improve the manufacturing of sturdier and more versatile warp, and Crompton's mule combined Hargreaves and Arkwright's designs, allowing better control of the process and was able to spin finer, more expensive threads.

As in textile manufacturing, improvements in iron and steel production were largely a result of trial and error. In 1709, Abraham Darby, a Quaker metalworker, substituted wood charcoal for coke obtained from coal in iron smelting. His son Abraham Darby II improved the process three decades later by carefully selecting ores with fewer impurities and better controlling the blast furnace. Progress in ironworking allowed the production of the mechanical parts with strict tolerances required for steam engine manufacturing.

In contrast with the empirical approach of English iron makers, Antoine Ferchault de Reaumur, a member of the French Academy of Sciences, experimented with iron and steel to determine their composition and properties. In 1722, he published *L'art de convertir le fer forge en acier*, a state-of-the-art manual, and won a prize of 12,000 livres per year for his pioneering studies on converting iron into steel.

Aiming to imitate and substitute Chinese porcelain, European artisans improved ceramics production in the early eighteenth century. Delft and Dresden were among the cities where white-and-blue porcelain was produced using secret materials and processes. England caught up and surpassed the Continent by the mid-eighteenth century, when Josiah Wedgwood started his first pottery factory in Staffordshire. In 1769, Wedgwood opened Etruria Works, one of the most efficient factories of its time, where he continued to innovate in product design, raw materials, production methods, and factory organization.

Wedgwood adopted the division of labor advocated by Adam Smith, emphasized quality control, trained and paid well his workers, and conducted experiments to identify the most suitable inputs, improve furnaces, and reduce impurities. He also pioneered retailing and marketing innovations, including the endorsement of royal patrons, well-arranged displays of dinnerware, printed catalogs, free delivery of goods, money-back guarantees, traveling salesmen and periodic sales at reduced prices.

An overview of developments during the Industrial Revolution indicates that experienced artisans, craftsmen, and practical engineers were responsible for the majority of technical innovations made in the eighteenth century. Improvements in clock making, construction, waterworks, metalworking, steam engines, iron, and ceramics did not directly arise out of scientific research, but rather from systematic experimentation. As science historian J. D. Bernal put it, "until the end of the eighteenth-century science drew far more from industry than it could yet give back" (Bernal, 1971, p. 491).

Engineering, Growth and Social Transformations

As technical improvements broadened production possibilities, lowered costs, and helped satisfy the demand for more and better-quality goods, economies and societies experienced profound transformations. During the eighteenth century, the annual growth rate of industrial output in England more than doubled to about 2%. In most of Europe, population and life expectancy increased, working and middle classes expanded, incomes and consumption grew, and urbanization and migration to cities intensified. Luxury consumption stimulated both imitation and product differentiation, prompting Hume to justify "the increase and consumption of all the commodities, which serve to the ornament and pleasure of life" (Hume, 1826a, pp. 307, 312).

The factory system transformed small cottage industries, in which artisans owned their equipment, into large mass-production factories with salaried workers, and with machinery and buildings owned by industrialists. This changed the interactions between workers, financers, merchants, suppliers, and consumers of industrial goods; altered social relations, family structure, and conceptions of work, leisure and the good life; and also increased the role of the market in resource allocation.

Changes in the conception of time accompanied the transformation of work patterns. Fixed working hours and the use of mechanical clocks to control attendance modified the centuries-old habits of task-oriented peasant agriculture and home manufacturing, leading to frequent misunderstandings and conflicts between workers, supervisors, and factory owners.

Institutional innovations underpinned the expansion of industrial and commercial ventures. According to Peter Gay, "the same practical philosophy that produced mechanical innovations produced the institutions that made their widespread use feasible and profitable. The factory, the minute division of labor, industrial discipline for workers and managers, improvements in credit and transport were all inventions as deliberate and rational as the steam engine or the flying shuttle" (Gay, 1995, p. 10). Falling transport costs and expanding markets boosted trade and demand for manufactured goods, increasing competition and pressures to improve organization, techniques, and productivity.

Nonetheless, in its early stages, the Industrial Revolution was not a widespread movement. Newcomers using more efficient and less skill-intensive techniques threatened both owners and experienced workers, which made older and independent manufacturers resist technical and organizational innovations. Wool spinning and weaving devices, the flying shuttle, power looms, and mechanical sawmills generated hostility, riots, and arson from spinners, weavers, and woodworkers. Luddite protesters following the supposed example of Leicester weaver Ned Ludd, who, enraged, destroyed two stocking frames in 1779, rioted in the English Midlands in the early nineteenth century. As Mokyr put it, "technological advance in the period of the Industrial Revolution was a minority affair; most of the entrepreneurs of the time were not like Boulton and Wedgwood and had no knowledge or interest in science or even innovation" (Mokyr, 2005, p. 301).

Formal technical education was not a dominant feature of the Industrial Revolution, which relied more on apprenticeship and learning-by-doing, but part-time training for mechanical skills became gradually available and popular. Toward the end of the eighteenth century, engineering became a distinct profession and rigorous discipline, requiring knowledge of advanced mathematics. Professional engineers built roads, ports, canals, bridges, water supply, fortresses, and buildings of all types. They were also in charge of designing and operating increasingly complex machinery to provide new sources of energy, substitute human labor, improve accuracy in manufacturing, and undertake tasks beyond the capabilities of the human body.

The teaching and practice of engineering, which involved conducting mechanical, physical, and chemical experiments, was institutionalized in the second half of the eighteenth century and became widespread in the following decades. The first civil engineering school, the *École Nationale des Ponts et Chaussées*, was established in Paris in 1747. Mining academies were established in Germany in the 1760s and 1770s, and the Smeatonian Club for Engineers was founded in 1771 in London. The French *Conservatoire des Arts et Metiers* was established in 1794 as a museum of science and technology to keep models of inventions. The same year saw the creation of the *Ecole Polytechnique*, which quickly became the elite school of France, training not only highly qualified engineers and scientists, but also the political elite.

Benjamin Thompson, Count Rumford, drew a proposal for creating the Royal Institution of Great Britain with the purpose of "diffusing the knowledge, and facilitating the general introduction, of useful mechanical inventions and improvements; and for teaching, by courses of philosophical lectures and experiments, the application of science to the common purposes of life" (James, 2000, p. 3). The Royal Institution was founded in 1799 at the London house of Joseph Banks, President of the Royal Society, with 58 wealthy patrons providing the initial funding. During the first half of the nineteenth century, the Royal Institution hosted the most important chemical and electrical research laboratories and became the institutional base of leading scientists such as Humphry Davy and Michael Faraday.

Other institutional innovations included standardized weight and measures to facilitate research, production, and trade, prizes to stimulate and reward inventors, and a strengthened patent system to protect intellectual property. The design of the universal metric system in revolutionary France during the 1790s, and its gradual adoption by other countries, addressed the lack of standard measures of length, area, weight, and volume, among others.

The increasingly visible convergence of science, technique, and production, which Bacon anticipated would improve the human condition, was clearly articulated by David Hume in 1752: "industry, knowledge and humanity are linked together by an indissoluble chain, [they] are not advantageous in private life alone; they diffuse their beneficial influence on the public, and render the government as great and flourishing as they make individuals happy and prosperous" (Hume, 1826a, pp. 306, 307). Coupled with the expansion and consolidation of capitalism, these new technologies would reshape production, economy, and society, and lay the ground for the deliberate deployment of the Baconian Program a century later.

Articulating Bacon's Implicit Program

As the eighteenth century advanced, the scientific method and the experimental verification of theories became standard practice in the study of natural and social phenomena. Rigorous research was gradually put at the service of practical ends, human progress was seen as indefinite and inexorable, and the place of humanity at the center of creation unequivocally restated. New institutional arrangements were devised to foster knowledge generation, dissemination, and utilization.

Increased literacy and the availability of printed material broadened access to ideas, opinions, and sources of knowledge. Encyclopedias, books, pamphlets, and newspapers reached an increasingly literate public, and publishers, literary societies, and lending libraries help them circulate widely. In parallel with the spread of literacy, education became an important pursuit for the middle and upper classes, and also a matter of public policy. Philosophers like Locke and Rousseau wrote extensively on how to shape young minds through education. Frederick the Great of Prussia made education of all children compulsory in 1769, established teacher-training programs, provided public funding for primary education, regulated school activities, and standardized exams.

Discoveries, innovations, and continuous change brought uncertainty and exhilaration, shaking firmly held beliefs. Looking back at the eighteenth century, in 1798, Thomas Malthus listed some of the forces that shaped the spirit of the age: "the great and unlooked for discoveries that have taken place in late years in natural philosophy, the increasing diffusion of general knowledge from the extension of the art of printing, the ardent and unshackled spirit of inquiry that prevails throughout the letter and even unlettered world, the new and extraordinary lights that have been thrown on political subjects which dazzle and astonish the understanding" (Malthus, 1798, p. 1).

A more effective secular and rational outlook gained ground over occult, spiritual, or religious explanations of natural and social phenomena. Divine providence faded from the scene, particularly for the learned elites, and faith in God as ultimate and incomprehensible cause was superseded by faith in science, a source of provisional but continuously improving understanding of nature and society. Humanity was the protagonist of its own advancement; progress became a human responsibility, not a divine gift.

The separation of knowledge from faith cleared the ground for scientific inquiry to advance without bounds. Reason offered theoretical explanations of natural phenomena; experiments provided the empirical evidence to accept or reject them. Standardized measuring units, more accurate observations, new scientific instruments, and meticulous research procedures helped to consolidate modern experimental science.

The replication of experimental results by other scientists became the way to corroborate findings and establish scientific facts, and as Malthus put it, "it is an acknowledged truth in philosophy that a just theory will always be confirmed by experiment" (Malthus, 1798, p. 2). Knowledge was seen to multiply and accumulate indefinitely. Even the apparently useless scientific advances were seen to eventually yield practical benefits, as Condorcet stated in a 1781 letter to d'Alembert: "one sees in the sciences many brilliant theories which have remained unapplied for a long time suddenly becoming the foundation of most important applications" (Condorcet, as cited in Kline, 1972, pp. 623–624).

Sharing research results to be replicated and confirmed by other scientists, and publishing to obtain recognition and establish priority, became widespread among the members of increasingly internationalized scientific communities. The idea that knowledge is a public good captures the spirit prevailing at this time, which Thomas Jefferson articulated well: "if nature has made any one thing less susceptible than all others of exclusive property, it is the action of the thinking power called an idea, … He who receives an idea from me, receives instruction himself without lessening mine; as he who lights his taper [candle] at mine, receives light without darkening me" (Jefferson, 1813, para. 4).

Shorn of its Millenarian overtones and religious underpinnings, the idea of progress, of continuous material and moral improvements in the human condition, integrated the purpose, direction, and focus of the Baconian Program. For Turgot, it was clear that "already Bacon has traced out for posterity the road which it must follow," and that the "host of facts, experiments, instruments, and ingenious exercises which the practice of the arts has accumulated over centuries" (Turgot, 2011, p. 341) provided a foundation for humanity to advance indefinitely. He had an unshakable faith in the goodness of humanity: "everything which draws men away from their present condition, and everything which puts varied scenes before their eyes, extends the scope of their ideas, enlightens them, stimulates them, and in the long run leads them to the good and the true, toward which they are drawn by their natural bent" (Turgot, 2011, p. 357).

Turgot thought that government could help advance economic growth "by means of education, … by encouraging the research of men of science and craftsmen who tend to perfect the craft, and, above all, by extending the knowledge of the practical processes which greed seeks to keep as so many secrets" (Turgot, 2011, p. 250).

Condorcet agreed with Turgot and helped to give definite shape to the Enlightenment idea of progress, particularly in his *Outlines of an Historical View of the Progress of the Human Mind*, written while in hiding from French revolutionary opponents a few months before he died in prison. For Condorcet, "the moral goodness of man … is, like all his other faculties susceptible of an indefinite improvement." He fully expected that "the human race will be meliorated by new discoveries in the sciences and in the arts, and, as an unavoidable consequence, in the means of individual and general prosperity; by farther progress in the principles of conduct, and in moral practice; and lastly, by the real improvement of our faculties, moral, intellectual and physical." Condorcet anticipated there would come a "moment in which the Sun will observe in its course free nations only, acknowledging no other master than their reason; in which tyrants and slaves, priests and their stupid or hypocritical instruments, will no longer exist but in history and upon the stage" (Condorcet, 1802, pp. 211, 216, 233).

Diderot's 1755 article for the Encyclopedia used almost the same words as Bacon to underscore the central place of humanity in the order of things: "if we banish man, the thinking or contemplating being from the face of the earth, this moving and sublime spectacle of nature will be nothing more than a sad and mute scene. The universe will cease to speak; silence and night will seize it. Everything will be changed into a vast solitude where unobserved phenomena take place obscurely, unobserved. It is the presence of man which makes the existence of beings meaningful" (Condorcet, as cited in Gay, 1995, p. 162).

Geologist James Hutton expressed a similar view in his 1788 *Theory of the Earth*: "the globe of this earth is evidently made for man. He alone, of all the beings which have life upon this body, enjoys the whole and every part; he alone is capable of knowing the nature of this world, which he thus possesses in virtue of his proper right; and he alone can make the knowledge of this system a source of pleasure and the means of happiness" (Hutton, 1788, p. 8).

Major institutional changes accompanied the unfolding of Bacon's program during the eighteenth century. Universities were joined by numerous scientific academies, technical schools, research institutions, museums, botanical gardens, publishing ventures, public libraries, lecture halls, coffee houses, and informal societies to create a rich and diverse array of organizations devoted to the generation and dissemination of knowledge.

Scientific academies spread through Europe rapidly during the eighteenth century. They gathered scientists, published journals, organized lectures, conducted experiments, arranged demonstrations, and awarded prizes. The Royal Prussian Academy of Sciences was established in 1700 and Leibniz was appointed as its first president. Similar institutions were created in St. Petersburg, Dublin, Edinburgh, Stockholm, Copenhagen, Göttingen, and Munich in the following decades. The publication of scientific journals, which had replaced books as the main vehicle for reporting research results, was one of the main tasks of these academies. The number of journals grew at a rapid pace and increased tenfold during the eighteenth century to reach about one hundred in 1800.

Several of these academies received official support, particularly when engaging in studies and research that required extensive fieldwork and the mobilization of large-scale resources. Astronomical observations from distant lands, attempts to establish longitude at sea accurately, modern mapmaking and botanical expeditions relied on centralized support of science and technology, often channeled through scientific academies. In contrast with James I, who ignored Francis Bacon's pleas for research support, King George III agreed to fund the construction and running costs of Herschel's forty-foot-long, five feet in diameter, reflective telescope, the largest in the world, and appointed him his personal astronomer and telescopemaker.

Informal societies gathered intellectuals and practitioners, particularly from industry, to discuss matters of mutual interest. The Lunar Society, established in Birmingham in 1766, was a group of progressive businessmen, intellectuals, and scientists who met regularly during the last decades of the eighteenth century. It had among its members Mathew Bolton, James Watt, Joseph Priestley, Josiah Wedgwood, John Wilkinson, and Benjamin Franklin as corresponding member. Some of these were also members of the Royal Society, which put them in contact with the leading natural scientists and allowed them to publish in its *Transactions*.

The Industrial Revolution gave rise to the first of several long waves of economic growth that would regularly intertwine the evolution of techniques, and later of science-based technologies, with the transformation of production activities. Technical and technological innovation and diffusion played a key role in the dynamics of these long-term fluctuations of economic activity.

At the turn of the nineteenth century, the soundness and validity of Bacon's ideas were reaffirmed by leading intellectuals and acknowledged by society at large. As the implicit Baconian Program would continue to unfold during the nineteenth century, the closer links between scientific research and practical pursuits led to the emergence of science-based technologies that superseded trial-and-error techniques. Coupled with the expansion and consolidation of capitalism, these new technologies reshaped production, economy, and society, and laid the ground for the deliberate deployment of Bacon's program.

References

Bacon, F. (2011). In J. Spedding, R. Ellis, & D. D. Heath (Eds.), *The works of Francis Bacon: Vol. 5: Translations of the philosophical works 2* (Digitally printed version). Cambridge University Press.

Bentham, J. (1907). *An introduction to the principles of moral and legislation*. Clarendon Press. Retrieved from http://oll.libertyfund.org/titles/278

Bentham, J. (1952). The philosophy of economic science. In W. Stark (Ed.), *Jeremy Bentham's economic writings. Critical edition based on his printed works and unprinted manuscripts* (Vol. 1, pp. 79–119). George Allen & Unwin.

Bernal, J. D. (1971). *Science in history; Vol. 2: The scientific and industrial revolutions*. MIT Press.

Cavendish, H. (1771). An attempt to explain some of the principal phænomena of electricity, by means of an elastic fluid. *Philosophical Transactions of the Royal Society of London, 61*, 584–677. https://doi.org/10.1098/rstl.1771.0056

Condorcet, J.-A.-N. (1802). *Outlines of an historical view of the progress of the human mind*. J. Frank.

Crosby, A. W. (1969). *The Columbian exchange, biological and cultural consequences of 1492*. Greenwood Press.

Gay, P. (1995). *The enlightenment: An interpretation. The science of freedom* (Vol. 2). Norton.

Gibbon, E. (1845). *The history of the decline and fall of the Roman Empire*. Christian Classics Ethereal Library. Retrieved from https://www.ccel.org/ccel/g/gibbon/decline/cache/decline.pdf

Herschel, W. (1802). Catalogue of 500 new nebulae, nebulous stars, planetary nebulae, and clusters of stars; with remarks on the construction of the heavens. *Philosophical Transactions of the Royal Society, 92*, 477–528.

Hume, D. (1826a). Essays II: Of refinement in the arts. In *The philosophical works of David Hume* (Vol. 3, pp. 302–316). Adam Black and William Tait. Retrieved from https://oll.libertyfund.org/titles/hume-the-philosophical-works-of-david-hume-vol-3-essays-moral-political-and-literary-1828-ed

Hume, D. (1826b). Essays: Moral, political, and literary. Part I (1742). In *The philosophical works of David Hume* (Vol. 3). Adam Black and William Tait. Retrieved from https://oll.libertyfund.org/titles/hume-the-philosophical-works-of-david-hume-vol-3-essays-moral-political-and-literary-1828-ed

Hutton, J. (1788). *Theory of the earth*. Sacred Texts. Retrieved from https://sacred-texts.com/earth/toe/index.htm

James, F. A. J. L. (2000). *Guides to the Royal Institution of Great Britain 1: History*. Royal Institution of Great Britain. Retrieved from https://www.google.com/url?sa=t&source=web&rct=j&opi=89978449&url=https://www.researchgate.net/profile/Frank_James2/publication/265521966_Guides_to_the_Royal_Institution_of_Great_Britain_1_HISTORY/links/55097f020cf2d7a2812ce3ed/Guides-to-the-Royal-Institution-of-Great-Britain-1-HISTORY.pdf&ved=2ahUKEwij07auyIiOAxWZFLkGHRdEES4QFnoECB0QAQ&usg=AOvVaw22LvlcViXlCSHb5lYiswwg

Jefferson, T. (1813, August 13). *Thomas Jefferson to Isaac McPherson*. Founders Online, National Archives. Retrieved July 7, 2025, from https://founders.archives.gov/documents/Jefferson/03-06-02-0322

Kline, M. (1972). *Mathematical thought from ancient to modern time*. Oxford University Press.

Lavoisier, A. L. (1789). *Traité élémentaire de chimie: Présenté dans un ordre nouveau et d'après les découvertes modernes; avec figures*. A Paris, Chez Cuchet, libraire, rue et Hôtel Serpente. Retrieved from https://archive.org/details/traitlmentairede01lavo

Linnaeus, C. (1806). *A general system of nature: Through the three grand kingdoms of animals, vegetables, and minerals, systematically divided into their several classes, orders, genera, species, and varieties, with their habitations, manners, economy, structure, and peculiarities*. Printed for Lackington, Allen. Retrieved from https://archive.org/details/generalsystemna5linn

Locke, J. (1881). *Conduct of the understanding*. Clarendon Press. Retrieved from https://archive.org/details/lockesconductofu00lock

Locke, J. (1999). In P. H. Nidditch (Ed.), *An essay concerning human understanding*. The Pennsylvania State University.

Malthus, T. (1798). *An essay on the principle of population*. J. Johnson. Retrieved from https://math.uchicago.edu/~shmuel/Modeling/Malthus,%20An%20essay%20on%20the%20principle%20of%20population.pdf

Millar, J. (2006). In D. R. Smith & M. S. Philips (Eds.), *An historical view of the English government: From the settlement of the Saxons in Britain to the revolution in 1688*. Liberty Fund. Retrieved from https://oll.libertyfund.org/titles/phillips-an-historical-view-of-the-english-government#lfMillar_label_634

Mokyr, J. (2005). The intellectual origins of modern economic growth. *The Journal of Economic History, 65*(2), 285–351.

Montesquieu, C. L. D. S. (1777). *The complete works of M. de Montesquieu: Vol. 1: The spirit of laws*. T. Evans. Retrieved from https://oll.libertyfund.org/titles/montesquieu-complete-works-4-vols-1777

Pomeranz, K. (2000). *The great divergence, China, Europe and the making of the modern world economy*. Princeton University Press.

Ramsay, D. (1801). *A review of the improvements, progress and state of medicine in the XVIIIth century: Read on the first day of the XIXth century, before the Medical Society of South-Carolina, in pursuance of their vote, and published at their request*. Printed by W.P. Young. Retrieved from https://collections.nlm.nih.gov/catalog/nlm:nlmuid-2568009R-bk

Robinson, E., & McKie, D. (Eds.). (1970). James Watt letter to John Robinson. In *Partners in science* (pp. 229–231). Harvard University Press.

Smith, A. (1776/2007). *An inquiry into the nature and causes of the wealth of nations*. Harriman House.

Stahl, G. E. (1730). *Philosophical principles of universal chemistry*. Printed for J. Osborn and T. Longman. Retrieved from https://archive.org/details/philosophicalpr00shawgoog/page/n4/mode/2up

Thompson, E. P. (1967). Time, work-discipline, and industrial capitalism. *The Past and Present Society, 38*. Retrieved from http://www.jstor.org/stable/649749

Turgot, A. R. J. (2011). In D. Gordon (Ed.), *The Turgot collection*. Ludwig von Mises Institute. Retrieved from https://cdn.mises.org/The%20Turgot%20Collection%20Writings,%20Speeches,%20and%20Letters%20of%20Anne%20Robert%20Jacques%20Turgot,%20Baron%20de%20Laune_2.pdf

Vico, G. (1948). *New science* (T. G. Bergin & M. H. Fish, Trans.). Cornell University Press.

Voltaire. (1999). In N. Cronk (Ed.), *Letters concerning the English nation*. Oxford University Press. Retrieved from https://books.google.gy/books?id=E6z1uvRf8psC&printsec=frontcover&source=gbs_ge_summary_r&cad=0#v=onepage&q&f=false

Chapter 7
Science-Based Technologies and Socioeconomic Transformations

We are living at a period of most wonderful transition ...
science discovers
the laws of power, motion, and transformation:
industry applies them to the raw mater.

Prince Albert Of Saxe-Coburg and Gotha (1849)

Modern large-scale industry is everywhere demolishing national barriers
and increasingly blurring local peculiarities of production, society and national character among all peoples.

Karl Marx and Frederick Engels (1850)

The unfolding of the Baconian Program accelerated during the nineteenth century. Hand-in-hand with the worldwide spread of capitalism and the consolidation of an international division of labor, its main features became increasingly visible as the pursuit of science became an established profession, research results led to practical applications, and science-based technologies gave rise to entirely new economic activities. A large and growing cast of leading, supporting, and character actors began to crowd the knowledge stage, while a progressively denser plot of interdependent events made it difficult for them to appreciate the full scale and enormous impact of scientific and technological advances.

Members of the emerging scientific and engineering communities of the early nineteenth century had at their disposal new mathematical procedures and tools, observation and measuring instruments, systems of units and catalogs of findings to generate, accumulate, retrieve, and apply knowledge. The growing variety of conceptual and empirical methods of inquiry increased their Baconian power to interrogate and dominate nature through understanding. As the century wore on, technologies developed through rigorous experimentation, incorporated research results, and replaced or upgraded trial-and-error techniques. The unfolding of Bacon's program ceased to be mostly a British and French cross-channel affair, spreading first to Germany, other European countries and the United States, and later a more widely but attenuated occurrence to other regions.

F. Sagasti, *Knowledge is Power*, Innovation, Technology, and Knowledge Management, https://doi.org/10.1007/978-3-032-20668-8_7

Advancing the transition from technique to technology, during the nineteenth century, trial and error gave way to rigorous experimentation in industry, mining, agriculture, transport, communications, medicine, and many other fields. Engineers and inventors, who combined theoretical and practical knowledge of how things worked and how to design all kinds of machinery and equipment, would become the leading exponents of the Baconian ideal of improving the human condition through the power of knowledge.

Reshaping the World Economic and Social Context

The transition from unfolding to deliberate deploying of the Baconian Program took place at a time when the Enlightenment, the French Revolution, American Independence, colonial ventures, institutional reforms, and the spread of capitalism had created a setting propitious for the accumulation of wealth and knowledge. Writing in 1845, German polymath Friedrich Engels popularized the phrase "industrial revolution" to characterize "the history of English industrial development in the past sixty years, a history which has no counterpart in the annals of humanity" (Engels, 1845/2020, p. 15).

As American historian and philosopher Laura Snyder put it: "It was a time of great change and great optimism in London. By the summer of 1815 the long war against France had finally ended and Britain was a peace, with energy and resources to spending its own growth and modernization" (Snyder, 2012, p. 59). During what British historian Eric Hobsbawm called "the long nineteenth century" that extended to the beginning of World War I, science and technology became the pillars of national economic growth for European nations and the United States.

As an indication of the newly acquired prominence of Europe, in 1820, Asia accounted for about 60% of the world's Gross Domestic Product, Europe for 27%, and other regions the remaining 14%. By the end of the century, the share of Asia more than halved to 28%, while that of Europe increased to 39%, and that of other countries, including primarily the United States, more than doubled to 32%.

During this period, England, which had the highest growth rate of industrial output in the world (2.5–3.0%), together with France, Germany and, later the United States, was the leading country in the unfolding and subsequent deployment of Bacon's program. Others were left behind, although Japan made a strenuous effort to catch up with its Western counterparts toward the end of the nineteenth century (Osterhammel, 2014, p. 239). The extent to which the introduction of new industrial techniques and technologies rebalanced world economic power is illustrated by some remarks by English industrialist and social reformer Robert Owen, who calculated that between the 1790s and 1850s, the price of a yard of cotton cloth manufactured using water and steam power went down a staggering 60 times, wiping out highly skilled local producers in colonial India (McNeill, 1980, p. 16).

In spite of these differences, material life standards improved noticeably in most regions of the world. Newly consolidated States began to provide basic social services to their populations. The rise of public education and public health measures would make an enormous difference toward the end of the nineteenth century, especially in urban settings. Public schools competed with church and private education, literacy expanded, and urbanization made these services more accessible to growing populations, even in colonial settings. The benefits of scientific research and technological knowledge extended life spans and improved living standards; public sanitation measures reduced mortality rates and fueled population growth.

All of this was celebrated at the time as a source of wonder. But nineteenth-century progress had its dark side: rising inequalities and concentration of wealth, worker exploitation and child labor, air pollution and environmental destruction, slavery and the expansion of rapacious European colonial ventures. However, some of its undesirable social effects, vividly described by writers like Charles Dickens, were seen as a temporary condition, a function of personal character, or as an inevitable consequence of the survival of the fittest.

The creation of national integrated markets for goods, capital, and labor was well advanced by the mid-nineteenth century. What Austrian economic sociologist Karl Polanyi called "the great transformation," involving forceful state intervention to create self-regulating and widely extended market transactions, first in England and then elsewhere, paved the way for large increases in the production, distribution, and purchase of goods and services (Polanyi, 1970). Mass consumption expanded as new and less expensive products became available, helped by shifting fashions, advertising campaigns, planned obsolescence, and the emergence of middle classes with greater incomes (Osterhammel, 2014, pp. 230–233).

These transformations took place at the same time European explorers aimed at leaving no blank spaces in the maps. The opening of new frontiers led to colonization ventures that incorporated other lands into a worldwide division of labor (Osterhammel, 2014, pp. 79–81, 908). Colonizing ambitions were often cloaked in a civilizational mission grounded in a sense of European superiority and religious zeal. Private–public partnerships ensured the economic and political viability of colonial ventures, with states providing security for corporations to earn profits. Colonial rulers often endowed themselves with Godlike powers in distant lands, deciding over life and death, administering punishment, dispensing favors, and forging alliances with local authorities to consolidate their power and seek profits (Williams, 2013; Holmes, 2010).

When trade and diplomacy were not enough to secure economic advantage, access to resources and political dominance, imperial powers resorted to coercion and war to impose conditions and bend colonies and weaker states to their will. The Opium Wars between England and China are a prime example of colonial powers inflicting social ills on the peoples over which they ruled or subjected. A similar approach prevailed in the American conquest of the West, which exterminated and encircled native populations in reserves and appropriated their lands. Together with slavery and racial segregation, these patterns of domination led to several violent conflicts that accompanied the worldwide expansion of markets and capitalism.

Mass migrations created long-distance networks of interaction, particularly between Europe and North America, but also within Europe and to a lesser extent with other lands. Steamships and railroads facilitated the transport of goods across borders and spurred international travel and tourism. The first global commercial brands emerged in the second half of the nineteenth century to distribute goods widely, a task facilitated by the launch of department stores in urban centers.

The socioeconomic and political context that emerged during the nineteenth century fostered an international division of labor that, with some recent exceptions mainly in Asia, has prevailed until the early twenty-first century. The endogenous capacity to generate scientific and technological knowledge, and to apply it in production and service activities, characteristic of the leading powers in Europe and North America, did not emerge in other lands. Most former colonies, either recently or long liberated, were not able to independently develop scientific capabilities and link them to technology and production. They largely relied on knowledge and technologies generated elsewhere, or on indigenous trial-and-error techniques for their productive and service activities.

From Natural Philosophy to Scientific Research and Engineering

The broad and ambiguous term "natural philosopher," used to describe the knowledge and intellectual activist of the eighteenth century, was superseded by the term "scientist" during the nineteenth century. At the 1833 meeting of the British Association for the Advancement of Science, poet Samuel Taylor Coleridge complained that, by calling themselves natural philosophers, science practitioners and empirical researchers "who studied material nature" were venturing beyond the confines of their call, trampling on lofty philosophical grounds (Morrel & Thackray, 1982, p. 20). Philosopher and historian of science William Whewell responded by coining the slightly derisive word "scientist," comparable to "artist" or "journalist," to differentiate them from the companionship of the supposedly more enlightened natural philosophers (like himself).

Living *for* science, as was mostly the case in previous centuries when commitment and independent means or access to patronage were necessary for gentlemen of science to pursue rigorous inquiry, became by the end of the nineteenth century living *from* science as dedicated scientist-professionals earned their keep from research in academia, industry, and government. The scientific community grew by leaps and bounds in England, other European countries, and, later, in the United States. The number of British scientists doubled every 15 years during the century; from about a thousand scientists in 1800, it increased tenfold by 1850 and a hundredfold by 1900. Between 1800 and 1850, the number of scientific societies increased from ten to a hundred, and the number of international scientific congresses grew from less than ten in the early 1850s to more than 350 by the end of the century (Greenway, 1966, pp. 33–34; Broadberry & O'Rourke, 2010; Morrel & Thackray, 1982, tables A-1 and A-2).

Advances and discoveries began to establish the foundations for modern scientific disciplines. As the number of professional scientists increased, a more crowded field of potential discoverers vied for recognition and prestige, heightening disputes about precedence and originality. Defying pigeonholing attempts, many of the leading scientists worked on more than one field: physicians became physicists, chemists worked on biological issues, mathematicians explored physical phenomena, and physicists made contributions to astronomy and geology. The predominance of narrow specialization would wait till the later decades of the nineteenth century.

Several conceptions of scientific activity—gentlemanly, romantic, people's, practical—coexisted during the first decades of the nineteenth century.[1] Well-to-do members of the upper classes and clerics with secure income considered scientific research as a vocation that should not be sullied by practical or profit motives (Morrel & Thackray, 1982, p. 33). However, even John Herschel, who began thinking that "men of science should support their own researches" would eventually join other members of the budding scientific professional establishment in soliciting government funds for projects that required costly equipment and data gathering in far-flung places (Snyder, 2012, pp. 42, 360).

Romantic science was the province of inspired, creative, disinterested, solitary individuals, who viewed nature as a source of "infinite wonder, of invisible powers and mysterious energies, of fluidity and transformations, of growth and organic change" (Holmes, 2010, p. xviii).[2] They occupied a small niche that would fade gradually toward the end of the nineteenth century. People's science was the purview of artisans, craftsmen, farmers, and mechanics who were shunned by the scientific establishment but made useful contributions to the study of nature and incremental improvements to production activities (Conner, 2005, p. 423).

Science became a popular spectacle. Entertaining, widely attended public lectures, and experimental demonstrations, together with the circulation of scientific pamphlets and textbooks, made research results and discoveries available to the educated middle classes. As Scottish scientist and writer Mary Somerville, who published the widely acclaimed *On the Connection of the Physical Sciences* in the 1830s, wrote, "a sufficient skill in analysis to follow the general outline … to comprehend by what means the most extraordinary conclusions have been arrived at … is within the reach of many who shrink from the task, appalled by difficulties, no more formidable than those incident to the study of the elements of every branch of knowledge" (Yeo, 1984, pp. 5–31; Somerville, 1858, p. 2).

As the century wore on, a practical conception of scientific inquiry, directed not only at uncovering the secrets of nature, but at providing the ways and means of making use of them, would ultimately prevail. Their practitioners took note of the real-world problems of industry, transport, construction, and other economic

[1] According to Snyder, in the early nineteenth century, "there was no agreed-upon 'scientific method,' no one process of discovering theories that was sanctioned above any other. … men of science and the public hardly ever explicitly argued about what kind of scientific method should be used" (Snyder, 2012, pp. 3–4).

[2] See also Secord (2014).

activities, and set to solve them. Organizations like the English Royal Institution hosted leading scientific researchers and inventors, such as chemist Humphry Davy who discovered several chemical elements and engineered a safe lamp for miners, and experimental chemist and physicist Michael Faraday, who invented electrical devices and discovered the electric induction effect.

The extent to which science captured people's attention can be inferred from the popularity of novels of imaginative writers. Taking cues from experimental results and theoretical speculations, novelists and poets extrapolated their human and social consequences. From Mary Shelley's Frankenstein monster (1818) to Jules Verne's captain Nemo (1870), scientific and technological advances were dreaded and celebrated, fixing their double-edged character in the minds of educated people.

Mary Shelley's (1826) apocalyptic novel *The Last Man* began describing a world of abundance and happiness, in which "the arts of life, and the discoveries of science had augmented in a ratio which left all calculation behind; food sprung up, so to say, spontaneously—machines existed to supply with facility every want of the population" (Shelley, 1826, p. 45). A deadly plague would destroy this idyllic state of affairs, making the narrator bid:

> farewell to the giant powers of man,—to knowledge that could pilot the deep-drawing bark through the opposing waters of shoreless ocean—, to science that directed the silken balloon through the pathless air,—to the power that could put a barrier to mighty waters, and set in motion wheels, and beams, and vast machinery, that could divide rocks of granite or marble, and make the mountains plain! (Shelley, 1826, p. 134).

During the first decades of the nineteenth century, scientific research remained rather independent of international politics; scientists moved with ease between hostile nations. In 1808, Humphry Davy was awarded the Napoleon Prize for research in electrochemistry by the Institute of France, despite England and France being at war (Encyclopaedia Britannica, 2025). The use of scientific knowledge for political, strategic, and military ends would come later.

The Crystal Palace Great Exhibition

A pivotal event in the transition from unfolding to deploying the Baconian Program was the 1851 *Great Exhibition of the Works of Industry of all Nations*, which took place in London's Crystal Palace, a prefabricated steel and glass structure built in a short time. Gathering thousands of exhibitors and tens of thousands of objects, it became a showcase for the progress of British industry and, to a lesser extent, of other nations. It provided an opportunity for technological entrepreneurs to display their inventions to businessmen and investors.

The *Great Exhibition* was the first of international fairs held in London (twice), Paris (five times), Vienna, Philadelphia, and Chicago during the second half of the nineteenth century, with the last of these taking place in Paris in 1900 and drawing more than 50 million visitors. These exhibitions "embodied in an effective way the universal character of the incipient capitalist industrial and commercial system"(Snyder, 2012, pp. 294–295; Plum, 1977, p. 60). They bore testimony to the fading of the gentlemanly, romantic, and popular approaches to science, while highlighting the professionalization of scientific research and technology development.

Several lectures delivered around the exhibition clearly stated the debt that industry had with scientific research. William Whewell indicated that:

> arts … employed in obtaining materials, are the most ancient; … the arts of manufacturing chemical products on a large scale, are among the most modern which exist. In the former … Art existed before Science; … in the second, Science has not only overtaken Art but is the whole foundation … here Art is the daughter of Science. The great chemical manufactories … owe their existence entirely to a profound and scientific knowledge of chemistry (Whewell, 1852, pp. 28–29).

The Great Exhibition gave scientists the opportunity to exalt the benefits of basic research and the importance of creating a strong domestic scientific community. Scottish chemist Lyon Playfair stated unequivocally that "the progress of abstract science is of extreme importance to a nation depending upon its manufactures. It is only the overflowings of science, arising from the very fullness of its measure that benefits industry. … It is abstract and not practical Science that is the life and soul of Industry." He further argued that "a competition in Industry must, in an advanced stage of civilization, be a competition of intellect. The influence of capital may purchase you for a time foreign talent. … but is all this not a suicidal policy, which must have a termination, not for the individual manufacturer, … but for the nation" (Playfair, 1852, pp. 190, 196).

Against the background of political turmoil in continental Europe, and coddled by the stability of the Victorian age, the *Great Exhibition* gave rise to diverging reactions. For Albert, Prince Consort, it was an occasion to show that:

> We are living at a period of most wonderful transition, which tends rapidly to the accomplishment of that great end to which, indeed, all history points—the realization of the unity of mankind. … The distances which separated the different nations and parts of the globe are gradually vanishing … science discovers the laws of power, motion, and transformation: industry applies them to the raw mater, … The Exhibition of 1851 is to give us a true test and a living picture of the point of development at which the whole of mankind has arrived in this great task, and a new starting point from which all nations will be able to direct their further exertions (Of Saxe-Coburg and Gotha, 1849, paras. 2, 3, 6).

Not surprisingly, while acknowledging the importance of the Great Exhibition, Karl Marx and Frederick Engels viewed it in a different light:

> Industrial prosperity will be further increased by … the great industrial exhibition of 1851 … announced by the English bourgeoisie already in 1849, with the most impressive cold-bloodedness, at a time when the whole Continent was still dreaming of revolution. … This exhibition is a striking proof of the concentrated power with which modern large-scale industry is everywhere demolishing national barriers and increasingly blurring local peculiarities of production, society and national character among all peoples (Marx & Engels, 1850, para. 24).

Prince Albert's royal hopes for the "unity of mankind" paralleled efforts by the leaders of the British Association for the Advancement of Science, established in the 1830s, to create a neutral ground where religious and political differences could be put aside while engaging in loftier knowledge pursuits. Adhering to eclectic religious views, they succeeded to a significant extent, replicating the feat of the moderate Anglicans who ran the Royal Society a century earlier and opened spaces for rigorous scientific inquiry mostly free of religious and political interferences. However, as events in the late nineteenth and early twentieth centuries would show, such hopes were woefully naïve and tragically dashed.

Scientific Research and Its Impact

The transition from the unfolding to the deployment of Bacon's implicit program would not have been possible without a wide range of advances in mathematics, physics, chemistry, geology, and biology, among other fields. These findings laid the ground for the introduction of new technologies in industry, agriculture, energy, mining, and communications.

Mathematics

Mathematics provided the tools for abstracting, organizing, and processing the key features of natural phenomena and the properties of materials, for establishing relations between their characteristic variables and parameters, and for describing all of these in succinct, quantifiable, and computable equations. Mathematical calculations enabled researchers to manipulate abstract representations of natural phenomena and the interactions between their constituent parts and contexts. This allowed them to anticipate their trajectories and future states, uncover their hidden properties and potentials, and explain anomalies and unusual behaviors. Without them it would have been impossible to understand and harness the power of physical and chemical phenomena.

Building on the work of eighteenth-century giants such as Swiss polymath Leonhard Euler and Italian-French mathematician Joseph-Louis Lagrange, Friedrich Gauss, Augustin Cauchy, Niels Henrik Abel, William Rowan Hamilton, Evarist Galois, George Boole, Georg Friedrich Bernhard Riemann, and Georg Cantor, among other outstanding mathematicians, were responsible for a wide array of advances in analytical geometry, group theory, symbolic logic, set theory, number theory, and many other fields during the nineteenth century.

As anticipated by Condorcet in 1781, apparently useless mathematical discoveries would eventually become useful in other branches of science. For example, complex numbers (which have a real and an imaginary component i that is the square root of -1) were formalized in the first decades of the nineteenth century and found practical applications in electromagnetism and fluid dynamics during its second half. Riemann's non-Euclidean geometries and *n*-dimensional surfaces were advanced in the mid-1800s and would help Einstein develop the relative theory half a century later (Condorcet, 1802, chapter 6, note 52; Asimov, 1972; Hellemans & Bunch, 1988; Bynum & Browne, 1981; Mason, 1956, p. 546).

Statistical methods, developed in earlier decades, were increasingly used in scientific research and technological development during the nineteenth century. Sampling methods and other statistical procedures became an established feature of the social sciences, as shown by Belgian statistician, astronomer, and sociologist Lambert Adolphe Jacques Quetelet's work on the Belgian census; in physics with the work of Scottish mathematician and physicist James Clerk Maxwell, Austrian mathematician and philosopher Ludwig Boltzmann, and American engineer J. Willard Gibbs on statistical thermodynamics; and in astronomy with physicist Edward Charles Pickering's statistical treatment of spectrographic star data (Asimov, 1972; Hellemans & Bunch, 1988; Laurendeau, 2005).

Chemistry

The study of the properties and behavior of gases under different conditions of pressure, temperature, mixtures, and combinations, led to a revival and refinement of the atomic theory of matter, which had a very long history extending back to pre-Socratic philosopher Democritus. Following several years of meteorological observations and atmospheric studies, in the early 1800s, John Dalton proposed that gases were made of atoms that repelled each other. Experiments with different mixtures of gases led Dalton to conclude that each gas was made of different atoms behaving in their own particular ways. In his *A New System of Chemical Philosophy*, he summarized his experiments and those of Gay-Lussac, Davy, and others, to identify and give estimates of the weight, specific gravity, and diameter of the atoms of 36 elements, and the constituent elements and their proportions for 24 compounds, providing symbols for each (Dalton, 1808, pp. 560–561; Ronan, 1982, pp. 438–439).

Following developments in the theory of matter, chemistry advanced at a firm pace in the early decades of the nineteenth century. German chemist Friedrich Wohler was the first to produce an organic compound from its inorganic elements, synthesizing urea in 1828. His compatriot, chemist Justus von Liebig, became interested in the industrial and agricultural applications of chemistry and established a laboratory at the University of Giessen. One of his students, William Perkins, followed in his steps and, in 1856, discovered a way of producing synthetic aniline, instead of the natural product derived from indigo, which laid the foundations for the synthetic dye industry in Germany (Ronan, 1982, pp. 439–443; Gribbin, 2003, p. 371; DeWitt, 2010, p. 95).

Thermodynamics

By the beginning of the nineteenth century, the study of heat had made significant progress thanks to steam engine improvements, but the theoretical foundations for the behavior of heat still remained to be laid. Scientific advances in what William Thomson, Lord Kelvin, would later call "thermodynamics," established the laws that govern energy transformations. Benjamin Thompson, Count Rumford, one of the founders of the Royal Institution, discovered there was an equivalence between heat and mechanical motion. French academician Jean Baptiste Fourier elaborated mathematical representations of heat flows taking into account thermal differences, the conductivity of materials, and shape of the objects (Fourier, 1878, p. 23).

In his *Reflections on the Motive Power of Heat* (1824), French army engineer Sadi Carnot stated that "the motive power of heat is independent of the agents employed to realize it; its quantity is fixed solely by the temperatures of the bodies between which is effected" (Carnot, 1897, pp. 7, 46, 68). While Carnot focused on steam engines, a few years later British engineer James Prescott Joule worked on the efficiency of electromagnetic engines. He was able to demonstrate that "the heat evolved by any voltaic pair is proportional, *ceteris paribus*, to its intensity or electromotive force; and … that the heat evolved by the combustion of a body is proportional to the intensity of its affinity to oxygen," concluding that "I thus succeeded in establishing relations between heat and chemical affinity" (Joule, 1850, p. 82).[3]

The equivalence of different forms of energy—motion, heat, electrical, magnetic, light, and chemical—began to be firmly established by physical and chemical researchers. German scientists Friedrich Mohr and Hermann Helmholtz approached the transformation of energy from chemical and biological perspectives. Mohr, a pharmacist and chemist, argued in a 1837 short article that in addition to the more than 50 known elements, "there exists in nature only one agent more and this is called 'force' ['energy' or 'Kraft' in German]," which "can come to the fore under the appropriate circumstances as motion, chemical affinity, cohesion, electricity, light heat and magnetism, and from each of these kinds of phenomena all the others can be produced" [Mohr, as cited in Gregory (1977, note 118)].

Hermann Helmholtz, a physician turned physicist later in his career, provided a clear statement of the "Law of the Conservation of Force, …[which] asserts, that the quantity of force which can be brought into action in the whole of Nature is unchangeable, and can neither be increased nor diminished." He further stated that "this law might also be expressed in the practical form that no perpetual motion is possible, that force cannot be produced from nothing; something must be consumed" (Eliot & von Helmholtz, 1909, pp. 2, 19, 20).

The laws of energy conservation and transformation were given final form by German theoretical physicist Rudolf Clausius and versatile Scottish academic, William Thomson, Lord Kelvin. Building on the work of Carnot, Joule, Holtzmann, and Thomson, starting in the mid-nineteenth century, Clausius developed a

[3] See also Mason (1956, p. 486), Gribbin (2003, p. 382), and Bowler and Morus (2005, p. 80).

mathematical treatment of the relations between heat and work arguing that "heat can be transformed into work, or work into heat, by a cyclical process," but that complete cyclic reversibility was an unattainable ideal.

Clausius coined the term "entropy" to characterize "the transformational content" of a body. He applied his conception of entropy together with "the axiom that is impossible to create a moving force out of nothing, ... that perpetual motion is impossible" to "the entire universe" considered as a "single body" (closed system) to deduce a couple of universal laws: "the energy of the Universe is constant," and "the entropy of the universe tends to a maximum" (Clausius, 1867, pp. 18, 21, 217, 219, 269, 357, 358, 364, 365). Based on Carnot's propositions in 1852, Lord Kelvin concluded: "there is ... a universal tendency to the dissipation of mechanical energy" that cannot be restored. This led him to speculate "within a finite period of time past, the Earth must have been, and within a finite period of time to come the earth must again be, unfit for the habitation of man" (Thomson, 1852, paras. 14, 16).[4]

Electricity

The discoveries that electric currents create magnetic fields by Danish chemist and physicist Hans Christian Ørsted and the work of Michael Faraday on induction spurred German mathematician and astronomer Carl Friedrich Gauss to study electric circuits and electromagnetism, leading him to develop a prototype electromechanical telegraph in the 1830s. Among several other fields, he made significant contributions to statistics, including the development of the method of least squares to reduce statistical errors and estimate the best fit of a curve to a set of data. He proposed the widely used normal or Gaussian distribution to represent the dispersion and frequency of the values of variables when the underlying structure of their values is not known.

James Clerk Maxwell's mathematical treatment of statistical thermodynamics and his electromagnetic theory of light changed the understanding of relations between electricity, light, and magnetism. Building on a long series of experimental findings of Faraday and Gauss, he was able to derive equations that represented the behavior of magnetic and electric fields in an accurate way, paving the way for devising a variety of electromagnetic devices such as dynamos, generators, and engines (Weinberg, 2015, pp. 258–260; Williams, 1962; Kline, 1972).

A direct link between physics and chemistry was established in 1800 by British chemist and inventor William Nicholson and surgeon Anthony Carlisle, who used electricity to decompose water into hydrogen and oxygen. Michael Faraday coined the term electrolysis to describe the use of a direct electrical current to stimulate chemical reactions. Fractional distillation, a process separating liquid chemical

[4] See also Gribbin (2003, pp. 386–388), Ronan (1982, p. 447), Mason (1956, pp. 493–494), and Bowler and Morus (2005, pp. 92–94).

compounds by raising the temperature to the different levels in which each of them would vaporize, was already known to Islamic alchemists in the ninth century. Systematic experimentation during the late 1700s and early 1800s by Justus von Liebig and other experimenters improved its efficiency by altering the shape of the condenser that turned these vapors into liquid again. Fractional distillation is still widely used in petroleum refineries to produce gasoline, diesel oil, kerosene, and other compounds.

Geology

Geology was another field in which scientific rigor and systematic inquiry produced results of practical use. Geographical expeditions and explorations in the first decades of the nineteenth century provided a plethora of data and information that allowed accurately estimating the age of the Earth and how geological changes had affected life on it. This led to a better understanding of different landscape features, the exploitation of valuable minerals, and the improved construction of infrastructure works. Much as had earlier happened with celestial mechanics, which made the heavens obey physical laws rather than divine designs, geological science cast aside the role of God in shaping the evolution of the Earth (Asimov, 1972, pp. 236–237; Bowler & Morus, 2005, pp. 114–116; Fara, 2009, pp. 226–227; Ronan, 1982, p. 423; Sarukhán, 2013, pp. 73–81; Secord, 2014, p. 140).

The study of fossils in different geological layers showed our planet had passed through various stages over a long time, punctuated by catastrophic events like floods and meteorite strikes. British geologist Charles Lyell's *Principles of Geology* (1830–1833) argued that geological change was gradual and very slow and obeyed the same set of laws at all times, which led him to identify distinct eras in the evolution of the Earth and its ecosystems. He pioneered the use of statistical methods to estimate the ages of geological strata based on the frequency distribution of fossils found in them. He was familiar with Bacon's inductive research method and empirical approach and appreciated the guidance it gave to his research (Lyell, 1881, p. 33). Lyell's developments in geology would become most useful in mining exploration, helping to identify sources of valuable minerals to be used in industrial production (Rudwick, 1970, pp. 24–26; Sarukhán, 2013, pp. 71–73).

Scientific research had already expanded notions of space, comprising all the range from cosmic to microscopic. Geology expanded the ideas of time and history, showing that the Earth had evolved over exceedingly long periods of time, which suggested that living creatures could have done the same, thus laying the ground for the concept of biological evolution. There was no shortage of religious objections to this view, but they would gradually recede from a staunch defense of Christian biblical accounts of creation and shift toward a more diffuse deism that viewed God as a distant and removed creator.

Evolution

French biologist Jean-Baptiste Lamarck's *Zoological Philosophy* (1809) stated that environmental factors determine the changes taking place in living organisms, which became more complex over time. This contradicted the view of his contemporary paleontologist George Cuvier, who staunchly adhered to the idea that species are fixed (Mason, 1956, p. 343). Several decades later, English biologist Charles Darwin would develop his theory of evolution, overturning Lamarck's ideas and arguing that inherited rather than environmental factors were the main cause of evolutionary changes.

Darwin sailed on the HMS Beagle in 1831 and returned to England 5 years later, after gathering all kinds of live specimens and fossilized remains, making detailed observations and taking copious notes. All of these allowed him to detect numerous and large variations in biological life. Spending the next half-decade refining his notes and drawings, Darwin developed the idea that species were not immutable and experienced transformations over time as a result of the "struggle for existence," which could act as a variety filter, culling those organisms that were less fit to survive in a particular biophysical environment:

> [If] variations useful in some way to each being in the great and complex battle of life, should occur in the course of many successive generations … individuals having any advantage, however slight, over others, would have the best chance of surviving and procreating their kind … On the other hand, … any variation in the least degree injurious would be rigidly destroyed. This preservation of favorable individual differences and variations, and the destruction of those which are injurious, I have called Natural Selection, or the Survival of the Fittest (Darwin, 1958, pp. 87–88).

By the late 1800s, there were two main conceptions of biological evolution of how traits are passed on from one generation to another. For Darwin, inherited features were a blend of those of the progenitors, and for Lamarck, new traits acquired in response to environmental stresses were passed to offspring. Experiments conducted by Gregor Mendel in the late 1850s and early 1860s with peas led him to develop an explanation of traits passed from one generation to another in terms of units of inheritance, later called genes, which combined and expressed themselves in different ways and led to variations in the characteristics of offspring. Mendel's work was unknown to Darwin and surfaced only in the early 1900s (Asimov, 1972, pp. 451–453; DeWitt, 2010, pp. 289, 304–305).

By the turn of the twentieth century, evolution was seen as a process of natural selection through which organisms survive and reproduce in a given environment. Darwin's evolution theory explained how more complex organisms emerged out of simpler life forms over long periods of time, by adapting and evolving as they surmounted environmental challenges one after another. Yet, evolution did not imply goal-directedness, let alone continuous improvement in the emergence of organisms; it had no particular direction or endpoint. Natural selection was just a struggle for existence, a result of putting together variations that emerge out of mutations or chance events with selection processes in particular environments. It allowed survivors to reproduce and pass on successful variations to their descendants.

Calculators

Mechanical calculation was another field of inquiry that made considerable advances during the nineteenth century. The first ideas for the design of calculating machines to replace routine human intellectual labor were put forward in the 1620s by Wilhelm Schickard, professor at the University of Tubingen, who reported to Johannes Kepler having built a "Calculating Clock" that could perform addition and subtraction. They were also designed independently by Blaise Pascal in the 1640s and improved by Gottfried Leibniz in the 1670s (Snyder, 2012, pp. 74–78).

However, the rough design for the construction of a general-purpose computing machine would wait till the 1830s when English mathematician Charles Babbage invented the Analytical Engine. Babbage began by designing a machine to play the paper game tic-tac-toe, identifying "what variety of combinations were required for all the possible variety of moves and situations," finding them to be "comparatively insignificant." He entertained the idea of designing an automaton to play the game that could become "a very popular and profitable exhibition," which would earn "in a moderate time, such a sum of money as would enable me to construct the Analytical Engine." While this may perhaps have been the case, Babbage concluded that "to conduct the affair to a successful issue it would occupy so much of my own time … that even if successful in point of pecuniary profit … it would be too late to avail myself of the money thus acquired to complete the Analytical Engine" (Babbage, 1989, pp. 154–156).

The interplay between ideas about how to process abstract mathematical calculations and the mechanical contraptions required to materialize them was clear in Babbage's mind. Referring to the 1851 Exposition at Crystal Palace in London, he said that "all its splendid contents owe their existence to tools as the physical means—to intellect as the guiding power … The contrivance and the constructions of tools, must therefore ever stand at the head of the industrial arts." Babbage concluded that "in order to succeed [in constructing Calculating Engines], it would become necessary to advance the art of construction itself," reporting that "the most enlightened employers and constructors of machinery … have expressed to me their opinion that if the Calculating Engine itself had entirely failed, the money expended by Government in the attempt to make it, would be well repaid by the advancement it had caused in the art of mechanical construction" (Babbage, 1989, pp. 322–323).

Mathematician Ada Augusta Countess of Lovelace, an associate of Babbage, translated into English Italian engineer Luigi Federico Menabrea's account of the Analytical Engine. Her annotations to the text provided detailed instructions for programming it to mechanically perform a variety of mathematical calculations. She famously stated that "the Analytical Engine weaves algebraic patterns just as the Jacquard-loom weaves flowers and leaves" (Menabrea, 1843, p. 30) and has been considered a pioneer of computer programming. Mechanical calculating machines became a common sight in the late nineteenth century and lightened considerably the task of processing numbers in mathematics, statistics, business, and government.

Together with English mathematician and philosopher George Boole, inventor of binary logic and of what he called the "laws of thought" in the 1850s, Babbage's design of the Analytical Engine provided the conceptual basis for the construction of the first digital computers. However, it would take another 100 years before Babbage's Analytical Engine designs and Lovelace's calculation procedures would be widely put into practice with the construction of the first programmable general computers.

Astronomy, Geography, and Social Sciences

There were several other fields of inquiry, such as astronomy, geography, and the social sciences, in which research made great strides that would find numerous practical applications in the following decades.

Astronomical findings continued to challenge conventional conceptions of the cosmos and to provide new methods of inquiry. In 1800, astronomer William Herschel discovered infrared radiation by detecting heat below the visible spectrum: "radiant heat will at least partly, if not chiefly, consist, if I may be permitted the expression, of invisible light." This was followed shortly thereafter by the discovery of ultraviolet rays by German chemist Johann Wilhelm Ritter, the study of radiation and the development of the spectrograph by German chemist and physicist Gustav Kirchhoff, and the invention of photography by French researchers and inventors Nicéphore Niépce and Louis Daguerre (Herschel, 1800a, p. 272; Herschel, 1800b, pp. 291–292; Caneva, 2001, pp. 11–12).

Geographic discoveries contributed to a better understanding of the Earth and its diverse ecosystems, allowing agricultural improvements and the medicinal and industrial use of newfound plants. German naturalist and polymath Alexander von Humboldt traveled extensively through the Americas, discovered new botanical and animal species, registered and disseminated geological, magnetic, and meteorological observations, examined the ethnic diversity of the populations, and studied climatic conditions and the impact of human activities on natural ecosystems (Wulf & von Humboldt, 2015). His findings combined cultural and natural aspects and would help considerably in developing a holistic approach to the study of nature. The diversity of flora and fauna found in these expeditions to different parts of the world stimulated efforts to describe and classify new information, as well as the creation of gardens by the Dutch and English India companies to supply ships with foodstuffs and to find medicines (Jardine, 2000, p. 224).

Economics, political science, history, philosophy, and the humanities made major strides throughout the nineteenth century. The social sciences began to employ mathematical and statistical tools to rigorously explain societal phenomena.

Sociology was recognized as a distinct and legitimate subject of inquiry; economics began to use mathematical formulations of concepts such as diminishing returns and general equilibrium. Anthropology and history saw the publication of major works by eminent researchers; archeological and linguistic discoveries changed conceptions of antique civilizations; and psychology stood as a new field of inquiry to explain human behavior.

From Techniques to Technologies

Toward the end of the nineteenth century, government officials, industrialists, entrepreneurs, managers, scientists, and engineers became fully aware of the potential of scientific knowledge and science-based technologies. Enlisting them in the pursuit of state, business, and social objectives, the gradual and haphazard unfolding of the Baconian Program shifted to deliberate deployment, which made "knowledge is power" an incontrovertible fact as the twentieth century approached.

Along the way, the Baconian idea of combining reasoning with experimentation became widely accepted and technology superseded technique. Scientific discoveries would eventually lead to the development of completely new technologies lying outside the scope of prior technical knowledge or experience, and also to their validation through scientific experiments. The consolidation and institutionalization of the engineering profession were closely associated with the rise of technology over technique, and with an increasing concentration of industrial production in the United States and several European countries (Osterhammel, 2014, p. 64).

Productivity in agriculture increased through the widespread use of natural (guano and saltpeter) and decades later synthetic fertilizers (ammonium nitrate, superphosphates), the dissemination of new world food crops such as the potato, the expansion of farming lands, and the invention of agricultural machinery. Processing innovations, such as canning, refrigeration, and the sterilization process invented by French microbiologist Louis Pasteur, allowed food products to last longer and become safer, and facilitated long-distance transport (Latour, 1988). Food production increased in the United States during the second half of the nineteenth century with the establishment of the Land Grant Colleges, the creation of a network of experimental agricultural stations, and the expansion of extension services.

Substantial increases in life expectancy were one of the major achievements of the nineteenth century. These were due to preventive health measures, medical treatments, clean water and sanitation, together with better anatomical descriptions and a better understanding of the functions of various organs. Widespread vaccination practices and the application of anesthetics in surgery also contributed to health improvements. During the second half of the 1880s, Pasteur studied fermentation, developed the germ theory of disease, identified diseases such as cholera and rabies and produced antidotes to fight them. About the same time, German physician and microbiologist Robert Koch discovered the bacilli that cause tuberculosis and anthrax, and German bacteriologist Friedrich Loeffler proposed the use of antitoxins to fight diphtheria (Pope, 1963, pp. 230–234).

Advances in organic chemistry led to the development of plastics, pesticides, synthetic fibers, and rubber, and many other products that became widely used. University, corporate, and independent research laboratories began to turn out new synthetic products that would rapidly find their way to large-scale manufacturing, distribution, and consumption. Experiments in metallurgy improved making and metalworking technologies and generalized the use of machine tools to fabricate other machines, prompting moves toward standardization and the use of exchangeable parts.

In 1856, British inventor Sir Henry Bessemer devised the steel-making open-furnace process that bears his name, which allowed the production of less expensive steel and made it available for general use in railroads, shipbuilding, high-rise construction, and the fabrication of high-precision machinery. The American Bethlehem Iron Company was founded in 1861 and soon began producing steel for railroad lines, armor plates for the United States Navy, and later steel beams for skyscraper construction.

Building on the theoretical and empirical work of Faraday and Maxwell, the electrical industry grew rapidly during the second half of the 1800s. Electricity generation and long-distance transmission made this source of energy increasingly available, particularly in large cities. Both industrial and domestic consumption of electricity grew by leaps and bounds in the later decades of the nineteenth century, particularly in the United States. It significantly altered life and work conditions, expanded nighttime activities, and facilitated the use of machinery to produce an ever-increasing range of goods.

American inventor and entrepreneur Thomas Edison created in Menlo Park, New Jersey, what is widely considered the first industrial research laboratory, Edison Electric, to systematically explore potential uses of mechanical, electric, and chemical technologies. Its efforts produced the first incandescent light bulbs, improved electrical transmission, and pioneered sound and motion recording. His aim was "to spend full-time in making new inventions" and he expected to make "a minor invention every ten days, and a big one every six months or so" (Noble, 1977, pp. 4, 8). Edison's approach to the generation and transmission of electricity relied on low-voltage direct current, which would eventually lose ground to the alternating current method championed by George Westinghouse. Using transformers to change the high voltage required for long-distance transmission to low voltage for domestic and industrial use, Westinghouse improved electricity distribution. He also manufactured alternating current induction motors after purchasing a patent from Serbian-born American inventor Nikola Tesla.

Advances in thermodynamics during earlier decades facilitated the design and construction of internal combustion engines, which relied on an increasing supply of oil and its derivatives. At the end of the 1870s, German engineers Nicolaus Otto and Gottlieb Daimler designed and patented a multiple-cycle engine that compressed the fuel before igniting it and transforming a linear displacement into a rotary motion. Inventors Karl Benz and Rudolf Diesel would subsequently refine the internal combustion engine, which began to power all kinds of industrial processes, automobiles, locomotives, and ship engines. The demand for oil and the byproducts of fractional distillation would soar with the invention of the internal combustion engine, prompting further innovations in refining and processing crude oil.

Telecommunications made great strides using the findings of research in electricity and magnetism. English entrepreneur and inventor William Cook and his associate academic scientist Charles Wheatstone devised the first electrical telegraph to send messages through wires at long distances in the 1830s. It was commercially used in railroads between several English towns, but shortly thereafter superseded by the telegraph invented by American inventor Samuel Morse, which used a system of relays to retransmit electromagnetic signals more efficiently over longer distances. Morse devised the code that bears his name to represent the letters of the alphabet by distinct combinations of short and long electrical pulses—dots and dashes—that could convey messages without delay or error. Morse's invention became the standard means of long-distance communication all over the world in a rather short time and lasted for several decades before the telephone and wireless radio communications became widely available.

Scottish-born Alexander Graham Bell invented the telephone after many years of tutoring persons with speech and hearing impairments in England, Canada, and the United States. In Bell's invention, the vibrations that sound produces in a membrane were used to modulate and transmit electrical signals, which another vibrating membrane transformed into sound at the receiving end. As other inventors were working on similar devices at the same time, disputes regarding priority and patent rights ensued, although Bell's claims prevailed finally. The highly successful Bell Telephone Company was created in the late 1870s; it expanded its reach by purchasing additional patents and became the publicly traded American Telegraph and Telephone (AT&T) Company at the turn of the twentieth century. Its laboratories became one of the leading industrial research outfits in communication technologies, holding thousands of patents and employing hundreds of researchers.

As the telephone became a widely used means for transmitting speech over long distances through wires, research on electromagnetic waves would lay the ground for wireless communications. German scientist Heinrich Hertz confirmed the validity of Maxwell's electromagnetism theory by producing radio waves that propagated without needing wires. His results were of great interest to many researchers, including Italian Guglielmo Marconi who anticipated the practical and commercial uses of radio waves and thought it unusual that "their application to useful purposes could have escaped the notice of eminent scientists." Marconi developed a wireless communication device and carried several demonstrations in England, which led him to create the Marconi Company in the late 1890s. Even though his newly founded corporation faced litigation from German and American competitors, it became highly successful in subsequent decades (Beauchamp, 2001, p. 186).

Engineers, managers, accountants, and financiers became interested in improving the efficiency of factories and companies. The expansion of railroads made it necessary to rationalize and synchronize train arrival and departure times, prompting the development of precise scheduling methods. Toward the end of the nineteenth century, American mechanical engineer Frederick Winslow Taylor, considered the father of scientific management, proposed four principles for management: employing scientific rigor and discarding empirical rules; fostering harmony and avoiding disagreements; promoting cooperation and leaving aside individualism; and developing the skills of each person to achieve maximum efficiency (Taylor, 1911). However, his rigid prescriptions for organizing factory work, with a strict definition of repetitive tasks and the times to perform them led to considerable labor unrest and elicited political opposition.

Time became a factor of production, a variable in the accumulation of financial assets, and a force to accelerate all kinds of endeavors. The 1884 International Meridian Conference in Washington, D.C., unified the way of determining times in different parts of the world, which facilitated the coordination of all kinds of economic and social activities, and simplified transport schedules across time zones. The old aphorism "time is money," attributed to Benjamin Franklin to scold idleness, acquired renewed currency as market forces placed a premium on being first to introduce products and services, and as interest and discount rates clearly recognized the time value of money (Osterhammel, 2014, pp. 69, 74–75, 260).

Uneven Unfolding: The West and the Rest

Toward the end of the nineteenth century, a broad process of economic integration into world markets was well under way in most regions, even though trade patterns were highly asymmetric. The more industrialized nations of Europe and North America exported manufactures and other knowledge-intensive goods and services, while colonies and independent nations in Asia, Africa, the Middle East, and Latin America exported mainly primary commodities.

According to American economic historian David Landes, rationality and activism, closely associated with the Baconian Program, were:

> … the crucial values that of that European culture and society that gave birth to the modern industrial world. But these alone will not account for the entire discrepancy between Western economic development and that of the leading centers of civilization elsewhere. There was also the element of differential violence—violence, first, in the sense of destructive incursions; and second, in the sense of dominion and exploitation of one society by another (Landes, 1969, p. 33).

The swift expansion of European empires in Africa, Asia, the Middle East, and Latin America starting in the seventeenth century made it impossible to consider the evolution of knowledge production, acquisition, distribution, and use in those regions without reference to the West. Traditional speculative knowledge confronted the challenge of religious ideas and the intellectual outlook of European missionaries, often with deadly results, as shown by the extirpation of idolatries in Latin America.

As summarized in one of my earlier books, "the repertoire of European technical and technological responses, particularly in the military field, would prove overwhelming to African, Indian, Meso-American, Andean, Chinese and Southeast Asian civilizations. At the same time, the exchange of plants and animals expanded considerably agricultural activities in Europe and the conquered lands. Production and trade in the colonies and in far-flung trading posts was organized as a function of the requirements of the European powers, as indicated by the spice trade, the mining of gold and silver, the establishment of plantations and large farms, the trade in textiles (cotton, silk and wool) and the infamous slave trade" (Sagasti, 2004, p. 22).

Traditional knowledge and technical practices did not disappear completely and in many cases, such as the Andean region, Africa, China, and India, coexisted uneasily for centuries with their transplanted Western European counterparts. In contrast with colonized lands, Japan adopted policies that allowed it to remain relatively isolated from European influence through the mid-nineteenth century, when deliberate efforts were made by the Meiji dynasty to acquire and adapt Western knowledge, technology, and institutions.

Whether as the result of an internal cumulative process (Western Europe) or of a transplant that grew its own roots (United States, Japan), in the industrialized countries the systematic generation of knowledge and the production of goods and services were closely linked through the development of science-based technologies. This was not the case in most Asian, African, Middle East, and Latin American countries that were incorporated into the international division of labor as suppliers of raw materials and as markets for European and North American manufactures. However, the interests of local elites, occasionally with support of European researchers, would eventually lead to the rise of what American scholar George Basalla defined as "colonial science" in the non-Western world (Basalla, 1967, pp. 611–622). Yet, their incipient scientific research activities and their productive processes would remain isolated from each other (Sagasti, 1980, 1988; Baark & Svedin, 1988).

Toward the Full Deployment of Bacon's Program

Resting on firm theoretical-empirical foundations, by the late nineteenth century, science-based technologies, closely interwoven with capitalist expansion, had created new economic activities, revitalized traditional ones, and spurred economic growth, primarily in Europe and North America. Expanding markets and competitive pressures placed a premium on developing new products, improving processes and achieving greater efficiency, tasks for which the results of scientific research would prove most useful. As innovation capabilities became a competitive advantage, technology theft, secrecy, and deception became corporate practices. Disputes on the priority of discoveries and conflicts on what patents covered led to long and contentious litigation.

Government agencies, private corporations, academic institutions, armed forces, professional associations, entrepreneurial inventors, workers' movements, and many other institutions became actively involved in the generation, mobilization, dissemination, and utilization of knowledge. As statesmen recognized the economic, military, social, and cultural advantages of leadership in the pursuit of knowledge, science and technology became a matter of public policy; scientific prowess would become a dimension of national power to underpin economic and military dominance. While this took place mainly in Europe and the United States, its effects and influence were felt all over the world.

As the transition to the twentieth century loomed on the horizon, the Baconian Program had fully unfolded and was consciously deployed: the results and impact of scientific research were clearly visible as the interplay between theories and experiments relentlessly advanced knowledge about natural and social phenomena; the ideas of indefinite improvements in the human condition and of humanity as the pinnacle of evolution were broadly shared; and the role of knowledge-generating institutions—laboratories, research institutes, academic centers, the patent system—was increasingly recognized.

But once it was fully unfolded, rips and tears were visible in the previously roughly crumpled paper of Sir Francis Bacon's implicit program. Innovations associated with science-based technologies, together with the worldwide expansion of markets and capitalism, would improve the standard of living for many people, but their reckless drive to dominate nature through understanding would leave a mixed legacy of challenging and potentially ominous consequences.

References

Asimov, I. (1972). *Asimov's biographical encyclopedia of science and technology: The lives and achievements of 1195 great scientists from ancient times to the present chronologically arranged* (2nd ed.). Avon.

Baark, E., & Svedin, U. (Eds.) (with Hagerstrand, T.). (1988). *Man, nature and technology: Essays on the role of ideological perceptions*. Macmillan.

Babbage, C. (1989). In P. Morrision & E. Morrison (Eds.), *On the principles and development of the calculator and other seminal writings*. Dover Publications. Retrieved from https://books.google.com.pe/books?id=FTXyAAAAQBAJ&pg=PR3&source=gbs_selected_pages&cad=1#v=onepage&q&f=false

Basalla, G. (1967). The spread of western science. *Science, 156*, 611–622.

Beauchamp, K. (2001). *A history of telegraphy*. The Institution of Engineering and Technology.

Bowler, P. J., & Morus, I. R. (2005). *Making modern science: A historical survey*. University of Chicago Press.

Broadberry, S., & O'Rourke, K. H. (2010). *The Cambridge Economic History of Modern Europe. Vol. 2: 1870 to the Present*. Cambridge University Press.

Bynum, W. F., & Browne, E. J. (1981). *Dictionary of the history of science*. Macmillan Press.

Caneva, K. L. (2001). *The form and function of scientific discoveries*. Smithsonian Institution Libraries. Retrieved from https://archive.org/details/formfunctionsci00Cane

Carnot, S. (1897). *Reflections on the motive Power of Heat*. John Wiley.

Clausius, R. (1867). *The mechanical theory of heat: With its applications to the steam-engine*. J. Van Voorst. Retrieved from https://archive.org/details/mechanicaltheor04claugoog/page/n5/mode/2up

Condorcet, J.-A.-N. (1802). *Outlines of an historical view of the progress of the human mind*. J. Frank.

Conner, C. D. (2005). *A people's history of science: Miners, midwives, and "low mechanicks"*. Nation Books.

Dalton, J. (1808). *A new system of chemical philosophy*. R. Bickerstaff.

Darwin, C. (1958). *Origin of the species*. Mentor Books.

DeWitt, R. (2010). *Worldviews: An introduction to the history and philosophy of science* (2nd ed.). Wiley-Blackwell.

Eliot, C. W., & von Helmholtz, H. (Eds.). (1909). On the conservation of force: Introduction to a series of lectures delivered at Carlsruhe in the winter of 1862–1863. In *Scientific papers: Physics, chemistry, astronomy, geology* (E. Atkinson, Trans.) (Vol. 30). P.F. Collier & Son. Retrieved from https://www.bartleby.com/lit-hub/hc/scientific-papers-physics-chemistry-astronomy-geology/on-the-conservation-of-force/

Encyclopaedia Britannica. (2025, December 13). Sir Humphry Davy. *Britannica.com*. Retrieved December 15, 2025, from https://www.britannica.com/biography/Sir-Humphry-Davy-Baronet

Engels, F. (1845/2020). *The condition of the working-class in England in 1844* (F. K. Wischnewetzky, Trans.). Project Gutenberg. https://www.gutenberg.org/cache/epub/17306/pg17306-images.html

Fara, P. (2009). *Science, a four-thousand-year history*. Oxford University Press.

Fourier, J. B. J. (1878). *The analytical theory of heat*. Cambridge University Press. Retrieved from https://archive.org/details/analyticaltheory00fourrich

Greenway, F. (1966). *John Dalton and the atom*. Heinemann Educational Books.

Gregory, F. (1977). *Scientific materialism in nineteenth century Germany*. Springer Science and Business Media.

Gribbin, J. (2003). *Science a history*. Penguin Books.

Hellemans, A., & Bunch, B. (1988). *The timetables of science: A chronology of the most important people and events in the history of science*. Simon and Schuster.

Herschel, W. (1800a). Investigation of the powers of the prismatic colours to heat and illuminate objects; with remarks, that prove the different refrangibility of radiant heat. To which is added, an inquiry into the method of viewing the sun advantageously, with telescopes of large apertures and high magnifying powers. *Philosophical Transactions of the Royal Society of London, 90*, 255–283. https://doi.org/10.1098/rstl.1800.0014

Herschel, W. (1800b). XIV. Experiments on the refrangibility of the invisible rays of the sun. *Philosophical Transactions of the Royal Society of London, 90*, 284–292. https://doi.org/10.1098/rstl.1800.0015

Holmes, R. (2010). *The age of wonder: How the romantic generation discovered the beauty and terror of science* (1st Vintage Books ed). Vintage Books.

Jardine, L. (2000). *Ingenious pursuits: Building the scientific revolution*. Anchors Books.

Joule, J. P. (1850). On the mechanical equivalent of heat. *Philosophical Transactions of the Royal Society of London, 140*, 61–82. https://doi.org/10.1098/rstl.1850.0004

Kline, M. (1972). *Mathematical thought from ancient to modern time*. Oxford University Press.

Landes, D. S. (1969). *The unbound Prometheus, Technological change and industrial development in Western Europe from 1750 to the present*. Cambridge University Press.

Latour, B. (1988). *The pasteurization of France* (A. Sheridan & J. Law, Trans.). Harvard University Press. Retrieved from https://archive.org/details/pasteurizationof0000lato_e1l2

Laurendeau, N. M. (2005). *Statistical thermodynamics: Fundamentals and applications*. Cambridge University Press.

Lyell, C. (1881). Letter to his father, November 1837. In *Life, letters and journals of Sir Charles Lyell, Bart* (Vol. 2). John Murray, Albemarle St. Retrieved from https://ia601300.us.archive.org/29/items/cu31924012129544/cu31924012129544.pdf

Marx, K., & Engels, F. (1850). *Review: May–October 1850*. Neue Rheinische Zeitung Revue. Retrieved April 11, 2017, from https://www.marxists.org/archive/marx/works/1850/11/01.htm

Mason, S. F. (1956). *A history of the sciences* (9th ed.). Collier Books.

McNeill, W. H. (1980). *The human condition: An ecological and historical view*. Princeton University Press.

Menabrea, L. F. (1843). *Sketch of the Analytical Engine invented by Charles Babbage, Esq.* (A. A. Lovelace, Trans. & Notes). Project Gutenberg. Retrieved from https://www.gutenberg.org/files/75107/75107-h/75107-h.htm

Morrel, J., & Thackray, A. (1982). *Gentlemen of science, Early years of the British Association for the Advancement of Science*. Clarendon Press.

Noble, D. F. (1977). *America by design: Science, technology, and the rise of corporate capitalism*. Alfred A. Knopf.

Of Saxe-Coburg and Gotha, A. (1849). *Albert Prince Consort's speech given at a banquet at the Mansion House on 21 March 1849*. Napoleon.Org. Retrieved from https://www.napoleon.org/en/history-of-the-two-empires/articles/albert-prince-consorts-speech-given-at-a-banquet-at-the-mansion-house-on-21-march-1849/

Osterhammel, J. (2014). *The transformation of the world: A global history of the nineteenth century*. Princeton University Press.

Playfair, L. (1852). On the chemical principles involved in the manufactures of the exhibition. In *Lectures on the results of the great exhibition of 1851*. David Bogue.

Plum, W. (1977). *Exposiciones Mundiales en el siglo XIX: Espectáculos del Cambio Socio-cultural*. Friedrich Ebert Stiftung.

Polanyi, K. (1970). *The great transformation: The political and economic origins of our time*. Beacon Press.

Pope, C. G. (1963). Development of knowledge of antitoxins. *British Medical Bulletin, 18*(3), 230–234. https://doi.org/10.1093/oxfordjournals.bmb.a070062

Ronan, C. (1982). *Science, its history and development among the world's cultures*. Facts on File.

Rudwick, M. J. S. (1970). The strategy of Lyell's principles of geology. *Isis, 61*(1), 4–33.

Sagasti, F. (1980). Towards endogenous science and technology for another development. *Technological Forecasting and Social Change, 16*, 321–330.

Sagasti, F. (1988). Reinterpreting the concept of development from a science and technology perspective. In E. Baark (Ed.), *Man, nature & technology* (pp. 37–56). Harvard University Press.

Sagasti, F. (2004). *Knowledge and innovation for development: The Sisyphus challenge of the 21st century*. Edward Elgar.

Sarukhán, J. (2013). *Las musas de Darwin*. Fondo de Cultura Económica.

Secord, J. A. (2014). *Visions of science: Books and readers at the dawn of the Victorian age* (1st ed.). Oxford University Press.

Shelley, M. (1826). *The last man*. Henry Colburn. Retrieved from https://www.gutenberg.org/cache/epub/18247/pg18247-images.html

Snyder, L. J. (2012). *The philosophical breakfast club: Four remarkable friends who transformed science and changed the world*. Broadway Books.

Somerville, M. (1858). *On the connection of the physical sciences*. J. Murray. https://archive.org/details/connexionofphysi00somerich

Taylor, F. W. (1911). *The principles of scientific management*. History of Economic Thought Books, McMaster University Archive for the History of Economic Thought. Retrieved from https://ideas.repec.org/b/hay/hetboo/taylor1911.html

Thomson, W. (1852). On a universal tendency in nature to the dissipation of mechanical energy. *Proceedings of the Royal Society of Edinburgh*. Retrieved from https://zapatopi.net/kelvin/papers/on_a_universal_tendency.html

Weinberg, S. (2015). *To explain the world: The discovery of modern science*. Harper.

Whewell, W. (1852). The general bearing of the great exhibition on the progress of art and science. In *Lectures on the results of the great exhibition of 1851*. David Bogue.

Williams, L. P. (1962). The physical sciences in the first half of the nineteenth century: Problems and sources. *History of Science, 1*(1), 1–15. https://doi.org/10.1177/007327536200100102
Williams, R. H. (2013). *The triumph of human empire: Verne, Morris, and Stevenson at the end of the world*. University of Chicago Press.
Wulf, A., & von Humboldt, A. (2015). *The invention of nature: The adventures of Alexander von Humboldt, the lost hero of science*. John Murray.
Yeo, R. (1984). Science and intellectual authority in mid-nineteenth century Britain: Robert chambers and 'vestiges of the natural history of creation'. *Victorian Studies, 28*(1), 5–31.

Chapter 8
Ambiguous Success

Science Finds, Industry Applies, Man Conforms: A Century of Progress International Exposition Chicago World Fair, 1933–1934

Mumford, (1969, p. 213)

The twentieth century witnessed the full deployment and success of the Baconian Program. Its components—method, purpose, direction, focus, and institutions—intertwined knowledge, technology, and production to herald the emergence of a "knowledge society" qualitatively different from the agricultural or industrial societies of older times. Scientific research, technological development, and innovation became the main determinants of economic growth and social improvements (UNESCO, 2005). There was a steady increase in the share of knowledge workers involved in education, research, and development, government and private services, information processing and exchange, media and the arts. In contrast, there was a significant reduction in the proportion of people employed in agriculture, mining, and industry, and in addition these activities became more knowledge intensive.

The close interconnection between scientific research and technological development was fully recognized and increasingly accepted. As German physicist Werner Heisenberg put it:

> The connection between natural science and technical science has from the beginning been that of mutual assistance: The progress in technical science, the improvement of tools, the invention of new technical devices have provided the basis for more, and more accurate, empirical knowledge of nature; and the progress in the understanding of nature and finally the mathematical formulation of natural laws have opened the way to new applications of this knowledge in technical science (Heisenberg, 1962, p. 188)

As the deliberate deployment of the Baconian Program took hold, the pace of advances in science and technology accelerated. Discoveries and inventions became more frequent and consequential, leading to new products and services and ways to provide them. At the same time, there were major changes in the ways scientific research, technological development, and innovation are carried out; there emerged a need to govern the acquisition and use of knowledge, and the world context

F. Sagasti, *Knowledge is Power*, Innovation, Technology, and Knowledge Management, https://doi.org/10.1007/978-3-032-20668-8_8

changed as a result of the ways in which the Baconian Program was put into practice and its ambiguous success.

Science Forges Ahead

The staggering breadth and pace of scientific discoveries during the twentieth century is hard to summarize. A few examples from mathematics, physics, and evolution theory suggest the impact of these discoveries on the development of new technologies and the ways they would alter the human condition.

Mathematics continued advancing in the early twentieth century with contributions of, among others, British philosopher Bertrand Russell, Austrian philosopher Ludwig Wittgenstein, and German logician Kurt Gödel. They underscored both the potential and the limitations of formal logic and mathematics, preparing the ground for more balanced and rigorous approaches to their applications. Hungarian mathematician and computer scientist John von Neumann developed the theory of games, helped to create the initial design for a digital computer, and joined the Manhattan Project team that built the first atomic bomb.

American mathematician and electrical engineer Claude Shannon applied Boole's digital logic to the design of electric circuits. He also laid the foundations of the field of information theory, and his contributions helped to separate signal from noise in the transmission of information. Going well beyond Babbage's early attempts a century earlier, English mathematician and computer scientist Alan Turing, who worked during World War II on breaking German ciphers, designed the basic structure of modern digital computers and of the software to program them (Turing, 1950).

Building on three centuries of research results, new statistical methods were developed starting in the second decade of the twentieth-century to extract the maximum possible amount of information from limited data. British statistician Karl Pearson developed sampling methods, test of hypothesis, and functions to describe the various properties of statistical distributions, thus easing the use of experimental data to accept or reject scientific hypotheses.

Two major advances in physics in the early decades of the twentieth century—general relativity and quantum physics—would alter the prevailing conceptions of the physical world in a fundamental manner. In Einstein's recasting of physical reality, space and time were no longer considered an immutable, all-encompassing universal stage, independent of the forces and bodies that dwell on it. They were rather conceived as space-time, a four-dimensional construct that interacts with mass and energy. These interactions distort the fabric of space-time, and gravity is no longer considered a force acting between masses at a distance, as Newton had postulated, but as a curvature of space-time caused by the presence of bodies and forces in it.

In 1905, in what has been called his "miraculous year" German and naturalized American physicist Albert Einstein published three papers that changed our understanding of time and space, explained how atoms generate random movements of particles suspended in a liquid, and discovered the photoelectric effect in which light generates an electric current. All of these had major implications, with the latter finding its way to a myriad of practical devices used daily throughout the world. Although he was not involved in the development of the atomic bomb and later opposed its use, Einstein's theoretical discovery of the equivalence between energy and mass ($E = MC^2$), complemented with contributions from many other physicists, paved the way for the Manhattan Project, the construction of the atomic bomb, and its use with horrifying effect in Hiroshima and Nagasaki toward the end of World War II.

The transition from classical to quantum physics in the early decades of the twentieth century ushered in a further revolution in our conceptions of matter, physical reality, and the relation between the scientific observer and the phenomena under observation. Classical physicists, including Newton and Einstein, considered that it was possible, at least in principle, to define the state of a mechanical system with precision, subject only to measurement errors. The quantum mechanics conception of the universe introduced the idea of probability into the basic structure of matter and energy. It was no longer possible—not even in principle—to know with certainty both the position and the momentum of a particle at a given instant in time: Heisenberg's uncertainty principle states that the more precise the measurement of the position, the less exact the measurement of its momentum must be.

The difference between classical and quantum physics was clearly stated by Danish theoretical physicist Niels Bohr: "While within the scope of classical physics … the interaction between the measuring instruments and the subject under observation neglected, or at any rate compensated for, … such interaction." (Bohr, 1966, p. 4). As American physicist Evelyn Fox Keller clearly stated, quantum mechanics questions the idea of physical reality as something fixed, immutably and fully knowable in a deterministic sense. American historian of science Russell McCormmach's novel *Night Thoughts of a Classical Physicist* describes beautifully and rather accurately the conundrums and wrenching dilemmas experienced by traditional physical scientists when facing the ambiguities and uncertainties of quantum physics (McCormmach, 1982; Keller, 1985, p. 139).

Regardless of the indeterminacy quantum mechanics introduced in our conceptions of reality, it provided the theoretical foundations for the invention of semiconductors and the development of integrated circuits, making possible major advances in microelectronics that would lead to the information revolution. Quantum mechanics also allowed us to examine the structure of molecules and atoms in chemistry, and to construct lasers that emit light in a narrow wavelength with numerous medical and industrial applications.

Evolution theory experienced significant changes during the twentieth century. American paleontologist George Gaylord Simpson joined Darwin's natural selection and mutation theories with Austrian biologist Gregory Mendel's discovery of genes and the laws of heredity. He was one of the creators of what English biologist Julian Huxley called the "modern synthesis" of evolution. While in Victorian England, Darwin's terms "struggle for existence" and "survival of the fittest" had ideological repercussions that extended to sociology, economics, and other fields,

Simpson put forward the more neutral conception of "differential reproduction." This implied that organisms best adapted to their environment, or that can best adapt to changing conditions, are likely to have better reproductive success, but does not mean they are the fittest in a general sense. Taking issue with the idea of struggle, he thought "differential reproduction is usually a peaceful process in which the concept of struggle is really irrelevant" (Simpson, 1967).

Some deeply religious scientists have seen evolution as an expression of God's will. For Australian neurobiologist and Nobel Prize winner Sir John Eccles, the improbable emergence of life and of humanity "is in fact a design, a divine design. The whole thing was wonderfully organized and planned to give the immensity, to give the size, to give the opportunity, for the Darwinist evolutionary process that gave rise to us ... all life and, of course, all human beings ... are part of the great creation plan" (Eccles, 1993, pp. 162–164).

However, most evolutionary biologists do not see any divine intervention in the process of evolution and consider it the result of blind stepwise processes of natural selection leading to biological structures which, as American cognitive psychologist Steven Pinker put it, "look as if they are engineered for a purpose" (Pinker, 1996, p. 49). Yet, Chilean biologists Humberto Maturana and Francisco Varela argued that notions of purposes or aims are unnecessary for the understanding of living systems and organizations (Maturana & Varela, 1980, p. 117). American physicist Murray Gell-Mann, a Nobel Prize winner who turned his attention to the study of complexity and self-organization, views the emergence of human beings as a fortuitous event: "each of us human beings ... is the product of an enormously long sequence of accidents, any of which could have turned out differently" (Gell-Mann, 1996, p. 320).

The controversies surrounding the changing interpretations of evolutionary theory and evidence lasted through the whole twentieth century and are unlikely to be settled any time soon. Indeed, evolution itself is now seen as evolving over time. American political scientist Walter Truett Anderson has pointed out that "evolution has many mysterious, fascinating aspects; the most mysterious and fascinating aspect of all is that evolution evolves" (Truett Anderson, 1987, p. 148).

Development and Diffusion of New Technologies

The transition from the unfolding to the full deployment of Bacon's program followed and reinforced a trend established during the nineteenth century: scientific research, even in subjects apparently remote from practical use, continued to find applications in a variety of fields.

Medicine advanced and life spans increased with the discovery of antibiotics to combat infections, synthetic drugs to treat disease and regulate fertility, the development of prostheses to repair and replace body parts, the discovery of painkillers and with a better understanding of genetic diseases and conditions. Synthetic fertilizers, hybrid seeds, and genetically modified organisms led to growth in food supply and reduced hunger and malnutrition.

Energy sources diversified as hydrocarbons-replaced coal, gasoline, and diesel fueled the rise of the automotive industries; improvements in electricity generation and transmission led to more efficient and less expensive electric motors; and renewable energy sources became economically viable. Nuclear energy generation was employed commercially in the mid-1950s, although high costs and potential dangers limited its application.

Assembly lines for the mass production of automobiles, together with the development of airplanes and high-speed railways, revolutionized transport in the early decades of the twentieth century. Long-distance travel became common and the movements of cargo and passengers economical and efficient. Improvements in equipment for industry (machine tools), agriculture (mechanical harvesters), construction (cranes, bulldozers, concrete mixers), and administration (electric calculators, typewriters) led to productivity growth. Automation made inroads in numerous industrial activities and the invention of the semiconductor opened new possibilities for a wider range of electronic devices.

Information and communications technologies made great leaps to alter most work and life processes. Vacuum tubes that powered large unwieldy computers in the mid-1950s were replaced a decade later by small, reliable, and more efficient semiconductors. Punched cards for inputs, large mechanical printers for outputs, and magnetic tapes for data storage were substituted by integrated circuits and microprocessors, disk and solid-state devices, keyboards, and visual and tactual screens for controlling operations.

The advent of the first personal computers in the 1980s put desk and laptop workstations within easy reach for business and private uses, although large computers continued being built for government and corporate applications requiring massive data storage, fast processing, and a huge number of calculations. The manufacture of microchips to power computers became a high-technology business requiring considerable investments. Programming languages evolved from machine language with zeros and ones in the 1950s to more accessible and convenient programming languages like Fortran IV and COBOL and later C++, Python, and Java. Spreadsheets became a tool for automating tasks that required repetitive calculations; beyond performing simple mathematical operations they became capable of running programs that employ a variety of arithmetic, algebraic, and statistical formulas.

Further developments would lead to cellular telephones and their supporting infrastructure, putting long-distance communication within the reach of most people. From unwieldy devices transmitting voice unreliably in less than two decades, they evolved into digital smartphones capable of voice and image transmission, recording sounds and video, providing digital storage, hosting multiple applications, and putting all their owners in contact with each other all over the world. These new means of transmitting and storing vast amounts of information across time and space altered human interactions in ways that are rapidly changing and still being explored.

The Space Age began in 1957 when the Soviet Union put in orbit Sputnik, the first artificial satellite, which launched a scientific and technological space race with the United States. The number of orbiting satellites increased to more than 100 by 2000 and would grow exponentially in the following two decades. Communications satellites facilitated the worldwide exchange of digital information, provided infrastructure for the Internet, allowed the exchange of electronic mails and made possible geolocation systems. The first of five American astronaut crews landed on the Moon in 1969 and was followed in subsequent decades by unmanned Moon missions from the Soviet Union, China, and India.

Throughout history, technical and technological development has been associated with the conduct of war. However, the scale and impact of the mobilization of technology and science for military purposes during the twentieth century were unprecedented. Aircraft, developed a few years earlier, were used in World War I for reconnaissance, bombardments, and aerial combat. Sonar, an echolocation device, was developed in England shortly before the war and widely used in submarine warfare.

Chemical weapons, which included toxic gases such as chlorine, phosgene, and mustard gas, were used by all sides during World War I, killing tens of thousands of soldiers and wounding many more. The German Chemical Warfare Service involved prominent scientists and engineers in the development of weapons, and other nations would soon turn to scientific research to expand their arsenals.

The impact of World War I on scientific research in the United States went far beyond the development of weapons. According to historian of engineering Ronald Kline:

> the topic [of scientific and industrial research] became a matter of national defense when the United States was cut off from German dyes, fine optics, and other products early in the war, ... The country did not lack necessary facilities. The research laboratory founded by the German-trained chemist Willis Whitney at General Electric in 1900 had proved its worth by the start of the war; AT&T had established a research group to improve long-distance telephony in 1911; and Eastman Kodak and Du Pont had spent considerable sums on industrial research before the war (Kline, 1995, pp. 194–221).

What emerged was a new "gospel of industrial research" that involved numerous chemists and engineers who aimed to persuade corporations to engage in scientific research and technological development.

Guided missiles, radar, jet engines, deciphering machines, among other science-based military equipment, would determine the course of World War II. The massive destruction and loss of life caused by the Allied bombing of German urban areas, and by the guided rockets launched by Germany to London and other English cities, would be eclipsed by the terrifying power of the American atomic bombs that obliterated the Japanese cities of Hiroshima and Nagasaki.

World War II forged close relations between research, industry, and the military in all countries involved in the conflict. As British historian Eric Hobsbawm put it:

> The Second World War fused political and scientific decisions and turned science fiction into reality, sometimes nightmare reality. The atom bomb was the social application of a political judgment against Hitler made in 1939 by the purest nuclear theorists and

> experimenters. … War and only war was to give science and technology—nuclear, spatial, computer-generated—the resources and the support structure that propelled both disciplines into the second half of the century. And because it put new and limitless powers into human hands, war escaped from control and reversed the relation between sorcerer and apprentice (Hobsbawm, as cited in Bernal, 1967, p. xxi; Hobsbawm, 2014, pp. 178–179).

The extent to which World War II stimulated interest and support for science and technology can be clearly seen in a statement of American President Franklin Roosevelt in the preface of a report, *Research: A National Resource*, submitted to Congress in May 1944: "One of the greatest resources in the arsenal of democracy is our national ability and interest in industrial research. For the vigorous prosecution of our defense program and for the assurance of national progress after the emergency we rely heavily on the continued vitality of research by industry in both pure and applied science" (United States National Research Council, 1941, p. 3).

Vannevar Bush, the Director of the US Office of Scientific Research and Development, would further develop this argument in his 1945 report *Science: The Endless Frontier*: "without scientific progress no amount of achievement in other directions can insure our health, prosperity, and security as a nation in the modern world" (Bush, 1945, p. 11).

World War II also prompted the creation of the new field of "operations research" to improve the performance of the British armed forces. Physicist Patrick Maynard Blackett recruited a group of diverse scientists to support the war effort. Known as "Blackett circus," this motley crowd of researchers used mathematical, statistical, and behavioral science methods to make significant contributions in various areas of warfare: deciphering coded messages, improving air raids and the safety of naval convoys, making radars and their use more effective, and helping organize the landing of the Allied Forces on the French coast.

Operations research approaches and methods would soon spill over from military to civilian business and government operations, and lead in subsequent decades to new management science methods and practices. As science historian John D. Bernal put it at the end of World War II:

> The original implications of operational research are already making themselves felt in peacetime economy. In principle it amounts to the statement that any human activity and any branch of that activity is a legitimate subject for scientific study, and subsequently for modification in the light of that study. Once this is accepted in practice, which implies the provision of research workers to carry out these studies, the way is open to a new level of man's control of his environment, one in which economic and social processes become scientific through and through (Bernal, 1967, p. xxi).

Dominating nature through understanding would become a national objective and a cornerstone of public policy for the United States, the Soviet Union, and later for other countries, signaling the pervasive acceptance and success of the Baconian Program.

However, Sir Francis Bacon's anticipation that scientific research can provide instruments of war and destruction became a disturbing reality during the two World Wars of the twentieth century. His warning was echoed by Heisenberg, who thought the use of science to produce arms would be disastrous, and Bohr, who argued "the rapid progress of science and technology in our days entails unique promises for the promotion of human welfare and at the same time imminent menaces to universal security, [which] presents our whole civilization with a veritable challenge" (Heisenberg, 1962, p. 206; Bohr, 1966, pp. 15–16).

All the scientific and technological advances of the knowledge society ended up modifying our understanding of the world and our living conditions. Scientific research, technological development, and innovation activities experienced major transformations, gave rise to the field of science and technology studies, and led to shifts in the worldwide distribution of economic and social activities.

The Changed Character of Scientific Research

According to Canadian science historian Benoit Godîn, "the emergence of the industrial research laboratory is without doubt one of the major innovations of the late nineteenth and early twentieth century. In the United States alone, there were three hundred such laboratories in 1920." What animated their work was what was called "the linear model of innovation," in which "technological innovation starts with basic research, then moves to applied research and then development. Once development is completed, the technology is produced on a large scale by industry then diffuses through the economy" (Godîn, 2009, pp. 5–6).

As the century advanced, instead of viewing research findings leading directly to new technologies and their subsequent incorporation into production and service activities, the complex interactions between science, technology, and innovation began to be recognized. Technological developments influenced scientific research agendas and supported economic and social innovation; production and service activities identified problems requiring technological solutions and stimulated scientific creativity; research methods and findings enabled technology development and opened new possibilities for social and economic innovators. Unlike what was assumed in the linear model, it was accepted that multiple interactive loops of scientific research, technological development, and innovation processes shape each other in often unexpected ways.

The institutional settings for the conduct of science, technology, and innovation activities shifted. Private enterprises, rather than public institutions, became the main performers of scientific and technological activities. The dominant role of profits and stock valuations shifted corporate research priorities and funding sources toward short-term profits, away from long-term undertakings aiming at social benefits. The private sector became responsible for more than half of research and development investments in most of the high-income countries, and in Japan, the Republic of Korea, Australia, Germany, Spain, Finland, and Italy, this proportion was even higher. Universities accounted for about a fifth of investments in science and technology, and public research institutes for the rest.

Links between universities and private firms strengthened in high-income countries, with corporations often setting the research agendas of academic institutions.

Collaborative industrial research and technological alliances became an imperative in the more advanced technological fields. Venture capital firms and specialized government agencies turned into a source of risk capital for science-based technology businesses.

Alliances between universities and private corporations became a major feature of the research landscape. The 1980 Bayh–Dole Act passed by the United States Congress allowed the results of publicly funded university research to be patented by the universities and their researchers. Instead of placing research results in the public domain, this led to the private appropriation of economic benefits from work carried out with taxpayer resources. The Bayh–Dole Act was initially considered a success because of the increased number of patents registered by universities and their researchers, and the numerous commercial ventures it led to. However, several downsides of the Bayh–Dole Act were soon identified: it fostered a culture of research for short-term pecuniary gains, promoted competition instead of collaboration, encouraged secrecy and limited the exchange of scientific information, and made it more difficult to use publicly funded research results as a basis for further scientific efforts.

Institutional settings for the conduct of scientific and technological activities changed also in response to major increases in the cost of basic and applied research, which led to greater concentration in fields where large teams and facilities were needed, and results could take a long time. Certain fields of inquiry (particle physics, genetics, molecular biology, astrophysics, among others) became increasingly dependent on highly expensive instruments and equipment that, as in the case of particle physics, chemical synthesis, and frontier microelectronics research, combined advances in electronics, materials science, optics, analytical techniques, and information processing. In spite of research being conducted largely by the private sector and academic institutions, public funds played a key role in the development of new technologies that would lead to the electronic revolution. In the United States, the Defense Advanced Research Projects Agency (DARPA) and the Department of Defense were behind many of the developments that led to, among other products and technologies, the iPhone and the Global Positioning System (GPS).

The accelerated pace of scientific progress required continuous efforts to keep up with advances in the state of the art. The stock of knowledge and the capabilities acquired through training and research became obsolete rather quickly. This had important implications for human resources development and for training researchers in advanced scientific fields.

The time span between scientific discovery and economic exploitation of research results shortened considerably as the Baconian Program shifted from unfolding to deployment. During the nineteenth century, it took 50 years between Faraday's discovery that a moving magnetic field can produce electricity and the first practical system for the generation and distribution of electric energy. Forty years elapsed between Einstein's early twentieth-century discovery of the fundamental relations between matter and energy and the detonation of the first atomic bomb. Twenty years were necessary for Watson and Crick's mid-twentieth century discovery of the structure of DNA to be applied in the first transplant of genes. It took only 6 years between the discovery of the electron tunneling effect by Japanese physicist Leo Esaki in 1957 and the first commercial application of semiconductor diodes.

The Systemic Nature of Technological Innovation

As scientific research and technological development were experiencing major transformations, the process of innovation acquired a systemic character. Putting new findings in practice became an increasingly complex task that combined advances in different fields, required a variety of complementary inputs, demanded greater management capabilities, and intensified both collaboration and competition.

A host of innovations emerged as a result of integrating previously unrelated scientific findings and technologies. It was seldom the case that individual advances in information technology, new materials, medical diagnoses and treatment, biotechnology, chemical synthesis, electronics, computer science, among others, could be applied on their own without integrating research results from different fields. The technological convergence implied by the more systemic character of innovation made it necessary for innovators to develop expertise in a broader array of science and technology disciplines.

In the health and medical field, small bio-electronic prostheses joined sensors monitored biological activity in the human body, registered and processed variations in real time with microelectronic chips that administered chemical drugs in predefined doses. Similar devices restored or replaced damaged body parts; pacemakers, artificial limbs, and hearing aids combined small long-lasting power supplies, electronic sensors, and new materials that could be safely inserted into the human body. Developments in biotechnology, molecular biology, and advanced electronic instrumentation transformed the food-processing and pharmaceutical industries.

Automation and computer-aided manufacturing put together advances in microelectronics, optoelectronics, digital computers, telecommunications, programming languages, and artificial intelligence to create integrated technology systems that vastly improved productivity in industry, agriculture, mining, and other sectors of the economy.

The systemic character of innovation altered the concept of critical mass in scientific research, technological development, and innovation. In addition to quantitative critical mass (amount of resources, number of people, size of facilities) and qualitative critical mass (type of resources and equipment, personnel qualifications), it became necessary to acquire an "interface critical mass" of competencies and capabilities in adjacent and indirectly related fields.

A larger number of parties became involved as a result of the greater complexity of the innovation process. In addition to suppliers of materials, energy, equipment, and other inputs, the development and introduction of new products and services required the support of quality control laboratories, intellectual property rights lawyers, management consultants, educational and research institutions, and specialized financial organizations. Government agencies in charge of safety, competition, labor standards, and other regulations complemented this larger cast of characters.

This has led to concerns about the slowing pace of technological innovation and the diminishing returns to investment in research and development. A report by McKinsey Consulting staff members pointed out that "innovation is becoming harder and more expensive" indicating that "research and development productivity has been declining." They point out this has been happening in many different fields, from microelectronics to drug discovery and agriculture. At the same time, they suggest that the use of artificial intelligence may increase the speed and the range of new technology options to explore, primarily by accelerating the conduct of research and development and by helping to focus efforts on the most promising candidates (Singla et al., 2025).

Policy Imperatives

The deployment and success of the Baconian Program made the governance of knowledge generation and utilization a main concern for public institutions, private enterprises, civil society organizations, and higher education institutions. How to acquire and consolidate science, technology, and innovation capabilities became a key subject for government policy, leading to a host of interventions that ranged from measures to strengthen higher education institutions to incentives for enterprises to adopt new technologies (Sagasti, 1972).

During the centuries-long Baconian epoch, there was a recurrent interest in finding ways to support the generation and utilization of knowledge. Bacon's pleas to Queen and King to support research, efforts by Royal Society members to create space for science and experimentation, Colbert's State policies to support useful science, and the renewal and expansion of higher education in the United States were some of the interventions aimed at strengthening science and technology capabilities.

Shortly before World War II, British scientist and historian John D. Bernal's *The Social Function of Science* paved the way for a new area of intellectual endeavors—science and technology studies—which emerged in full view following the successful mobilization of science to support the war effort (see Bernal, 1967). From initial concerns centered on the growth and conduct of scientific research, during the following decades science and technology studies focused on technological development, technology transfer, appropriate technologies, and the implementation of innovation policies.

Several science and technology policy research and teaching programs were established in European and American universities in the 1960s. Historians, sociologists, anthropologists, and philosophers applied the scientific method to examine the conduct of science itself, the means to foster technology development, and how to promote innovation. The concept of "national systems of innovation" advanced in the 1980s aimed to describe and examine how new knowledge is generated and utilized (Sagasti, 1972).

The "science wars" of the 1990s were an example of the controversies arising in this new area of study. According to British humanities professor Steven Goldman, the received conceptions of scientific knowledge as objective, neutral, and verifiable were questioned by the "critics of science, who argued that science was a socially empowered belief system or ideology … and became actively hostile to the practice of science as well as to the putative knowledge that scientists produced, denouncing both as ideological, patriarchal, sexist, racist, and pretenders to truth." As he pointed out, "the implications for how we are to understand the nature of scientific knowledge remain profound for formulating effective science-based public policies" (Goldman, 2021, p. 243).

Science and technology studies also covered questions of policy design and implementation, which became a primary concern of countries with limited knowledge generation capabilities. Among other issues, findings led to a distinction between explicit and implicit science, technology and innovation policies. Explicit policies are directly aimed at influencing decisions on knowledge generation and utilization. The concept of implicit policies refers to the impact that policies in other fields have on science, technology, and innovation decisions.

Financial, credit, educational, labor, tax, trade, and regulatory policies lie outside the conventional boundaries of science and technology policy. However, their collateral effects and second-order consequences may stimulate or discourage the generation and utilization of knowledge; may create either a favorable or a hostile environment for rigorous inquiry, experimentation, and risk-taking. Therefore, they have an implicit content of science, technology, and innovation policies. It is not enough to focus just on explicit policies, but necessary to align them with a wider range of other policies to ensure they reinforce and not undermine each other (Sagasti, 1979).

The high cost of advanced scientific facilities, equipment, and personnel, together with financial constraints, puts many fields of research out of the reach of the majority of middle and low-income countries. Yet, advances in microelectronics, information processing, and telecommunications allow researchers from all parts of the world to undertake joint research projects. They make possible accessing remote libraries and sources of information, holding real-time videoconferences with peers in distant places, instantly sending test results to centers with advanced facilities to analyze them, and using personal computers and specialized software as virtual laboratory instruments.

It was recognized that building science, technology, and innovation capabilities are long-term and arduous tasks, and that for the foreseeable future public support will be essential to help manage research risks. Hard-won achievements appeared to diminish at the rapid pace of advance at the frontiers of scientific research and technological innovation. In many cases, investments were made, researchers trained, institutions built, and policies designed and implemented, only to see them fall apart a few years later. Lack of persistence, twists and turns in the paths of scientific advances, strategic mistakes in the selection of priorities, and political indifference all led to wasted efforts, resources, and time.

Jorge Sábato, the Argentinean physicist who pioneered science and technology policy studies in Latin America, used to say: "it takes fifteen years of hard work to build a world-class research facility, but only two years for incompetent politicians to destroy it" (J. Sábato, personal communication). Nonetheless, as the examples of the Republic of Korea and China show, determined efforts sustained over decades make it possible to build science, technology, and innovation capabilities, to become internationally competitive in key economic sectors, and to significantly improve domestic living standards.

A Changed World Context

Sir Francis Bacon thought that the perfect use of reason—the scientific method—would allow dominating nature through understanding and lead to indefinite improvements in the human condition. Yet, as pointed out clearly in *New Atlantis*, he also anticipated that advances in the generation and utilization of knowledge could lead to harmful outcomes. This became clear as the deployment of the Baconian Program intertwined with the expansion of world markets, the logic of capital accumulation, and the eruption of international wars and other violent conflicts. While fostering economic growth and improving living standards, this entanglement also had negative consequences, as it became obvious during the two World Wars.

The context for human endeavors changed radically during the twentieth century. Population increased nearly fourfold to about 6.3 billion, doubling the growth rate observed between 1750 and 1900, and increasing tenfold the rate that prevailed in the millennia prior to 1750. The world production of goods and services grew at a rapid pace; in 2000, it was almost 20 times larger than at the beginning of the century. According to the International Monetary Fund:

> … technological change has driven an enormous increase in the production of goods and services, sufficient to support both vastly higher living standards and vastly larger populations than ever before in history. The increase in productivity has been accompanied by greatly increased specialization in production, leading to the rising importance of markets that have facilitated the exchange of goods and the diffusion of technology, both within and between national economies. By greatly reducing transportation costs, technical progress has contributed to the geographical expansion of markets (International Monetary Fund, 2000, p. 149).

The growth and diversification of productive and service activities took place in parallel with changes in international trade and finance. Liberalization and deregulation gave a greater role to market forces in determining the volume, content, and direction of the international flow of products, capital, technology, information, knowledge, and labor. International trade and financial transactions grew at a higher rate than economic output, and the nature of the international financial and monetary system changed significantly and repeatedly in the course of the twentieth century (International Monetary Fund, 2000, p. 151).

These changes led to the emergence of a tight web of global financial transactions involving securities trading, arbitrage in multiple markets and currencies, futures trading with exotic financial instruments, automated securities trading platforms, portfolio investment through a bewildering array of international funds, and massive transborder capital movements. Financial transactions acquired a life of their own and became largely uncoupled from the production of goods and services.

The expansion and greater sophistication of financial markets and instruments had an important influence on the creation and acquisition of science, technology, and innovation capabilities, particularly in high-income countries. Numerous venture capital firms supported startups working at the frontiers of knowledge, although the pressure to exhibit short-term returns and maintain high equity valuations was often incompatible with the long-term task of acquiring and maintaining advanced research capabilities, and even less with directing them to the improvement of the human condition in its widest sense. The consequences were several waves of acquisitions, mergers, and bankruptcies that increased corporate concentration, strengthened the market power of large technology firms, and limited the entry of new players.

Another important feature of the international trade scene at the end of the twentieth century was the adoption of "Trade-Related Aspects of Intellectual Property Rights" (TRIPS). Technology-advanced countries pressured for stricter regulations that strengthened the bargaining power of corporate technology owners. In addition to increasing technology costs, TRIPS limited opportunities for technology adaptation, imitation, copying, and reverse engineering, which were used earlier by firms in high-income countries to acquire technology and innovation capabilities, often with strong government support.

The consequences of more restrictive intellectual property rights were described by the United Kingdom Commission on Intellectual Property Rights:

> developing countries should not be deprived of the flexibility to design their intellectual property systems that developed countries enjoyed in earlier stages of their own development, and higher intellectual property standards should not be pressed on them without a serious an objective assessment of their development impact. We need to ensure that the global intellectual property systems evolve so that they may contribute to the development of developing countries, by stimulating innovation and technology transfer relevant to them, while also making available the products of technology at the most competitive prices possible. We need to make sure that the intellectual property system facilitates, rather than hinders, the application of the rapid advances in science and technology for the benefit of developing countries (Commission on Intellectual Property Rights, 2002, p. 8).

The relentless pursuit of new and more effective ways of satisfying human needs had its drawbacks. The greater diversity of products and services associated with economic growth, together with innovations in marketing and advertising, planned obsolescence, short manufacturing cycles, and slightly differentiated products, created demand for many superfluous goods and services. This intensified the use of materials and energy consumption, prompted searches for new supply sources, and increased the burden of disposing of waste, residues, and discards. Their consequences—global warming, climate change, air and water pollution, biodiversity loss, and inordinate stresses on the natural ecosystems—would become acute in the twenty-first century.

In a review of developments during the twentieth century, the International Monetary Fund underscored that "the fruits of economic growth have been distributed unevenly among countries, ... Inequality between the world's rich and poor regions, measured by output per capita, has increased dramatically over time," (International Monetary Fund, 2000, p. 149), as it has done within countries. Widespread poverty, inequality, and the concentration of wealth, together with frustrated expectations and unfair access to economic and social benefits, prevent many people from living a satisfactory and meaningful life, which often leads to social unrest.

In his essay *Of Sedition and Troubles*, Bacon argued that poverty and discontent are the main causes of uprisings: "want and necessity" create "danger that is imminent and great ... rebellions from the belly are the worst" (Bacon, 1985, p. 103). In his view, suffering and fear lead to perilous discontent, exhaust patience, and lead to violence. This stern warning, made four centuries ago, appears quite timely.

Success and Its Downsides

As the deployment of the Baconian Program intertwined with the expansion of world markets and capital accumulation, the twentieth century witnessed a widespread adoption of science-based technologies and significant transformations in the conduct of scientific research. Technological innovation acquired a systemic character, science and technology became issues for government policy, and the international economic, social, and political landscape changed to an extent unimaginable in the early 1900s.

The Baconian Program of dominating nature through understanding succeeded to an extraordinary degree. Its gradual unfolding and deliberate deployment would create new settings for the exercise of human faculties. Its components—method, purpose, direction, focus, and institutions—wove themselves into the social fabric, initially in Europe and North America and later unevenly throughout the world. Scientific research, technological development, and innovation entangled with each other at the frontiers of knowledge.

However, unlocking the secrets of nature to improve the human condition had unexpected downsides that cast gloomy shadows on the success of the Baconian Program. While the scientific method was generally accepted as the most effective and useful way to generate knowledge, its limitations began to be recognized and acknowledged. Seeking to revive outdated and misleading ways of acquiring and using knowledge, resistance to science kept on simmering and occasionally erupting, seeding mistrust and skepticism, questioning the conduct of science and its results.

The purpose, direction, and focus of the Baconian Program evolved in a paradoxical way. While creating extraordinary opportunities to improve the human condition, they also had increasingly deleterious effects. Advances in knowledge allowed us to build deadly weapons and awesome means of destruction that endanger the survival of our species. The notion of indefinite progress was put on hold as improvements in living standards coexisted with widespread poverty, hunger, destitution, and rising inequalities between and within countries.

Bacon's Promethean notion that "the whole world works together in the service of Man" encouraged a quest that ended up degrading the natural ecosystems that support life. Institutional arrangements for the generation and utilization of knowledge shifted away from public entities toward private corporations. Instead of regarding research results as widely available public good, they were increasingly appropriated for private gain. Profit-making corporations became the main supporters of technological development and innovation, with public sources relegated to a second plane.

Was the unfolding, deployment, and success of the Baconian Program a Promethean achievement or a Faustian bargain? Was it a way of elevating humanity toward Godly powers, or a pact with the devil that will end up annihilating our species? The shadows cast during the twentieth century by the ambiguous success of Bacon's Program herald the twilight of his epoch. They set the stage for even more momentous changes in the human condition, even deeper and wider-reaching than those experienced in the transition from Medieval to Modern times. As we began to tread unsteadily further into the twenty-first century, the twilight of Bacon's epoch forced us to urgently reassess the prospects for humanity.

References

Bacon, F. (1985). In J. Pitcher (Ed.), *The essays*. Penguin Books.

Bernal, J. D. (1967). *The social function of science*. MIT Press.

Bohr, N. (1966). *Essays 1958–1962 on atomic physics and human knowledge: The most important essays written by Niels Bohr in the last years of his life*. Vintage.

Bush, V. (1945). *Science: The endless frontier. A report to the president on a program for postwar scientific research*. National Science Foundation. https://ia601304.us.archive.org/29/items/scienceendlessfr00unit/scienceendlessfr00unit.pdf

Commission on Intellectual Property Rights. (2002). *Integrating intellectual property rights and development policy*. Commission on Intellectual Property Rights.

Eccles, J. (1993). A divine design: Some questions on origins. In H. Margenau & R. A. Varghese (Eds.), *Cosmos, bios, Theos* (pp. 162–164). Open Court Publishers.

Gell-Mann, M. (1996). Plectics. In J. Brockman (Ed.), *The third culture*. Touchstone.

Godîn, B. (2009). *The linear model of innovation (II): Maurice Holland and the research cycle* (No. Working Paper No. 3). Project on the Intellectual History of Innovation. https://espace.inrs.ca/id/eprint/9914/1/Godin_2009_linear.pdf

Goldman, S. L. (2021). *Science wars: The Battle between knowledge and reality*. Oxford University Press.

Heisenberg, W. (1962). *Physics & philosophy: The revolution in modern science*. Harper & Row.

Hobsbawm, E. (2014). *Fractured times: Culture and society in the twentieth century*. Abacus.

International Monetary Fund. (2000). *World economic outlook, may 2000: Asset prices and the business cycle*. International Monetary Fund. https://doi.org/10.5089/9781557759368.081

Keller, E. F. (1985). *Reflections on gender and science*. Yale University Press.

Kline, R. (1995). Construing “technology” as “applied science”: Public rhetoric of scientists and engineers in the United States, 1880-1945. *Isis, 86*(2), 194–221.

Maturana, H., & Varela, F. J. (1980). *Autopoiesis and cognition: The realization of the living*. Reidel Publishing Company.

McCormmach, R. (1982). *Night thoughts of a classical physicist*. Avon Books.

Mumford, L. (1969). *The pentagon of power: The myth of the machine*. Harcourt Brace.

Pinker, S. (1996). Language is a human instinct. In J. Brockman (Ed.), *The third culture*. Touchstone.

Sagasti, F. (1972). A systems approach to science and technology policymaking and planning. .

Sagasti, F. (1979). *Science and Technology for Development: Main comparative report of the STPI project*. International Development Research Centre.

Simpson, G. G. (1967). *The meaning of evolution: A study of the history of life and of its significance for man*. Yale University Press.

Singla, A., Sukharevsky, A., Berteletti, E., Yee, L., & Chui, M. (2025). The next innovation revolution powered by AI. *McKinsey Quarterly*. https://www.mckinsey.com/capabilities/quantumblack/our-insights/the-next-innovation-revolution-powered-by-ai

Truett Anderson, W. (1987). *To govern evolution: Further adventures of the political animal*. Harcourt Brace Jovanovich.

Turing, A. (1950). Computing machinery and intelligence. *Mind, 49*, 433–460.

UNESCO. (2005). Towards knowledge societies. In J. Bindé (Ed.), *UNESCO world report*. UNESCO Publishing. http://specialcollections.nust.na:8080/greenstone3/library/sites/localsite/collect/unesco/index/assoc/HASH013b.dir/Towards_knowledge_societies.pdf;jsessionid=899AFA380E14272B300A4DEF07159438

United States National Research Council. (1941). *Research: A National Resource: Industrial research*. US National Printing Office.

Part III
The Twilight of Bacon's Epoch

Introduction to Part III

The unfolding, deployment, and extraordinary success of the Baconian Program changed humanity's understanding of itself and its place in the cosmic order, increased the repertoire of technological responses to the challenges of the biophysical and social environments, and multiplied products and services to satisfy individual and collective needs. The fusion of science, technology, and production it led to opened new possibilities for improving the human condition but also increased enormously the impact of human activities on the planet.

Yet, in ways that were not anticipated centuries ago, the success of Sir Francis Bacon's program ended up displacing the worldview that gave rise to it. The foundations on which it initially stood—articulated in Bacon's conceptions of method, purpose, direction, focus, and institutions—shifted; they no longer can support, on their own and as they were implicitly formulated, the approaches now required to make sense of the situations it generated. The Baconian Program requires an urgent update, a complete reformulation that preserves what may still be useful but rethinks and reshapes its components. Whatever such an exercise may lead to must be placed within the broader framework of what humanity is becoming at the twilight of Bacon's epoch.

Disregarding Bacon's admonition to avoid the all-too-human tendency to assume greater similarities where there may be none, we may be tempted to draw parallels between Bacon's life and the fate of its program. His professional and political career unfolded slowly during the long years of Queen Elizabeth's reign; his considerable intellectual gifts and courtier skills were consciously employed during the first decade of King James I's reign. He succeeded spectacularly during the following 5 years, becoming Chancellor, viscount of St. Albans and rising to the highest possible positions in the realm, but only to fall precipitously from grace, accused of corruption, of subverting the very laws he fought to uphold, and of betraying royal trust.

As we witness the twilight of Bacon's epoch, as advanced earlier, we may indulge in drawing parallels between, on the one hand, his slow rise to fortune, unrelenting search for royal favors, determined exercise of political power and his eventual fall from grace and, on the other, the unfolding, deployment, success, and twilight of his program. In the same manner he reinvented himself in exile during the last years of his life, we face the task of reinventing his program, of rethinking its premises, content, consequences, and future prospects. We may take a cue from Hungarian-American philosopher Agnes Heller's *Renaissance Man*, a treatise that describes the social and individual impacts of the transition from the Middle Ages and the Renaissance to Modernity, which radically changed our understanding of the human condition. The twilight of Bacon's epoch, whether dusk or dawn, brings even greater seismic shifts in our assessment of the human prospect.

The third part of this book appraises the consequences of the success of the Baconian Program, examines the unprecedented situation of extreme vulnerability and great opportunity it has created, and explores how we could cope with the transition to a post-Baconian epoch.

Chapter 9 describes the new context for human endeavors in the first decades of the twenty-first century. It reviews briefly current conceptions of the cosmos, matter, time, evolution, consciousness, and interrelations with ecosystems. It then focuses on advances in information technology, cyberspace and virtual reality, and artificial intelligence, viewing them as new realms for the exercise of human faculties that transcend the dualistic mind/matter Cartesian distinction of the Baconian epoch. The chapter ends with an appraisal of the new "domain of the global," a new planet-wide setting for human action that, together with the domains of the local and of the networks, has created a paradoxical fractured global order.

Chapter 10 offers a reappraisal of the Baconian Program and its self-undermining consequences, examining how each of its components—method, purpose, direction, focus, institutions—has been altered by their relentless pursuit during 400 years. It reviews current challenges to the scientific method and the conduct of science; argues that the concept of development is the latest and last reinterpretation of the idea of progress within the framework of the Baconian Program; and provides an overview of the emerging institutional arrangements for the generation and utilization of knowledge.

Chapter 11 reflects on the transition to a post-Baconian epoch, exploring some of its possible features and offering a few hints on how to cope with it. As put forward in the introduction to this volume, twilight can mean dusk or dawn; whether it is one or the other will depend on how we deal with the ambiguous legacy of Sir Francis Bacon's program.

Chapter 9
A New Setting for Human Endeavors

Man will take his own evolution in hand, with the aim...of modifying it by improvements of his own design. Whether we have the right to do it,...is the most serious question that can be posed.

Hans Jonas

The success of Bacon's program radically altered the human condition and its prospects. It shifted the ways we perceive and understand the world, dislodging humanity from its supposedly privileged place in the order of things. It led to the emergence of a paradoxical fractured global order that puts people all over the world in contact with each other, while simultaneously creating and maintaining deep fissures between them. At the twilight of Bacon's epoch, we are in a new setting for the pursuit of human endeavors.

The fusion of science, technology, and production emerging from the unfolding, deployment, and success of the Baconian Program opened possibilities for better health, higher life expectancy, improved material comfort, rewarding intellectual pursuits, deeper understanding of societies, pleasing artistic endeavors, and diversified leisure activities. However, its unquestionable success also brought undesirable consequences, distributed its benefits unevenly, and threatened the existence of our species.

Shifting Worldviews

Scientific research led to new findings about the universe, the structure of matter, and the concept of time. The nature of the physical world has been challenged by strange probabilistic notions of matter, which is now seen as made up of fields of possibilities rather than as something stable; by speculation about the existence of multiple universes, impossible for current science tools to confirm or deny; and by

F. Sagasti, *Knowledge is Power*, Innovation, Technology, and Knowledge Management, https://doi.org/10.1007/978-3-032-20668-8_9

the displacement of absolute linear time, which no longer constitutes a fixed backdrop for the flow of events.

Humanity ceded its Promethean centrality, acknowledging reciprocal give-and-take interactions with the ecosystems that support all kinds of living organisms; it wrestled away from nature the haphazard conduction of biological evolution, placing it under its guidance and control.

Advances in information sciences, communications technology, digitalization, and artificial intelligence created new realms for the exercise of human faculties, transformed our individual and social selves, and created artificial intelligence devices that complement and even substitute human reasoning.

The swift emergence of virtual reality and cyberspace challenged the mind/matter dualism that underpinned the modern worldview since the times of Bacon and Descartes in the seventeenth century. It created an intermediate realm of virtual entities that are less physical and real than tangible ones, but more concrete and capable of visualization than concepts or ideas. As the virtual realm of cyberspace is explored and settled, a mind/virtual/matter triad has laid the ground for novel expressions of human creativity.

Global communication networks have speeded up information access and exchanges, reduced distance and time constraints, and created new ways of living, learning, and working. The proliferation of these networks, together with the worldwide environmental impact of individual decisions and actions, has led to the emergence of the domain of the global, a new wide-reaching field of intensified and continuous human interactions, and of humanity with the ecosystems all over the world. While this new domain creates new opportunities for collaboration and collective action, it also magnifies the undesirable impacts of individual decisions and local actions.

Matter, Cosmos, and Time

Scientific research findings have sown doubts about the nature of the physical world. Decades of work on quantum mechanics theory provide baffling accounts of the atomic and subatomic phenomena that constitute matter. Experimental results have prompted theoretical speculation and interpretations, bequeathing on us a proliferating zoo of subatomic particles.

The Standard Model of particle physics explains how different combinations of quarks, leptons, bosons, gluons, bosons, and fermions, among other particles, make up protons, neutrons, electrons, neutrinos, photons, and gravitons, binding some of them together and creating fields that make up the material world in which we live. Different combinations of particles are kept together by four basic forces: the strong and weak force which act at the nanoscopic atomic and subatomic levels, and the electromagnetic force and gravity that work at longer distances.

Theoretical physicists have been searching for a unified theory—a “Theory of Everything”—to account for all of these particles and fields in a single framework.

They have been able to integrate three of these fundamental forces, the electromagnetic, the weak, and the strong forces, but incorporating the fourth, gravity, has proved elusive. String and superstring theories attempt to do so, postulating that spacetime is filled with tiny multidimensional string-like entities whose different vibrations generate all existing particles and forces, but their experimental verification is still a work in progress.

Entanglement is one of the unusual inferences derived from quantum theory. It postulates that two distant particles can occupy multiple states simultaneously, preserving the same properties in spite of being far apart. Instantaneous communication between the two separate particles gave rise to the hypothesis that they are linked by some type of space wormhole held together by gravity. Quantum entanglement has been experimentally verified and is finding applications in quantum computing and cryptography (Clavin, 2022).

To understand the origins of the Universe, it has been found necessary to combine general relativity with quantum mechanics. The result places our planet in a vastly expanded cosmic setting, infinitely greater and more complex than what could be imagined centuries ago. This challenges not only the central place we used to assign our species and our planet in the order of things, but also the uniqueness of the very universe we inhabit.

The foundations of modern cosmological theory were laid by Einstein's general relativity theory, which implied that the universe could be either expanding or contracting. Reluctant to accept this conclusion, he adjusted his equations to yield an unchanging universe. Edwin Hubble's 1929 discovery that galaxies are moving away from each other challenged Einstein's static model. A universe receding in all directions must have had an initial state of infinite density, a "singularity," in which all matter was crushed to zero size and temperature was infinitely high. From such a state, the universe began with an explosion, a "big bang," and has expanded, thinned out, and cooled in its 13.8 billion years of existence.

The extreme conditions of the very early universe made the laws of quantum mechanics applicable to it. Quantum theories of gravity explain what happened at that primordial time in the life of the cosmos. A major result of the marriage between cosmology and quantum mechanics was the formulation of the inflationary model of the universe. It claims that shortly after the big bang the infant universe went through a brief and extremely rapid expansion, after which it returned to a more leisurely rate of growth.

The discovery of the cosmic microwave background in the 1960s detected tiny variations attributed to fluctuations in the radiation released 380,000 years after the big bang. The particles released by this initial explosion began to combine into various elements as the universe cooled, eventually forming stars and galaxies, and ultimately creating the Earth we inhabit (European Space Agency, n.d.). One startling consequence of accepting the inflationary model of the universe is that, had different initial conditions prevailed, there may exist other universes we are not able to observe. This led Russian-American theoretical physicist Andrei Linde to postulate the "eternally existing, self-reproducing inflationary universe" (Linde, 1994,

p. 54) hypothesis, suggesting that our universe may be just one of many in an expanding sea of universes.

Recent findings have shown the limitations of earlier accounts of the origin of the Universe. Astrophysicists have had to consider that the evidence gathered through more refined observation methods does not coincide with theory, and have had, as British and American astrophysicists Adam Frank and Marcelo Gleiser put it:

> … to postulate the existence of components of the universe for which we have no direct evidence. The standard model today holds that 'normal' matter—the stuff that makes up people and planets and everything else we can see—constitutes only about four percent of the universe. The rest is invisible stuff called dark matter and dark energy (roughly 27 percent and 68 percent) (Frank & Gleiser, 2023, para. 11). See also (Cowen, 2013; Wood, 2025).

A conception of continuously flowing time from past to present, steadily marching toward the future, underpinned the idea of indefinite progress associated with Bacon's implicitly formulated program. An indefinite succession of instants of infinitely small duration was thought of as approaching the march of real time, which provided a background for the evolution of everything in the Universe and for human progress (Nisbet, 1980). This notion has been superseded by the work and findings of scientists on the relations between time and the configuration of language, the identification of culture-specific time narratives, and attempts to catalog the different kinds of time experience. Imagination has been stretched to apprehend time spans that extend from billionths of a second to billions of years, and to accept strange notions of imaginary time, time flowing backward, and entangled simultaneous events (Fraser, 1981; Hall, 1984; Hawking, 1993; Penrose, 2012).

Relativity theory questioned the idea of time flowing evenly throughout the whole Universe, forever leaving behind a trail of instantaneous nows that relentlessly transform the future into the past. The rate at which time passed varied with the velocity of motion and all motion was relative to a chosen frame of reference, implying that it is not possible to unequivocally say that one event happened before, after, or simultaneously with another. Time could no longer be considered to be immutable; observers in different places and moving at different speeds experienced the passage of time in distinct manners (Falk, 2020; Wolchover, 2014).

Evolution and Genetics

During the Baconian epoch, the boundaries and limitations imposed by the slow process of biological evolution were unquestionably accepted. This changed toward the end of the twentieth century with the discovery of the structure of Deoxyribonucleic acid (DNA), the molecule that carries genetic information. It made possible the development of genetic engineering and cloning technologies for selecting and recombining DNA molecules, which replicate and propagate to create genetically altered organisms.

The first large-scale application of genetic engineering was made in plant breeding. By the second decade of the twenty-first century, the process of creating Genetically Modified Organisms (GMOs), which involved identifying genes with desired traits from one plant and inserting them into another, superseded and complemented the selective breeding and crossbreeding of food crops, the traditional methods for increasing productivity and resistance to weather changes and pests. In spite of some reservations about their impact on biodiversity conservation, they were approved by food safety agencies and made widely available to consumers.

Advances in genetics and heredity research made it possible to apply similar approaches to the human body. The description of the complete human genome at the beginning of the twenty-first century made it possible to develop tests for genetic diseases and devise therapies to overcome them. The development of Clustered Regularly Interspaced Short Palindromic Repeats (CRISPR) technology allowed to target specific DNA sequences to be excised and replaced in the human genome, opening a way to remove harmful mutations that cause genetic diseases. While still in its initial stages, with potential unintended consequences and high costs, further developments in gene modification are likely to reduce the prevalence of genetic malfunctions.

Discoveries and advances in genetic engineering imply that humanity is no longer at the mercy of blind evolutionary forces. This raises complex and thorny ethical questions. The power to alter the essential characteristics of human beings introduces the possibility of making deliberate choices to direct the biological evolution of our species. Humanity has the capability of transforming mutation, natural selection, and adaptation into intentional design, into a process of augmenting the human body and crafting human beings with desired characteristics. We need to agree soon on the ethical principles, habits of thought, institutional frameworks, and everyday practices to help us discharge the newly acquired responsibility of directing human evolution.

However, recent studies suggest that biological evolution is not solely based on genetic modifications that are products of adaptive natural selection, and that it is possible for organisms to influence the selective pressures exerted on them by altering their environments. As American historian of science Jessica Riskin puts it, "organisms are not purely passive objects of transformation but actively take part in directing the course of evolution, … the best way of understanding evolutionary processes is not by reducing them to just one cause, but rather by trying to encompass the rich causal variety in evolution." (Riskin & Feldman, 2022, para. 6).

Knowledge of how the immune system and the various organs of the human body, coupled with advances in electronics and materials science, has led to the development of biosensors, artificial organs, synthetic tissues, and biomechanical prostheses. These devices allow us to repair or substitute damaged parts of our bodies; they have opened up the possibility of a symbiosis which—added to the developments in artificial intelligence—may be leading to the co-evolution of humans and machines. Progress in biomedical engineering and related fields may be in the process of transforming human beings into the "prosthetic gods" envisaged by Austrian psychoanalyst Sigmund Freud (Freud, 1930).

Researchers have shown how human beings construct conscious perceptions of themselves and the surrounding world. The separation between bodily and mental processes, characteristic of Cartesian dualistic mind/body interpretations of human nature, has given way to mind and consciousness as emergent processes underpinned by exceedingly dense and rich neuronal circuits. These processes integrate sense data, the state of the body, and past experience in complex and chaotic ways. They interact and condition each other to create conscious and unconscious manifestations of the self that control and coordinate bodily functions, give rise to emotions and behaviors, and place our minds and bodies in the context of the world we inhabit (Béjar, 2013; Feldman Barrett, 2021; Libet, 2004).

The realization that our species is the result of a long evolutionary chain, which began eons ago with exceedingly simple organisms, has had profound consequences for the way we view the place of human beings in the order of things. Darwin's challenge to the Promethean centrality of humanity has had a paradoxical character: as we displaced the human species from the center of creation, we also acquired the capacity to influence and control our biological destiny. We have learned to preserve health, extend life and regulate human fertility, and have acquired the capacity to manipulate our genetic endowment. In addition, we are now constructing a host of biomechanical and bioelectronic devices that are augmenting human faculties.

The implications of these scientific advances are far-reaching. While other organisms undergo biological evolution, only human beings are aware and conscious of their evolutionary processes. As Russian-American geneticist Theodosius Dobzhansky and Swiss population geneticist Ernest Boesiger anticipated:

> man has now arrived at a stage which gives him extraordinary powers over his own evolution. Neither stagnation nor regression are possible … man alone understands evolution better and better—both his own and that of other species. Not only is he able to act and to intervene in his evolution, but he does so, massively, for better or for worse—whether or not he wishes to do so." (Dobzhansky & Boesiger, 1983, p. 107)

Ecosystems and the Anthropocene

Human activities have greater impact on the biophysical environment than those of any other species. During most of the Baconian epoch, human activities did not pose insurmountable environmental challenges. Local disruptions created problems of water and air pollution, biodiversity loss, soil erosion, and waste disposal, among others, but most could be contained and in some cases reversed. As long as natural resources could be replenished and the production of waste could be absorbed by the regenerative capacity of natural ecosystems, the scale of human interventions did not pose global environmental threats. However, at the beginning of the twenty-first century, the magnitude of world economic and social activities had surpassed the capacity of the environment to sustain them indefinitely.

The academically controversial term "Anthropocene" has been coined to designate this new period in Earth's history, in which the footprint left by our species has altered its biophysical features. World population exceeded 7.8 billion in 2020, more than three times the figure in 1950, life expectancy increased from 46 to 73 years during the same period, and average income per capita grew from $3360 to US$15,400 (Ritchie et al., 2023). The associated increases in consumption, energy use, and waste generation, among other consequences, have had a major impact on the natural environment. Average figures mask deep inequalities; mean incomes per capita in Western Europe and North America are more than ten times higher than in Africa. Even with slower rates of population growth, it will not be possible for the whole world to reach the current levels of material welfare, consumption patterns, and energy use of the high-income countries without destroying the environment.

A review of the economics of biodiversity prepared under the direction of British economist Sir Partha Dasgupta underscores this:

> When looking at the wider scope of the economics of the biosphere … our economic possibilities are circumscribed—even if several steps removed via technological progress—by the Earth-System's workings. We are embedded in Nature; we are not external to it. No amount of technological progress can make economic growth as conventionally measured an indefinite possibility. Ours is inevitably a finite economy, as is the biosphere of which we are part (Dasgupta, 2021, pp. 27–28).

Climate change is one of the most troubling manifestations of the human overshoot of nature. Average world temperatures exceeded the 1.5 degrees centigrade threshold in 2024, which, according to the Intergovernmental Panel on Climate Change, causes major disruptions all over the world—droughts, floods, hurricanes, heat waves, cold spells, ocean warming, biodiversity loss, and farmland degradation, among others—that increase habitat vulnerability and heighten migration pressures (Intergovernmental Panel on Climate Change [IPCC], 2019).

Activities that overwhelm the ecosystems that support them will eventually cease. The question is when and how they will end. According to the Dasgupta review, the rate of extinction of biological species is an indicator of having passed the threshold of irreversible damage to the biophysical environment:

> Largely as a result of human activities, species are becoming extinct much more rapidly than in the past. As currently calculated, extinction rates are judged to be 100 to 1,000 times higher than their background rate over the past tens of millions of years (0.1-1 per million species per year) and are continuing to rise … Continued species extinctions will damage the biosphere irreparably, involving unknown numbers of tipping points, which should tell us that potential cascades cannot be staved off by mere technological fixes (Dasgupta, 2021, p. 32).

The wholesale disappearance in a short time of biological organisms that took long to evolve raises alarm and points toward the troubling possibility that the human species may also become extinct in the not-too-distant future. As Sean ÓhÉigeartaigh, Co-Director of the Center for Existential Risk at Cambridge University has put it:

> Human extinction may seem unlikely but cannot be ruled out as a possibility. We now know that there have been cataclysmic events in the past that might have wiped out humans were those events to occur now. Novel threats to human civilization are now posed by our own activities, both in the form of climate change and environmental degradation and in the

form of powerful weapons such as nuclear weapons and emerging technologies such as artificial intelligence (AI) and engineered biology (ÓhÉigeartaigh, 2025, p. 1).

Faced with such dire prospects, the debate between what were known as doomsayers, who decades ago predicted catastrophic events on our planet due to population growth, excessive consumption, and global warming, and the cornucopians, who argued that technology and ingenuity will always usher in new golden eras for humanity, has acquired a new twist with the rise of transhumanism (Simon, 1981). Contrary to the views of those warning about the possibility of human extinction, transhumanists anticipate that we shall take control of our continued evolution, primarily due to advances in geoengineering, cybernetics, nanorobotics, neural implants, artificial intelligence, and other technological forms of augmenting human capabilities.

Less gloomy assessments suggest that humanity may stave off the potentially catastrophic consequences of our relentless Baconian quest to dominate nature through understanding, but at a high cost. Rather than extinction or transhumanist mutation, a significant cutback in world population would reduce the impact of human activities on the environment, drawing us closer to a sustainable equilibrium with nature. British historian Peter Frankopan thinks "it is easy to answer how the question of how the problem of climate change is solved: it will be nature, rather than human action, that ultimately brings net emissions towards zero. It will do so through catastrophic depopulation, whether through hunger, disease or conflict," (Frankopan, 2023, p. 658), to which we could add the disastrous impact of climate change, rogue artificial intelligence, and a nuclear holocaust.

The paradoxical situation that our species finds itself at the twilight of Bacon's epoch requires major adjustments in the expectations of future generations and new leadership styles in all areas of human activity. Yet, we still do not glimpse adequate responses to this predicament. Reconciling expectations and demands, not to mention prejudices and atavisms, with the biophysical limitations of our planet is a gargantuan task that requires a wholesale adoption of new values, attitudes, and behaviors. Whatever happens in the rest of the twenty-first century, the Baconian premise that dominating nature through understanding always leads to improvements in the human condition is no longer tenable.

Information Technology and Virtual Reality

The ideas put forward by Descartes and Bacon in the seventeenth century allowed humanity to operate in two kinds of entities—abstract thoughts and material objects—and to link them in a systematic way through the scientific method. Early modern science connected them by contrasting theories and hypotheses with observations and experiments.

Advances in information technology, microelectronics, telecommunications, and artificial intelligence challenged the Cartesian dualism that underpinned the scientific method of Bacon's implicit program; they created a new kind of entity—cyberspace, virtual reality—that lies somewhere between abstract thoughts and material objects. Australian-American professor of visual communication Michael L. Benedikt considered this development as an "inevitable step toward providing the maximum number of individuals with the means of creativity, productivity and control over the shapes of their lives within the new information and media environment." He provided one of the early definitions of this new entity:

> "Cyberspace is a globally networked, computer-sustained, computer-accessed, and computer generated, multidimensional, artificial or 'virtual' reality. In this reality, to which every computer is a window, seen or heard objects are neither physical nor, necessarily representations of physical objects but are, rather, in form, character and action, made up of data, of pure information. This information derives in part from the operations of the natural, physical world, but for the most part it derives from the immense traffic of information that constitute human enterprise in science, art, business, and culture." (Benedikt, 1992, pp. 121–123)

Virtual reality is changing the nature of human experience in ambiguous ways. It has the paradoxical potential of providing a new range of sensorial experiences which may, at the same time, enrich our interconnections with the world that surrounds us and remove ourselves from physical and social interactions. As American professor Michael Heim put it, "cyberspace is more than a breakthrough in electronic media or in computer interface design. With its virtual environments and simulated worlds, cyberspace is a metaphysical laboratory, a tool for examining our very sense of reality." He warns that by trapping us in an electronic never-never land of symbols, alphanumeric characters, streams of data, computer simulations, and multimedia constructs, "cyberspace can cast a spell of passivity in our lives." (Heim, 1993, pp. 79, 82).

The divorce between virtual and physical realities may also foster delusions and distort our ethical systems. As Dutch cyberspace researcher Herman E. Van Bolhuis and his collaborator Vicente Colom highlighted: "Virtual environments are not bound anymore by physical laws. Things may appear very easy; houses might be built in hours, landscapes and (virtual) populations (human beings, animals and plants) destroyed in virtual wars, new beings created without problems." (Bolhuis & Colom, 1995, p. 32). Flexibility and freedom to engage and act in cyberspace are indelible rights acquired just by logging in; they are constrained only by the overall parameters of software, which can be tweaked by learning algorithms and user choices. In cyberspace, we can destroy all that we have created and—at the touch of a key, at the click of a mouse, or at the tap of a pad—reset initial conditions to start all over again. In such instances, the sense of responsibility for our creatures and actions may vanish.

The various digital expressions of cyberspace—social networks, data storage, games, simulation models, communication systems, among many others—are under the joint control of the designers who program them, the agents who engage with digital entities, and the open-ended autonomous processes of adaptation, learning, and self-organization built into their algorithms. As is the case with artificial intelligence, they can break loose from and surpass their initial design and programming restrictions, with unknown and possibly dangerous consequences.

Augmented reality, a technology that superimposes layers of intangible visual information on depictions of physical objects, infuses the perception of these objects with interpretations, meanings, and judgments. Perceptions of the augmented world are influenced by choices of what information to overlay, who does it and why, offering the possibility to shape and manipulate them. The same applies to the processing, interpretation, and uses of large amounts of information acquired from transactions and activities in cyberspace, which allow sending narrowly targeted and tailored messages. While there is always the choice of opting out of cyberspace transactions, the growing number, variety, and intensity of information exchanges, together with their perceived relevance and usefulness, make disengagement increasingly difficult and troublesome.

When amplified to span the whole planet, these vast seas and powerful waves of information plus interpretation overwhelm individual and collective perceptions of events, phenomena, ideas, behaviors, emotions, values, and myriad other aspects of human life, introducing unnoticed biases in our appraisals of what is real. The diversity of views available from mass and social media provides only a mild antidote, for they are increasingly targeted to shape and reinforce consumption habits, work patterns, and political inclinations of specific audiences, and to harden their preexisting beliefs, attitudes, and behaviors. By discouraging reaching out to others and restricting spaces for meaningful social interaction, this blunts empathy and stunts learning.

Artificial Intelligence

There are many definitions of intelligence and it may be useful to begin with the broad statement of American cognitive psychologist Howard Gardner, who considered it as "the ability to solve problems, or to create products, that are valued within one or more cultural settings." (Gardner, 1983, p. x). The combination of several innate and acquired faculties—ability to capture and store data, to reason and process it rapidly and efficiently, and to do so broadly and in different situations—is what may be said to confer intelligence in humans or in machines (Evans, 1981, pp. 182–227).

The possibility of creating computer programs mimicking human intelligence was advanced in 1961 by American computer scientist Marvin Minsky, cofounder of the MIT Artificial Intelligence Laboratory:

> I am confident that sooner or later we will be able to assemble programs of great problem-solving ability from complex combinations of heuristic devices multiple optimizers, pattern-recognition tricks, planning algebras, recursive administration procedures, and the like. In no one of these will we find the seat of intelligence. Should we ask what intelligence "really is"? My own view is that this is more of an esthetic question, or one of sense of dignity, than a technical natter! To me "intelligence" seems to denote little more

than the complex of performances which we happen to respect, but do not understand (Minsky, 1960, p. 54).

Fast forward half a century since the early speculations about the possibilities of reproducing and surpassing human intelligence. By the turn of the twenty-first century, artificial intelligence mounted an assault on the capacity to reason as an exclusive attribute of human beings, which raised both hope and alarm. After Copernicus made us yield our privileged central place in the cosmos, after Darwin forced us to acknowledge our evolutionary descent from the apes, and after Freud thrust upon us the awareness of our hidden drives, we still had the consolation of considering reason and intelligence as unique attributes of human beings. We clung to what Michael Polanyi called the "ambitious anthropocentrism of our reason" (Polanyi, 1962, p. 5) and thus found a justification to view ourselves as unique and continue adhering to the Promethean centrality of humanity. At the twilight of Bacon's epoch, this was simply no longer possible.

Advances in Artificial Intelligence (AI) surpassed the most optimistic expectations, to the extent that their newly discovered and baffling capabilities appear to be beyond human comprehension. By endowing a variety of artificial intelligence programs and platforms with capabilities that exceed human information processing and reasoning by several orders of magnitude, we have ventured into unknown territory. Whether Ali Baba's treasure or Pandora's box, we will probably soon know.

Byelorussian intellectual Evgeny Morozov has summarized the two Janus-like faces of AI. Among many other applications, it helps in medical diagnoses, business, and marketing; allows customizing educational materials, producing videos, podcasts, and texts; assists writers and researchers with a variety of tasks; and also automates coding and computer programming. But it is also upending teaching and learning by facilitating plagiarism and cheating, reproducing and perpetuating biases in decision-making, enabling widespread surveillance that curtails freedom, and also entering the fields of justice administration and warfare with yet unknown consequences (Morozov, 2024).

American artificial intelligence pioneer and entrepreneur Sam Altman argues that the improved reasoning and image-creation capabilities of his latest software move it closer to the creation of AI agents that can execute tasks done previously by humans, and that it could achieve genius-level intelligence (Khalaf, 2025). German-American artificial intelligence researcher Leopold Aschenbrenner is more sanguine but more concerned: "few have the faintest glimmer of what is about to hit them. … By the end of the decade [2030], they will be smarter than your or I; we will have superintelligence, in the true sense of the word. … The power—and the peril—of superintelligence will be dramatic." (Aschenbrenner, 2024, p. 3). This could lead to the problem of misalignment, which means that AI agents may pursue goals radically different from those defined by their human designers and handlers (Douthat & Kokotajlo, 2025).

Yet, early doubts were cast regarding whether the logical, sequential, parallel, and orderly approach of AI agents could be similar to human cognition processes. A few decades ago, Gardner pointed out that "human thought emerges as messy, intuitive, subject to subjective representations—not as pure and immaculate calculation—"associated with our intrinsic biological embodiment, leading him to conclude that although human rationality may be modeled by a computer it would bear scant resemblance to actual human thought processes (Gardner, 1987, p. 386).

In addition, researchers have pointed out that AI designers are finding it rather difficult to obtain real data to train them, which has led in some cases to the use of AI-generated texts and images as inputs to further train their models. As Sona Alemohammad and colleagues have found when training AI models with AI-produced data: "without enough fresh real data in each generation of an autophagous loop, future generative models are doomed to have their quality (precision) or diversity (recall) progressively decrease" (Alemohammad et al., 2024, p. 1). They have called this condition Model Autophagy Disorder (MAD) and show that after doing this several times AI models degenerate and produce rubbish.

A sober perspective of the use of AI and its relation to human intelligence would suggest that both of them are likely to evolve jointly as human beings learn to use this powerful new technology that amplifies rational judgments, complementing it with judgments of fact and judgments of value. As Blaise Agüera y Arcas, AI researcher and vice-president of technology and Society at Google argues, "AI is not distinct from humanity, but rather is a recent addition to a mutually interdependent superhuman entity we are all already part of. An entity that has long been partly biological and partly technological." (Agüera y Arcas, 2025, p. 850). The question is whether capabilities to employ AI to further such joint evolution will be equitably distributed among all human beings or will be concentrated in a few privileged ones.

In addition to the unequitable distribution of capabilities to develop and employ AI, Stuart Russell and his colleagues have called attention to the risks and harms associated with the unethical use of AI systems (Russell et al., 2025). They point out the growing danger of large-scale scams and fraud, the possibility of manipulation and dependency, and the fact that AI models have demonstrated deceptive behavior and resisted shutdown. Together with prominent global leaders they have launched a call for "red lines" that should not be trespassed to "prevent AI from inflicting serious and potentially irreversible damages to humanity" (AI Red Lines, 2025, para. 1), and that should stop both unacceptable AI uses and unacceptable AI behaviors. Both governments and international organizations must be actively involved in this initiative because AI risks are systemic and transcend borders, because unbridled competition and the race for profits between AI corporations are fueling what Russell and his colleagues define as a "race to the bottom," and because public trust is essential for good AI governance.

A further issue to speculate about is whether advanced artificial intelligence devices, which could be capable of improving themselves indefinitely, may evolve in autonomous directions, quite separate and independent from human or joint evolutionary processes, with the accompanying danger that may be associated. British science fiction writer James Hogan explored this possibility in the prologue to his book *The Code of the Life Maker*. He envisaged a parallel but quite distinct process of non-biological evolution over an exceedingly long time on a far-away planet, a consequence of sending autonomous and self-repairing robots and software programs into deep space. Their reproduction raised the possibility of non-biological evolutionary processes—perhaps "chipological"?—that would give rise to completely different non-organic life forms (Hogan, 1984).

A Fractured Global Order

The twilight of Bacon's epoch has created a world of turbulence, inconsistencies, and ambiguities that, in addition to shifting our worldviews, has changed the context for human activities. One of the consequences of the successful deployment of Bacon's program, and of the convergence of scientific knowledge, technology, and production associated with it, has been an accelerated, segmented, and uneven intensification of interactions between peoples, societies, and organizations all over the world. This process is creating a paradoxical fractured global order that simultaneously integrates and excludes, generates multiple exchanges and increases isolation, brings together and creates divisions, opens opportunities and closes options, and leads to a lopsided distribution of the costs and benefits of an increasingly interconnected world.

Three closely interconnected and partially overlapping domains—the local, the networks, the global—configure the fractured global order. They have emerged at different times in human history. Each has its own specific features, logic, and ways of interacting with the other two.

The domain of the local is made up of relations and transactions anchored in time and space, comprising the production, exchange, and consumption of tangible goods and services, and of information resources and personal interrelations, necessary for human beings and social groups to exist and evolve. The domain of the local has been in existence since the dawn of humanity. The social relations, transactions, and interactions in it are firmly embedded in the settings of concrete life experiences. Transactions are relatively easy to trace and patterns of contact are one-to-few, few-to-one, and few-to-few. It contains a rich range of face-to-face interactions that allow coordinated action, enable joint undertakings, and convey feelings, emotions, aspirations, and values.

The domain of the networks consists of multiple combinations of exchanges of tangible and intangible goods—products and services, power and influence, data and information, among many other forms of interaction—flowing through identifiable channels and nodes that connect social groups throughout the world. Over time, the proliferation of linkages between public agencies, private corporations, civil society associations, academic institutions, and other organizations, in addition to a mesh of interpersonal connections, has created a tangled web of overlapping networks of networks.

This domain is constantly changing as new channels and nodes appear, old ones vanish, and as connections are established and severed; social relations at a distance are partially embedded in and disembedded from time- and space-bound local contexts. Long in the making, the domain of the networks emerged in full view in the sixteenth century with the globe-spanning European expansion. It owes its present richness to recent transport and communications innovations that allow the establishment of various one-or-few-to-many and many-to-few-or-one patterns of contacts.

The domain of the global consists primarily of the intensive, dense, and nearly instantaneous exchange of intangible symbols on a planetary scale, and of the tangible manifestations of specific human actions that have worldwide impact. Information technology advances freed symbolic human interactions from the constraints of time and space, delinked them from their concrete experiential settings, and allowed them to be restructured at will in the ethereal dimensions of cyberspace and virtual reality that characterize the domain of the global. At the same time, human activities in the domains of the local and the networks have expanded and intensified, to the extent of increasingly crossing thresholds that make their effects, impacts, and consequences felt in the domain of the global.

In this domain, which took shape in the transition to the twenty-first century, social relations are lifted and disembedded from their local contexts and their extended networks. Patterns of contact are from many to many, and potentially from one-, few-, and many-to-all and vice versa, overwhelming the capacity of human beings to process information and make sense of increasingly interconnected events. These novel forms of interaction break identity into various partial selves that can be projected on a global stage, ushering in new sets of fluid social groups that coalesce and dissolve or harden with bewildering speed. The emerging domain of the global is creating awareness that individual and group actions have global consequences; it poses fresh challenges for collective action and demands globally shared values and institutional arrangements that should be congruent with improvements in the human condition.

Decisions taken and actions performed in the domains of the local and the networks may have undesirable consequences that find expression in the domain of the global. This is the case in areas such as climate change, global warming, biodiversity loss, pandemic spreads, and some aspects of global finance, among others, which are migrating from the domains of the local and the networks to the domain of the global and emerging as shared worldwide concerns. Emissions of greenhouse gases that lead to climate change take place anywhere but their impact and consequences are felt throughout the world, regardless of where they come from. Similar considerations apply to biodiversity loss, highly contagious diseases, and deadly conflicts.

The Dasgupta review of the economics of biodiversity argues this with clarity:

> societies until modern times were incapable of affecting the Earth System as a whole. Matters are different today. The human presence is so dominant that the Earth System is no longer as modular as it was until recently. Disturbance in one location today gets transmitted to other parts in short order. Movements of people and trade in goods have created a transmission mechanism with a long and quick reach. The mechanism's medium has, however, remained the same: Nature is *mobile*. We weaken the Antarctica ice sheet without ever going there; phosphorus discharge from farms in Minnesota contributes to a deadening of the Gulf of Mexico; emissions of soot from kitchens in the Indian sub-continent affect the circulation patterns of the monsoons; the Green Revolution's demand for water, fertilizers and pesticides

pollute the rivers and ground waters of the Indo-Gangetic Plain; fish in the North Sea eat microplastic originating in markets in the Bahamas; and so on (Dasgupta, 2021, pp. 30–31).

Similarly, financial transactions now take place on a global scale and at a rapid pace, with money moving constantly throughout the world's financial channels and hubs in a search for higher returns. While it may be possible in principle to identify the origin and to follow the sequence of transactions of financial instruments, a series of financial crises triggered by speculation, changes in expectations, automatic trading, and the proliferation of opaque money instruments makes it difficult to anticipate and trace the consequences of financial transactions. Once they move from the domains of the local and the networks and enter the domain of the global, it is extremely difficult to track them.

Internet straddles the domains of the networks and the global. The infrastructure of high-speed lines, towers, and satellites to transmit information belongs to the domain of the networks, but the messages that move through it are broken down into myriad packets, sent through multiple routes and reconstituted on arrival. Senders and receivers can disguise their identities and locations, and the speed and massive volume of exchanges make it difficult to follow, retrieve, and process the information they contain. Though interception is possible, it requires efforts whose scale is out of reach for all—excepting very few institutions.

Most social interactions span the domains of the local and the networks. International trade in goods and services takes place through identifiable routes, but they require localized production and involve localized consumption. The work of international public, private, and civil society organizations is at the intersection of these two domains, as are travel, migration, research, journalism, and similar undertakings involving physical displacement or traceable exchanges of ideas and information.

Activities once circumscribed in time and space can rise from the domain of the local, leveraged through the domain of the network, and reach the domain of the global. Some examples could be English as an international language, shared tastes for Italian and Chinese food, and preferences for rock and Brazilian music, neoliberal economic policies, artistic designs derived from local cultures, among many others. In reverse, activities that take place in the domain of the global filter down through the domain of the networks and reach the domain of the local—viral memes, video clips and podcasts, highly mobile financial assets invested in specific locations, junk-food eating habits. Portuguese sociologist Boaventura de Sousa Santos calls the former "globalized localisms," and the latter "localized globalisms" (Santos, 1995, p. 263).

Fault Lines

The fractured global order and its three domains are characterized by a multiplicity of fault lines of geopolitical, demographic, social, economic, cultural, political, scientific, and technological nature, which partially overlap, often shift direction, sometimes reinforce each other, and at other times work at cross purposes. Integration and exclusion coexist uneasily in all domains of the paradoxical fractured global order.

Geopolitical shifts during the second decade of the twenty-first century have altered the structure of international relations and power dynamics that prevailed since the end of World War II, which managed to maintain a semblance of stability and avoided a few potential global catastrophes. We are now witnessing the rise of violent conflicts, terrorism, and extortion, drug traffic and international crimes, cyber sabotage and warfare, proliferation of chemical and biological weapons, spread of small-scale nuclear devices, unabashed exercise of military power, and widespread violation of human rights at scales not seen in decades.

Demographic imbalances between regions and countries have become an additional source of global instability. Uneven fertility rates, access to contraceptive devices, changing patterns of non-communicable diseases, longer life expectancy, and better aging have modified the patterns of population growth. High-income countries have fertility rates below replacement levels and many low-income ones maintain high rates of population growth, which intensifies international migration pressures and exacerbates xenophobic reactions in countries with stagnant or diminishing populations. A larger proportion of aging non-workers, primarily in high-income countries, strains pension systems and burdens younger generations with care requirements.

Unsatisfied demands for education, health, food, housing, sanitation, jobs, among others, unlikely to be met in the short- and medium-term in the majority of low- and middle-income countries, have become sources of widespread social unrest. Large proportions of young people in countries at all levels of income are neither studying nor working. Increasingly drawn to social media usage, they are developing stunted habits of interaction with others, turning to illicit activities and degrading social cohesion.

The COVID-19 pandemic revealed the extent of global health fault lines. Access to vaccines that prevent contagion, mitigate symptoms, and avoid loss of life was restricted, for quite some time, to the mostly high-income countries in which they were developed. In September 2021, 9 months after they became widely available, 68% of the population of high- and higher-middle-income countries had been vaccinated, in contrast with the 3% of low-income and 29% of lower-middle-income countries (United Nations Development Programme, 2021).

Clashes between the determination to preserve cultural and ethnic homogeneity and the arrival of migrants with different beliefs, habits, and behaviors are becoming common and even violent in various parts of the world. They expose the cultural fractures and conflicts arising out of the increased personal mobility that characterizes a fully interconnected globe.

Religion, which faded to the background during the deployment and success of Bacon's program, has returned to center stage at its twilight. Spiritual concerns were largely absent in the secular conceptions of progress and development. However, religious fundamentalism, whether Christian, Islamic, Jewish, or Hindu, among other variants, has become a driving force for political action. In addition, the new emphasis on faith has revived old controversies between religious and scientific explanations of all kinds of phenomena.

Politics and governance issues have become contentious in many nation-states as democracy and authoritarianism vie for acceptance, support, and preeminence. Sources of legitimacy, matters of efficiency, questions of representation, ways of ascertaining the will of the people, institutional capabilities to process and respond to social demands, and styles of leadership are all becoming the subject of heated debates about how countries should be governed.

The roles of the public, private, and civil society sectors are being redefined at the national and international levels; new forms of citizen engagement are vying for recognition and acquiring greater importance. Information technologies and social network platforms now have a major impact on politics and governance, particularly because misinformation and fake news can weaken and even shatter societal bonds.

Faith in democracy is eroding, as democratic institutions and practices—still the most effective and least traumatic form of governance in turbulent times—appear to be inadequate for coping with the new challenges of the fractured global order. Breaking the barriers of disbelief and cynicism, reaching out and engaging citizens, generating and maintaining trust have become perhaps the most important task of democratic government authorities at the twilight of Bacon's epoch.

Ambiguities, contradictions, and inconsistencies, together with turbulence, confusion, and uncertainty, characterize the emergence of the fractured global order. Forces at play in each of its three domains and the fault lines that crisscross them have both positive and negative implications, depending on the structure of power relations, the perspectives from which they are viewed and the capacities to cope with them.

Hegemonic powers were able to instill some measure of lopsided and self-serving stability in international relations for a few decades after the end of World War II. However, as we move deeper into the twenty-first century, nobody is fully in charge of the contradictory processes of integration and fragmentation that characterize the fractured global order. In a jagged and paradoxical way, it is creating a few winners and many losers in all realms of human activity.

British sociologist Anthony Giddens' "juggernaut" metaphor of modernization could be aptly applied to describe the fractured global order as:

> a runaway engine of enormous power which, collectively as human beings, we can drive to some extent, but which also threatens to rush out of control and which could render itself asunder. The juggernaut crushes those who resist it, and while it sometimes seems to have a steady path, there are times when it veers away erratically in directions we cannot foresee. ... we shall never be able to control completely either the path or the pace of the journey (Giddens, 1990, p.139).

The juggernaut of the fractured global order has worn out the power of nation-states. Both external pressures and internal demands have reduced their capacity to design and implement policies and strategies. At present no country can, on its own, control its economic activities, protect its culture, withstand the impact of climate change, avoid pandemic contagion, or singlehandedly protect its citizens from organized crime, aggression, and weapons of mass destruction (Ogilvy, 2016).

In addition to limiting the spheres of action of nation-states, the advent of a fractured global order has also had a negative impact on the functioning of international organizations. Their effectiveness depends on the will and acquiescence of their national members; as these falter, they are losing their already limited ability to mediate conflicts, maintain peace, guarantee human rights, arbitrate disputes, and promote sustainable and equitable human development.

The erosion of nation-states, both because of external pressures and internal demands, has reduced their capacity to design and implement strategies and policies. The international rules-based order that prevailed, with ups and downs, since the end of the Second World War has disappeared. In its place international political actions and interventions are now based on a combination of economic and military power, narrow conceptions of the national interest, and the configuration of international alliances with specific purposes.

The power asymmetries inherent in the fractured global order make it difficult to envisage international governance structures that may be commensurate with the challenges faced. According to internationalist and Club de Madrid member Sean Cleary, "no overarching concept of the desirable principles of a future global order will soon emerge from the leading powers" (Cleary, 2017, p. 7). The rifts that are preventing the emergence of generally accepted international norms may have even more serious consequences. According to the Quincy Institute for Responsible Statecraft:

> Instead of birthing a multipolar world, a multi-order world risks coming into existence—one in which states will no longer differ over competing interpretations of existing laws and norms, but rather will proffer competing sets of rules and norms. The result would be a hollowing out of crucial universal norms, laws, and institutions, and, by that, a removal of the constraints that have helped make conflicts less likely (Quincy Institute for Responsible Statecraft, 2024, p. 2).

Acknowledging the difficulty of organizing global responses involving powerful countries increasingly at odds with one another, there have been fewer ambitious proposals. American diplomat Richard Haass argues that, despite its limitations and even if they are not universal in scale, multilateral interventions are preferable to unilateral actions:

> Multilateralism is far preferable to unilateralism, but narrow multilateralism is far more promising than universal or broad forms of collective action that rarely succeed; … Better to pursue realistic partnerships of the like-minded, which can bring a degree of order to the world, including specific domains of limited order, if not quite world order. … realism must trump idealism (Haas, 2022, para. 33).

For the foreseeable future, and in spite of the imminent perils, geopolitical fractures are likely to prevent broad multilateral initiatives. Coalitions of able and willing nations—what has been termed "plurilateralism"—may be more feasible; middle-size countries, too small to constitute a threat but too big to be ignored, may play a significant role in mobilizing international cooperative initiatives. In spite of their power limitations, their concerted interventions may help contain some of the global threats in the offing.

The knowledge divide is one of the key fault lines of the fractured global order. Differences between rich and poor countries in their capabilities to generate and utilize scientific and technological knowledge have been widening and deepening as the Baconian Program unfolded, was deployed and succeeded. Private corporations, government agencies, academic institutions, and civil society organizations in a small group of high- and middle-high-income countries concentrate most of the world's scientific research, technological development, and innovation capabilities. Low-income and most middle-income countries rely, to a large extent, on their stock of traditional knowledge and techniques, complemented by layers of imported modern technologies, products, and services.

Disparities between science, technology, and innovation capabilities are much larger than economic ones. In 2021, the ratio between the Gross Domestic Product (GDP) per capita of the high-income countries and that of the low-income countries (as defined by the World Bank) was about 57 to 1, and the ratios of gross capital formation and trade per capita were 46 to 1 and 64 to 1, respectively. However striking these disparities may be, they are dwarfed by the differences in their capacities to generate scientific knowledge, develop modern technologies, and produce high-technology goods and services. The ratio of scientific publications per 100,000 inhabitants in high to low-income countries is 81 to 1, the ratio between patent applications per 100,000 inhabitants is 709 to 1, and the ratio of high-technology exports per capita is 5974 to 1 (World Bank, 2025).

High-income countries account for more than 80% of investments in research and development, with private enterprises being responsible for three quarters of the total. Gaps in the capacity to generate and utilize scientific and technological knowledge have been accompanied by a concentration of investments in a few very large corporations, especially in fields like artificial intelligence, biotechnology, genetic engineering, new materials, and information technologies. The Baconian assumption that knowledge should be a public good, widely shared for the benefit of humanity, has been discarded. The economic value of scientific research results and of technological development has led to their private appropriation through intellectual property regimes, which have become increasingly rigid and exclusionary.

Asymmetries in the worldwide distribution of science and technology capabilities are even greater than the data suggest. The cumulative character of capacity building efforts in science, technology, and production means that, as abilities in these fields are acquired, it becomes easier to continue accumulating them. Countries that have a long history of doing so are in a much better position to reap the benefit of current and future scientific and technological advances. However, as shown by the recent experience of a few countries—the Republic of Korea, China, Singapore, Vietnam—at the twilight of Bacon's epoch, it is possible to overcome the knowledge fracture through appropriate public policies and strategies, sustained over long periods by political will and government determination.

Toward a New Epoch

Scientific findings and technological developments associated with the unfolding, deployment, and success of Bacon's program have led to major revisions of notions we took for granted during the last four centuries. They have forced a reconsideration of our conceptions of the universe and reality, of our planet and our place in it, and of evolution and the distinctiveness of humanity. They have made us aware of the distressing nature of intensified social media interactions that alter our notions of the social and the self. They have created a knowledge divide that threatens to become an impassable abyss.

Shifts in worldviews and the emergence of a fractured global order, which are ushering a new epoch in the history of humanity, demand significant adjustments in our mindsets. It is now essential to update and expand the repertoire of concepts and ideas with which we apprehend our human nature, the ecosystems that support our lives, and the ways we relate to each other. These new habits of thought should go beyond logical analysis and dialectic synthesis, which although necessary are not sufficient to cope with the challenges created by the ambiguous success of Bacon's program.

These considerations refer us to the concept of paradox, which describes what we perceive as incompatible or contradictory states. To apprehend and process opposing situations that do not admit resolution, at least in appearance and in a given time frame, it is necessary to adopt a paradoxical approach that makes it possible to tolerate ambiguities and identify ways to overcome contradictions. Paradoxical thinking leads us to discover and develop broad frames of reference that contain, absorb, and dissolve inconsistencies; recognizes that contextual changes and the awareness of our agency can alter the course of events; fully embraces ambiguity and contradiction while maintaining the capacity for purposeful intervention, for putting ideas into practice.

We must accept that it is possible to be coherent, although not necessarily consistent, and that our reasoning about ambiguous situations evolves gradually. We should realize and accept—as Canadian composer, poet, and thinker Leonard Cohen put it—that "there is a crack, a crack in everything, that's how the light comes in" (Cohen, 2019). The task at the twilight of Bacon's epoch is to find those cracks; to let the light in, to illuminate the darkness as we enter into a new period in the history of humanity.

References

Agüera y Arcas, B. (2025). What is the future of intelligence? The answer could lie in the story of its evolution. *Nature, 647*(8091), 846–850. https://doi.org/10.1038/d41586-025-03857-0

AI Red Lines. (2025). *Global call for AI red lines: What signatories say*. AI Red Lines. https://red-lines.ai/#call

Alemohammad, S., Casco-Rodriguez, J., Luzi, L., Humayun, A. I., Babaei, H., LeJeune, D., Siahkoohi, A., & Baraniuk, R. (2024, March 16). Self-consuming generative models go MAD. *The twelfth international conference on learning representations*. https://openreview.net/forum?id=ShjMHfmPs0

Aschenbrenner, L. (2024). *Situational awareness: The decade ahead*. https://situational-awareness.ai/wp-content/uploads/2024/06/situationalawareness.pdf

Béjar, M. (2013, November 12). La conciencia emerge de los procesos cerebrales. *Tendencias21*. https://www.tendencias21.es/La-conciencia-emerge-de-los-procesos-cerebrales_a26977.html

Benedikt, M. (1992). *Cyberspace: First steps*. MIT Press.

Bolhuis, H. E. v., & Colom, V. (1995). *Cyberspace reflections*. VUB Press.

Clavin, W. (2022). *Proving that quantum entanglement is real*. Caltech, California Institute of Technology. https://www.caltech.edu/about/news/proving-that-quantum-entanglement-is-real#:~:text=The%20Freedman–Clauser%20experiment%20was,2010%20Wolf%20Prize%20in%20physics

Cleary, S. (2017). Reconceptualising transnational governance: Making global institutions fit for purpose. *Economics, 11*(1), 20170021. https://doi.org/10.5018/economics-ejournal.ja.2017-21

Cohen, L. (2019, March 29). *Anthem (Official Live in London 2008)* [Video de YouTube]. Leonard Cohen. https://www.youtube.com/watch?v=c8-BT6y_wYg

Cowen, R. (2013). Cosmologists at odds over mysterious anomalies in data from early universe. *Nature*, 14368. https://doi.org/10.1038/nature.2013.14368

Dasgupta, P. (2021). *The economics of biodiversity: The Dasgupta review*. HM Treasury. https://assets.publishing.service.gov.uk/media/602e92b2e90e07660f807b47/The_Economics_of_Biodiversity_The_Dasgupta_Review_Full_Report.pdf

Dobzhansky, T., & Boesiger, E. (1983). *Human culture: A moment in evolution*. Columbia University Press.

Douthat, R., & Kokotajlo, D. (2025, May 15). The forecast for 2027: Total A. I. domination. *The New York Times*. https://www.nytimes.com/video/opinion/100000010157582/the-forecast-for-2027-total-ai-domination.html

European Space Agency. (n.d.). *Planck and the cosmic microwave background*. European Space Agency. Retrieved May 15, 2025, from https://www.esa.int/Science_Exploration/Space_Science/Planck/Planck_and_the_cosmic_microwave_background#

Evans, C. (1981). *The micro millennium*. Washington Square Press.

Falk, D. (2020, May 4). Arrows of time. *Quanta Magazine*.. https://www.quantamagazine.org/what-is-time-a-history-of-physics-biology-clocks-and-culture-20200504/.

Feldman Barrett, L. (2021). This is how your brain makes your mind. *MIT Technology Review*.

Frank, A., & Gleiser, M. (2023, September 2). The story of our universe may be starting to unravel. *The New York Times*. https://www.nytimes.com/2023/09/02/opinion/cosmology-crisis-webb-telescope.html

Frankopan, P. (2023). *The earth transformed: An untold history*. Alfred A. Knopf.

Fraser, J. T. (Ed.). (1981). *The voices of time: A cooperative survey of man's views of time as expressed by the sciences and by the humanities*. University of Massachusetts Press.

Freud, S. (1930). *Civilization and its discontents* (J. Strachey, Trans.). https://canvas.ou.edu/courses/26008/files/1307618

Gardner, H. (1983). *Frames of mind: The theory of multiple intelligences*. Basic Books.

Gardner, H. (1987). *The mind's new science: A history of the cognitive revolution*. Basic Books.

Giddens, A. (1990). *The consequences of modernity*. Polity Press.

Haas, R. (2022, October). The dangerous decade: A foreign policy for a world in crisis. *Foreign Affairs*.. https://www.foreignaffairs.com/united-states/dangerous-decade-foreign-policy-world-crisis-richard-haass.

Hall, E. T. (1984). *The dance of life*. Anchor Press.

Hawking, S. (1993). *Black holes and baby universes, and other essays*. Bantam Books.

Heim, M. (1993). *The metaphysics of virtual reality*. Oxford University Press.

Hogan, J. P. (1984). *Code of the life maker: A novel*. Del Rey Book.

Intergovernmental Panel on Climate Change (IPCC). (2019). *Global warming of 1.5°C: IPCC special report on impacts of global warming of 1.5°C above pre-industrial levels in context of strengthening response to climate change, sustainable development, and efforts to eradicate poverty*. Cambridge University Press. https://doi.org/10.1017/9781009157940
Khalaf, R. (2025, May 9). OpenAI chief Sam Altman: 'This is genius-level intelligence.' *Financial Times*. https://www.ft.com/content/a3d65804-1cf3-4d67-ac79-9b78a10b6dcc
Libet, B. (2004). *MindTime: The temporal factor in consciousness*. Harvard University Press.
Linde, A. (1994). The self-reproducing inflationary universe. *Scientific American*, 48–55.
Minsky, M. (1960). Steps toward artificial intelligence. *IRE Transactions on Information Theory, 6*(2), 1–65. https://people.cs.umass.edu/~barto/courses/cs687/Minsky60steps.pdf?utm_source=chatgpt.com
Morozov, E. (2024, December 4). The AI we deserve. *Boston 50 Review*. https://www.bostonreview.net/forum/the-ai-we-deserve/
Nisbet, R. (1980). *History of the idea of progress*. Basic Books.
Ogilvy, J. (2016, May 26). The second reformation: Transitioning to the economic era. *Forbes*. https://www.forbes.com/sites/stratfor/2016/05/26/the-second-reformation-transitioning-to-the-economic-era/?sh=58634dc741a4.
ÓhÉigeartaigh, S. (2025). Extinction of the human species: What could cause it and how likely is it to occur? *Cambridge Prisms: Extinction, 3*, e4. https://doi.org/10.1017/ext.2025.4
Penrose, R. (2012). *Cycles of time: An extraordinary new view of the universe*. Vintage Books.
Polanyi, M. (1962). *Personal knowledge: Towards a post-critical philosophy*. Harper Torchbooks.
Quincy Institute for Responsible Statecraft. (2024). *A reformed U.N. security council for a post-unipolar era* (No. Quincy paper 15). Quincy Institute. https://quincyinst.org/research/a-reformed-u-n-security-council-for-a-post-unipolar-era/#
Riskin, J., & Feldman, M. W. (2022, April 2). An evolving view of inheritance. *New York Review of Books Newsletter*. https://www.nybooks.com/online/2022/04/02/an-evolving-view-of-inheritance/
Ritchie, H., Rodés-Guirao, L., Mathieu, E., Gerber, M., Ortiz-Ospina, E., Hasell, J., & Roser, M. (2023). *Population growth*. Our World in Data. https://ourworldindata.org/population-growth
Russell, S., Segerie, C.-R., Iliadis, N., & Zoumpalova, T. (2025). *AI governance through global red lines can help prevent unacceptable risks*. OECD.AI Policy Observatory. https://oecd.ai/en/wonk/ai-governance-through-global-red-lines-can-help-prevent-unacceptable-risks
Santos, B. d. S. (1995). *Toward a new common sense: Law, science, and politics in the paradigmatic transition*. Routledge.
Simon, J. L. (1981). *The ultimate resource*. Princeton University Press.
United Nations Development Programme. (2021). *Global dashboard for vaccine equity*. Data Futures Exchange. https://data.undp.org/insights/vaccine-equity
Wolchover, N. (2014, April 16). Time's arrow traced to quantum source. *Quanta Magazine*. https://www.quantamagazine.org/quantum-entanglement-drives-the-arrow-of-time-scientists-say-20140416/
Wood, C. (2025, March 19). Is dark energy getting weaker? New evidence strengthens the case. *Quanta Magazine*. https://www.quantamagazine.org/is-dark-energy-getting-weaker-new-evidence-strengthens-the-case-20250319/
World Bank. (2025). *World development indicators*. https://databank.worldbank.org/source/world-development-indicators

Chapter 10
Rethinking the Baconian Program

Sitting on the ruins of failed paradigms
we are condemned to invent new ones
for the twenty-first century.

Ignacy Sachs (2009, p. 5)

The twilight of Bacon's epoch requires a reappraisal of the premises and components of his implicit program. Its fundamental tenet—knowledge is power—has not only stood the test of time but continuously and increasingly reaffirmed its unquestionable validity. However, while another premise—mobilizing knowledge to dominate nature through understanding—led to vast improvements in the human condition, their unequal distribution and undesirable consequences became obvious and increasingly ominous. The paradoxical consequences of the unfolding, deployment, and success of the Baconian Program ended up undermining its foundations.

The components of Bacon's implicit program—method, purpose, direction, focus, and institutions—have evolved in different trajectories, but the program as a whole succeeded beyond the wildest expectations of its architect, who at various times felt dejected and thought his ideas and proposals would fade without significant impact. Slide in time since its inception and it can now be seen that, for different reasons and to different extents, the premises and components of the Baconian Program require reexamination and updating.

Using knowledge to dominate nature was closely associated with the concept of human exceptionalism, the widespread Western idea that divine will had bestowed on our species a privileged position in the cosmos; that human beings are fundamentally different from all other creatures and that we can determine our own destiny. Furthermore, as Bacon argued forcefully in his recounting of the myth of Prometheus, it was also assumed that the world is vast and provides unlimited opportunities for exploiting its bounty as a God-given right; that human ingenuity—guided by divine grace—can surmount all problems to indefinitely improve our lot (and, for the virtuous ones, achieve eternal salvation).

The twilight of Bacon's epoch made us realize that humanity may be special but also flawed. As William Shakespeare put it aptly in his play Julius Caesar, "the fault,

F. Sagasti, *Knowledge is Power*, Innovation, Technology, and Knowledge Management, https://doi.org/10.1007/978-3-032-20668-8_10

dear Brutus, is not in our stars, but in ourselves, that we are underlings." The knowledge generated as a result of the unfolding, deployment, and success of the Baconian Program has given us a better hold on the possibilities and limitations of our species, and a more nuanced perspective of humanity in the cosmic order. The paradoxical awareness of our strengths—consciousness, self-awareness, inquisitive instincts, capacity to generate knowledge, and ethical pursuits, among many others—, and of our weaknesses—dependency on ecosystems that support life, mental and physical limitations, and ultimate mortality, to state a few—forces on us a sobering appraisal of the Baconian Program and its components.

Attempts to cope with the manifestations, consequences, and challenges of Bacon's program at the twilight of his epoch are creating confusion, anxiety, and a widely shared feeling that humanity has lost its bearings. Hans Jonas made this very clear:

> Bacon did not anticipate this profound paradox of the power derived from knowledge: that it leads indeed to some sort of domination over nature … but at the same time to the most complete subjugation under itself. The power has become self-acting, while its promise has turned into threat, its prospect of salvation into apocalypse. Power over the power is required now before the halt is called by catastrophe itself—the power to overcome that impotence over against the self-feeding compulsion of power to its progressive exercise (Jonas, 1984, pp. 141–142).

Wily, court savvy, Francis Bacon, instrumental in the ruin of several English high political figures of his time, knew how to exercise power but was unable to envisage his own downfall. Like its flawed illustrious author, Bacon's program, triumphant after four centuries of unfolding and deployment during the epoch that bears his name, would encounter its eventual twilight.

Reappraising Bacon's Implicit Program

The components of the Baconian Program—method, purpose, direction, focus, and institutions—have each morphed into something quite different from what the Lord Chancellor had in mind 400 years ago.

Method

The scientific method evolved gradually since the time of Bacon, Galileo, Descartes, and Newton, but is now experiencing wrenching transformations. The emergence of cyberspace and virtual reality, artificial intelligence and new modes of knowledge production, as well as the reflective and value-laden character of modern science, suggest the need for a reappraisal of the ways in which the scientific enterprise is conducted. As Sir James Frazer pointed out at the end of the nineteenth century, science may eventually be complemented with new ways of "registering the shadows on the screen" (Frazer, 1964, p. 740).

The scientific method is adapting to accommodate entities that lie somewhere in between abstract concepts, theories, and hypotheses on the one hand, and real phenomena, experimental findings, and empirical evidence on the other. These virtual entities exist in cyberspace as computer simulations, learning algorithms, visual representations, and artificial intelligence platforms, among other intangible objects that can be sensorially grasped, are capable of interacting with humans, and can be manipulated and controlled from the detached safety of electronic computing devices.

Virtual reality allows for the vicarious conduct of scientific research in situations that otherwise would be too costly, difficult, or even impossible. Climate changes under different conditions and deliberate interventions cannot be observed in practice, although it is possible to examine their trajectories and impacts with computer simulations. Software programs create dynamic interactive images that allow teaching and learning to take place in virtual worlds. Artificial intelligence and machine learning algorithms are capable of postulating scientific hypotheses, discovering new materials and protein structures, among other feats, and can also test them in cyberspace without conducting physical experiments. Artificial intelligence has accelerated the speed and space at which scientific research is conducted, as well as increased its scale. This poses challenges to human understanding and the capacity to keep up, process and utilize knowledge advances to an unprecedented degree.

These considerations raise epistemological questions about the nature of empirical versus virtual verification of theories and hypotheses, and about the intersubjective validation of research results. Virtual corroborations may not have the same standing as empirical ones, but they may be more reliable than the results of mental experiments.

Philosophers of science have recently reviewed the perennial question of objectivity in science, and the extent to which it is possible to detach the observer from the phenomena under study to achieve greater reliability. Beyond the accepted observer–phenomena interactions in particle physics, issues such as the uniqueness of training, experience, and perspective of the scientist cannot be fully extricated from the conduct of scientific research. Culture and socioeconomic factors play a role in the selection of research topics and the approaches to the formulation of theories and hypotheses.

David Bohm's ideas on quantum physics, the nature of reality, wholeness, and order, still speculative but gaining more attention in recent years, suggest the need to further explore the nature of the scientific method (Schmieke, 2022; Kakkuri-Knuuttila, 2025; Pylkkänen, 2025). His concepts of implicate and explicate orders at different and infinite recursive levels, developed over decades from his unease with the radical indeterminacy of the Copenhagen interpretation of quantum physics, led him to postulate an alternative view of how physical and mental phenomena interact and shape the ways humans perceive and act on the world.

Bohm argues that "there has been an overall fragmentation in our general attitude to reality" and that "we have to pause and consider the possibility of a fundamental and extensive change in what science means to us" (Bohm & Peat, 1987, pp. 12, 13). His notions of wholeness and of implicate and explicate orders provide a different vantage point from which to appreciate human life and experience, as well as the physical world we inhabit. Extending his notions to the social realm, he argues that genuine and open dialogue leads to the creation and evolution of meaning that involves shared significance, purpose, and value (Bohm, 2004, pp. 20, xxiii).[1] Bohm's ideas, developed through interactions with scientists, philosophers, and mystics, have the potential of altering the scientific method, the ways in which physical and social sciences attempt to make sense of the world.

Another consideration that prompts a revision of the methods of science is the prevalence of ancestral and traditional knowledge and practices, such as those of indigenous peoples in tropical forests, and the emergence of more comprehensive accounts of human evolution that those that have usually characterized Western thought (Graeber & Wengrow, 2021). Trial-and-error and more or less systematic experimentation allowed the development of conservation practices that have sustained their lifestyles for a long time. Non-Western modes of thinking and techniques can be combined with scientific approaches and technologies to devise more appropriate responses to challenges such as biodiversity conservation, use of native plants, water management, and coping with the effects of climate change, among other contemporary environmental challenges. In the words of Gregorio Mirabal, an Amazonian indigenous leader, "If indigenous knowledge were empowered with the tools of modern science, the result would be a relationship of mutual strengthening" (Val et al., 2025, p. 454).

Purpose, Direction, and Focus

These three components of the Baconian Program aimed at setting the broad course for the generation and utilization of scientific knowledge. The purpose was, as Bacon repeatedly stated and Hans Jonas rephrased, to "dominate nature through understanding for the improvement of the human condition." The direction pointed toward steady and indefinite advances in human welfare. The focus was sharply aimed at making nature subservient to human will. The trajectories followed by purpose, direction, and focus followed meandering and jagged paths, with advances and setbacks, although with a generally upward trend that may be coming to an end.

Judged as a whole, the results of the unfolding, deployment, and success of Bacon's implicit program are decidedly mixed. On the positive side of the ledger, there are the extraordinary gains in comprehending and taking advantage of a multiplicity of natural and social phenomena over which humanity acquired control. These led to improvements in material wellbeing, the extension of life spans, and greater security and comfort for a sizable contingent of the world's population. On

[1] For an early treatment of the consequences of Bohm's approach in the social real, see: Ravn (1989).

the negative side, domination of nature led to the degradation of ecosystems, the benefits of knowledge were unevenly distributed, wealth concentrated in a few hands, too many people remained in poverty, and scientific research results were used for destructive purposes. As we entered the twenty-first century, the negative effects began to outweigh the positive ones, tilting the balance in ways impossible to dismiss.

Unwittingly, the Promethean focus of Bacon's implicit program fostered an exploitative approach to the biosphere, leaving little room for careful and responsible uses of its riches, and no room at all for nurturing the regenerative capabilities of ecosystems to ensure our survival and that of other species. The Earth's response to the human compulsion to extract its secrets has been devastating. As Eric Hobsbawm put it, we are now "shedding the old belief in the possibility of improving the human condition" and witnessing "the rise of a new irrationality hostile to science [that] gives way to the fear of an inevitable environmental catastrophe" (Hobsbawm, 2014, p. 199).

Over time the purpose, direction, and focus of the Baconian Program crystalized in the ideas of progress and development, which guided human endeavors as it morphed and evolved over time. At the twilight of Bacon's epoch, purpose became distorted; direction, uncertain; focus, blurred.

Institutions

Sir Francis Bacon's visionary description of the House of Solomon as an institution for the creation of useful knowledge has stood the test of time. Even though his pleas for royal research support went unheeded during his lifetime, the decades and centuries that followed would see the creation of numerous research institutions, laboratories, technical colleges, and the expansion of university research, first in England and Europe, and then all over the world.

Support from government, wealthy patrons, and entrepreneurs increased gradually till the mid-nineteenth century and expanded rapidly thereafter as the economic value of research results was recognized by government officials, businessmen, and academics. The generation of useful knowledge became a corporate, governmental, and scholarly mission in Europe and North America.

The deliberate deployment of Bacon's program merged with the international expansion of markets and the spread of capitalism, leading to the rapid growth of industrial incomes and profits, which were subsequently invested in further research and technological development activities. Government policies and institutions aided the self-reinforcing processes of technology development, product diversification, and market expansion that furthered economic growth. Intellectual property rights were a key policy instrument for achieving these aims, evolving over decades to create almost impenetrable fortresses of legal rights that protect often frivolous claims to originality that keep potential competitors at bay.

Institutional arrangements at the twilight of Bacon's epoch have strayed away from the idea that knowledge is a public good, to be generated for the improvement of the human lot. They have morphed into laws, rules, regulations, and organizations that protect and prioritize the generation of knowledge for private profit and ceaseless accumulation. Institutional reforms are urgently needed, from regulations to protect the environment, confront climate change, and conserve biodiversity, to measures for making the results of scientific research and technological development more widely available, and to prevent the excessive concentration of knowledge-based economic power.

Reassessing Progress

The articulation, unfolding, and deployment of the Baconian Program provided a framework for the evolution of the idea of progress during the last four centuries; it permeated all aspects of social and human affairs in the West throughout the nineteenth century. According to British and Irish historian and classicist John D. Bury: "The idea of human Progress … involves a synthesis of the past and a prophecy of the future. It is based on an interpretation of history which regards men as slowly advancing … in a definite and desirable direction and infers that this progress will continue indefinitely." He underscored that Bacon had argued that "the proper aim of knowledge is the amelioration of human life, to increase men's happiness' and mitigate their sufferings" (Bury, 1932, pp. 5, 51, 52).

Conceptions of indefinite future progress characterized all the variants of the idea that became an article of faith in Europe during the Enlightenment. Numerous thinkers—Bernard de Fontanelle, Gottfried Leibniz, Giambattista Vico, Jeremy Bentham, Adam Smith, the French Encyclopedists, and Voltaire, among others—contributed to cement the notion of indefinite progress in the Western mindset. According to John Bury, Anne Robert Jacques Turgot, prominent French economist and statesman, provided "the first systematic, secular and naturalistic … statement of the 'modern' idea of progress," conceiving "history as the progress of the human race advancing as an immense whole steadily, tough slowly, through alternating periods of calm and disturbance towards greater perfection" (Bury, 1932, pp. 136–137, 143, 152, 155). Human exceptionalism, which viewed our species as destined to dominate nature no holds barred, was closely associated with and underpinned the idea of progress as an inevitable privilege of Man.

Further elaborations of the idea of progress informed the United States Declaration of Independence. American sociologist Robert Nisbet considers that for Benjamin Franklin, Thomas Jefferson, and Tom Paine, among others, "nothing was more important by way of generating and advancing American prosperity and well-being than security given to the creative mind." For Nicolás de Condorcet, French philosopher and politician who died in prison during the French Revolution, "science is the golden avenue to the future and to the final perfection and egalitarian spirit of the future." Barring a few critics, such as novelists Mary Shelley

(*Frankenstein*), Samuel Butler (*Erewhon*), and H. G. Wells (*The Time Machine*), belief in the inevitability of progress was a dominant feature of the intellectual landscape till the end of the nineteenth century.

Tracing the history of the idea of progress, Nisbet underscored its European origins and the way it was imposed in the rest of the world:

> the Western idea of progress has been (…) Eurocentric from the beginning. … the faith in human progress became a means of assimilating all the non-Western peoples into a single progressive series reaching its apogee in Western civilization. Belief in progress and in its premise of the humanity of mankind (…) made it possible to convert perceived heterogeneity into a conceptual homogeneity: [a] temporally ordered progression of all peoples in the world from the simplest to the most advanced (by advanced meant) Western Europe" (Nisbet, 1980, pp. 149).

However, faith in the inevitability of human progress eclipsed during the turbulent first half of the twentieth century. World War I, the Russian Revolution, the Russo-Japanese and Sino-Japanese wars, the rise of Fascism and Nazism, the Holocaust and other genocides, the Great Depression and economic crises, military coups, political upheavals, and the carnage of World War II, among other devastating events, forcefully challenged the idea of steady and unending human progress.

From Progress to Development

A renewed faith in the possibility of progress emerged at the end of World War II. The Allied triumph, based in large measure on an unprecedented mobilization of scientific knowledge, operational competence, and managerial skills, brought back the idea that deliberate interventions could help to improve the human condition. The idea of development emerged in the mid-1940s to revitalize the idea of progress. The notion that government strategies and policies would lead to economic and social advances gained ground in the post-World War II years, giving widespread currency to the need for development planning.

Firmly rooted in Bacon's program, development was the latest incarnation of the idea of progress at the mid-twentieth century. Improvements in living standards would be achieved through economic and social policy measures, boosted by technical assistance and financial aid. The success of the Marshall Plan to revive the European and Japanese economies, together with a quarter century of uninterrupted economic growth through the mid-1970s, appeared to prove conclusively that progress, relabeled development, was indeed possible—but only if poor countries did the right things with the assistance of the rich West. Largely understood in terms of improved material wellbeing, development was transformed into a universal objective. The zenith of the Baconian Program coincided with the emergence of the concept of development that carried within it the imperative of economic growth.

Two alternative systems for achieving development were postulated at the onset of the Cold War between the United States and the Soviet Union: one based on market economies and pluralistic democracies, and the other on centrally planned economies and single-party political systems. In both cases, the underlying assumptions were not only that development was possible and imperative for everyone, but also that economic growth and modernization were the only paths toward it. Development thinking and practice were primarily concerned with economic efficiency, resource allocation, production and consumption, savings and investment, and related economic policy issues.

The concept of development that emerged after World War II placed the evolution of all societies along the same continuum. As American economist Walt W. Rostow (1971) put it, all countries were supposed to advance linearly from a least-developed stage to become advanced mass-consumption societies through economic growth. Development was assumed to be a problem that could be solved by adopting the right strategies and policies, usually fashioned in the image of those prevailing in richer societies. This approach ignored that lack of development is not a problem, but rather a condition with multiple dimensions, complex interactions, indeterminate causalities, nonlinear responses, and difficult-to-trace sources of influence.

The first three decades of the post-World War II were the Golden Age of economic growth: during 1945–1975, the world economy grew continuously and everywhere at an unprecedented rate, which seemed to prove that development was not only possible, but indeed achievable for the world as a whole, especially as the Welfare State in European countries indicated that State intervention could lead to vast social improvements. This period also saw a surge in development assistance from rich to poor countries.

Ideas about how to bring about development changed continuously. Shortly after World War II, development thinking and practice were based on concepts such as the need for a big push of investment and capital to initiate self-sustaining economic growth (Paul Rosenstein-Rodin, Ragnar Nurkse), the priority of investments in human capital (Theodore Schultz, Hans Singer), and the importance of fostering import-substitution industrialization (Raul Prebisch).

During the following decades, notions such as unlimited supply of labor (Arthur Lewis), deterioration of the terms of trade (Hans Singer, Raul Prebisch), poles of development (Francois Perroux), development planning (P. Mahalanobis, Jan Tinbergen), circular cumulative causation (Gunnar Myrdal), unbalanced growth (Albert Hirschman), dependency theory (Fernando Henrique Cardoso, Osvaldo Sunkel), structural underdevelopment (Celso Furtado), unequal exchange (Arghiri Emmanuel), redistribution with growth (Hollis Chenery), basic needs (Hans Singer, Paul Streeten, Richard Jolly, Manfred Max-Neef), export-oriented industrialization (Ann Krueger, T.N. Srinivasan), small is beautiful (E.F. Schumacher), and ecodevelopment (Ignacy Sachs, Maurice Strong), among many others, were used to interpret the reality of developing countries and to offer policy recommendations.

With the end of the Golden Age of global economic expansion in the mid-1970s, a range of economic, social, political, and technological tensions surfaced (oil shocks, debt crises, financial and trade imbalances, increasing inequalities, demographic transitions, geopolitical shifts, new technologies). These tensions characterized the lost decade of the 1980s and presaged the turbulent post-Cold War decades of the 1990s and 2000s, which eventually led to the emergence of a fractured global order and geopolitical disarray.

The transition to the twenty-first century witnessed heated but inconclusive debates about the roles of the state, markets, and civil society in the conduct of economic and social activities, the advantages and limitations of capitalism and of socialism, the nature and social impact of neoliberal economic policies, the possibility of central planning in an information and computation-rich environment, and the relative merits of democratic and autocratic political systems. In the end, practically all countries ended up adopting some version of capitalist market economies, but with different political systems whose proponents have become increasingly strident and intolerant.

French and Polish ecological economist Ignacy Sachs has suggested that a sober and pragmatic approach to the organization of socioeconomic activities is expected to prevail:

> Political conditions for implanting non-capitalist alternatives are not likely to appear in the near future. The solutions are to be sought, again within the limits of reformed capitalism, which is not tantamount to going back to past solutions. These ought to be critically revisited as one source of inspiration. … The demise of real socialism and the impasses of the neoliberal market theology indicate that the prevailing institutional setting will be that of mixed economies with a strong, yet regulated market sector and a significant presence of the developmental state (Sachs, 2009, p. 11).

With notable exceptions, culture, religion, ethics, and ethnic loyalties, which can reinforce or enter into conflict with each other, did not figure prominently in development thinking and practice. Cultural factors were seen largely as prerequisites but not as an integral component of successful development efforts, which privileged increasing consumption and improving material comfort, both of which required an ever-growing use of natural resources and ecosystem services.

Barring acts of faith, largely based on the promise of technological advances, limitless growth is not possible in a finite world. The material wellbeing for all that has been the basic aspiration of the modern development idea since its inception, has been seen by those who oppose it more as a quest to tear apart the fabric of the planet than as a means of achieving freedom from want. As Frankopan highlighted, "when it comes to vulnerability, the principal sources of risk in every period of human history—and not just in the present day—have come above all from the problems caused by overexploitation and unsustainable consumption habits" (Frankopan, 2023, para. 12).

The idea of development as a march toward limitless material prosperity for all, along a single path for all of humanity to follow, is no longer tenable. From this perspective, development is the latest and last reinterpretation of the idea of progress.

We are still at the early stages of rethinking the ideas of progress and development in the uncertain transition to the post-Baconian epoch. This process requires a multiplicity of practical imagination exercises and collective learning processes, which should be capable of accommodating a variety of provisional and partial conceptions, and of gradually accumulating knowledge and experience. A potentially fruitful approach to this task involves focusing on the value systems that guide human actions.

Values and the Redefinition of Progress

Spanish philosopher Manuel García Morente defined progress as "the realization of the realm of values through human effort, (…) in essence progress signifies the realization of values" (García Morente, 1980, p. 45). For García Morente, human life and progress imply deliberate actions toward preferred ends that embody values:

> living is not just being; but, above all, engaging the world in the way dictated by our preferences; it is to be anticipating and wishing; it is to be building goods and destroying evils, in those things that nature creates impassible and beyond good and evil (García Morente, 1980, pp. 37–38).

From this perspective, development and progress in the post-Baconian age could be redefined as: *the open-ended process of reframing old, revitalizing existing and creating new values, of seeking to evolve shared perceptions of what humanity is and should be, of distinguishing between good and bad, and of devising the means for advancing, both individually and collectively, toward realizing these values and putting them in practice.*

As individual human beings, we all have the capacity to establish conscious distinctions between preferred and not preferred, between good and bad, situations, states, events, emotions, ideas, and things. However, the transition from individual to collective preferences is a problematic process, riddled with conflicts and paradoxes. Only to the extent that certain preferences become accepted, widely shared and institutionalized, can they transform into values, into collective perceptions of what is desirable.

The emergence of the domain of the global demands additional value sets to adequately confront the challenges of the fractured global order. The first is the imperative of respecting and preserving the ecosystems that nurture our species. It includes ethical obligations such as conserving biodiversity, reducing emissions that cause climate change, using natural resources sustainably, and avoiding the excessive use of materials and fossil energy that characterizes high-consumption societies.

A second set of values associated with the domain of the global focuses on the need to ensure a respectful and peaceful social coexistence in the times of massive and instant communications. Social networks and platforms, as well as communications media allow all of us to establish contact with all others instantaneously, something completely new in the history of humanity. We have at our disposal a wide range of socialization possibilities. New behavioral norms, new values, are indispensable to prevent this new situation from obliterating privacy, from spreading falsehoods, from destroying mutual trust and undermining social cohesion.

The third set of values refers to the impact of scientific and technological advances at the twilight of Bacon's epoch and the transition to a new period in the history of humanity. Discoveries and developments at the frontiers of scientific research and technological development are altering the human condition in fundamental ways, although we have not, as yet, developed the values and principles to guide their use and cope with their consequences.

A fourth set of values is related to the imperative of responsible consumption. According to a recent review by a group of scientists led by Australian civil engineer Thomas Wiedmann, this "implies the adoption of less affluent, simpler and sufficiency-oriented lifestyles ... consuming better but less. This also include addressing socially unsustainable underconsumption in impoverished communities in both less affluent and affluent countries, where enough and better is needed to achieve a more equal distribution of wealth and guarantee a minimum level of prosperity to overcome poverty" (Wiedmann et al., 2020, p. 4). In their view, this requires establishing both a floor and a ceiling strategy of sustainable consumption, and envisages reformist, radical, and green growth approaches. Yet they acknowledge that when both bottom-up and governmental initiatives appear to be rather limited, the task of overcoming the dynamics of market societies and capitalism to reduce overconsumption appears quite improbable.

There is no single interpretative scheme that could explain the realities of human societies and guide all of us unequivocally along a single path in the search for progress and the design of development strategies and policies. Cultural identities, ethnic loyalties, religious affiliations, and ethical principles can enter into conflict with each other and undermine efforts to collectively improve the human condition. This implies the need for accepting diversity and a multiplicity of viewpoints, the existence of potential conflicts and the need to resolve them without violence, and willingness to engage with others to begin sharing fundamental values.

The paradoxical lesson which can be derived from this is that if we are to accept the plurality of value systems and cultural perspectives to reframe, revitalize, create, and realize a diversity of values, we must of necessity recognize the primacy of certain universal values on top of which to build culture-specific ones that could reflect the diversity of the human condition. Values such as recognition, trust, respect, tolerance, transparency, empathy, solidarity, and willingness to engage with others need to be nurtured and consolidated as a basis for realizing other values.

American philosopher Sissela Bok provides a point for departure to explore the set of values that could improve mutual understanding and help to construct shared ways of improving the human condition. She has stated four propositions to support explorations into the realm of values:

> (1) Certain basic values necessary to collective survival have had to be formulated in every society. A minimalist set of such values can be recognized across societal and other boundaries. ... (2) These basic values are indispensable to human coexistence, though far from sufficient, at every level of personal and working life and of family, community, national, and international relations. ... (3) It is possible to affirm both common values and respect for diversity and in this way to use the basic values to critique abuses perpetrated in the name either of more general values or of ethnic, religious, political, or other diversity. ... (4) The need to pursue the inquiry about which basic values can be shared across cultural boundaries is urgent, if societies are to have some common ground for cross-cultural dia-

> logue and for debate about how best to cope with military, environmental, and other hazards that, themselves, do not stop at such boundaries (Bok, 1995, pp. 13–25).

Bok elaborates on the basic values required for collective survival:

> (A) All human groups, first of all, and all religious, moral, and legal traditions stress some form of positive duties regarding mutual support, loyalty and reciprocity … (B) The second category of fundamental values consists of negative duties to refrain from harmful action. All societies have stressed certain basic injunctions against at least a few forms of wronging other people—chief among these "force and fraud," or violence and deceit. (C) A third category of basic values worked out in all societies consists of norms of at least rudimentary fairness and procedural justice in cases of conflict regarding both positive and negative injunctions, prominently including those listed in the first two categories above (Bok, 1995, pp. 13–16).

For Bok, common values have to be viewed from a minimalist perspective, focusing on those that could be recognized and accepted by different societies and cultures. In her view, these minimalist values would be "limited in number, scope and degree of elaboration. … require no special erudition … to be understood. … concern primarily what people should do or not do, … start out from clear-cut cases, … call for no agreement as to their source, … may not be the only values necessary for collective survival, … no claim to universal acceptance need to be made for these values, … Nor, finally, are such minimalist values absolute in that they allow for no exceptions." She concludes: "given that minimalist moral values are so widely to be found, they offer a basis on which to build negotiation and dialogue about how to extent the scope within which they are honored" (Bok, 1995, pp. 18–19).

From an unusual combination of idealistic and pragmatic considerations, Bok provides a conceptual framework to begin exploring systematically how it may be possible to redefine progress and development as the reframing, revitalizing, creating, and realizing values that will be more appropriate for the new context of humanity at the twilight of Bacon's epoch. Swiss theologian Hans Kung has argued along the same lines, suggesting that "only and ethic of responsibility use for a new world order. It presupposes a conviction but realistically seeks the predictable consequences of a particular policy, … the art of politics … consists in combining political calculation (of modern real politics) convincingly with ethical judgements (ideal politics)" (Kung, 1998, p. 66).

French philosopher Edgar Morin tackled the question of individual and shared values from a different perspective, but ended up coinciding on the need to reconcile individual and collective values:

> Matters naturally change with the growth of autonomy and individual responsibility, since the imperative no longer proceeds from God, religion, the state or society but from the individual himself, in accordance with the Kantian categorical imperative. This imperative has become insular, self-generating and self-justifying, and this situation must evolve through recognition that the human being is not simply an individual, society or the human species, but rather an interdependent trinity comprising all three. From this standpoint, values relate not only to the individual, in terms of his sense of responsibility, dignity, virtue and honor, but also to the group and the species—particularly in a context of globalization (Morin, 2004, in Bindé, 2004, p. 43).

The relations between values and science and technology have been a subject of concern for philosophers and humanists during the last decades. British-American philosopher Peter Caws put forward in the mid-1960s the idea that humanity was facing a "crisis of value," largely a consequence of the impact of science and technology, but that "no *separation* of the range of activity of science and value is possible. The *distinction* between them nevertheless remains: they deal with the same phenomena but from different temporal perspectives" (his emphasis). In his view, science deals with the past, with explaining phenomena that have occurred; values refer to the future, to what should guide our actions. He considers the role of science and technology as that of expanding freedom because they expand the space for human activity.

Arguing along similar lines, Polish and British mathematician and humanist Jacob Bronowski maintained that science plays a creative part in the process of value changes by distinguishing what is true and what is false, thereby enhancing our sensibility and helping us distinguish what is acceptable from the unacceptable (Bronowski, 1953, 1956).

Stating like Caws that we are confronting a "contemporary crisis of values," (Caws, 1967, p. 16) French futurist Jerome Bindé raises the hope that "new values—both cognitive and future-oriented—seem to be emerging. They are not so much inherited as invented, not so much reproduced as created, not so much received as transmitted" (Bindé, 2004, p. 13).

Yet the difficulty of this much-needed collective enterprise should be soberly considered. The uncertainty and complexity of contemporary society, together with the dominant influence of ubiquitous social media, are creating what British social scientist Alice Evans calls an epidemic of "digital solitude." Meaningful dialogue and willingness to engage with others are shunned and rejected, hampering discussions to agree and disseminate shared values. The situation is even worse in the realm of politics. Venezuelan writer and former politician Moises Naim has clearly shown that populism, polarization, and post-truth are degrading political discourses, preventing sensible compromises, and sidelining the principled give-and-take that should be the norm in politics (Naim, 2022).

The task of reframing, revitalizing, creating, and realizing the values that will redefine what progress and development are is just at an early stage. Much more thought and work will be necessary to transform these ideas into operational guidelines capable of orienting human behavior.

Beyond agreeing on a new set of values, there remains the question of how to disseminate them to guide human actions. Education, communications, and example are the ways with which values are usually transmitted; they provide means to shape the behavior of those exposed to them, both for good and bad. In addition to transmitting knowledge, reasoning methods, and skills to access and process information, education instills values, promotes attitudes, and shapes patterns of social interaction. Family, social relations, schools, universities, and training programs, among many other institutions and organizations, are involved in educational activities that transmit values.

Media and social networks play a key role in the transmission and adoption of values. They could be privileged settings to promote notions such as the common good, harmonious social convivence, and shared visions of the future. But for this to happen, it will be necessary to revert the negative features they have acquired and are prevailing as fake news, distorted interpretations, false narratives, and doctored images, among many other lies that dull our senses and warp our minds. It is difficult to do, but not impossible with knowledge of how social networks and mass media operate, of how to shape messages that are appealing and persuasive, and of how to develop critical and reflexive skills for all of us who are at the receiving end of the messages, information, and stories they disseminate.

Example is perhaps the most immediate and effective way of transmitting values. The attitudes, affinities, preferences, aversions, interests, and emotional dispositions to which we are exposed when interacting with other people influence the evolution of our character and the way we perceive the actions of others around us. They give meaning to the concepts and evidence with which we appreciate situations. Although the example of the family environment is decisive during the early years, throughout our lives we meet people with whose qualities we wish to identify ourselves, whom we consider as models.

Consciously or not, we tend to imitate the behavior of prominent leaders, whatever their position in public, private, or social organizations at any level, local, national, and international. In particular, those who exercise political power and authority have a special moral obligation: to transmit values, to govern by example, to persuade by their conduct, to inspire by their behavior, to be worthy of imitation, to use their knowledge wisely, and to maintain the integrity and dignity of their investiture.

Knowledge Is Power: The Role of Governance

Beyond disseminating values, putting them in practice and bringing them down to Earth is an indispensable but difficult task. This is the art of governance, of transforming knowledge into power, of setting the course for any social group to follow, whatever its scope, nature, composition, or any other feature that defines it. Governance derives from the Greek *kybernetes*, which refers to the steerer, helmsman, or pilot of a vessel, who guides and directs and sets the framework for decisions and actions that lead to a desired destination.

As we stagger into the twilight of Bacon's epoch, we must adopt a paradoxical approach to governance. Ambiguity, uncertainty, and contradiction require the capacity to steer courses of action employing all knowledge resources available for exercising power and authority. Listening to multiple voices to articulate a coherent discourse, accommodating diverse demands to dissolve conflicts, creating structures for autonomous choices to converge, and reconciling individual freedom with collective action are what characterize good governance in turbulent times.

The processes of governance that transform knowledge into the power to act are deeply personal. Each of us has a unique set of experiences and learnings, acquired over our lifetimes, that together with the ways we perceive the world around us and the ways we instinctively feel about it, condition how we wield—and yield to—power and authority. Resorting to a stylized account of how these convoluted processes take place may be useful to examine, and possibly improve, the tasks of governance we are involved in, whether as leaders, followers, subjects, or concerned bystanders.

When approaching any situation, we make an initial approach to assess whether we are satisfied with it or not, or whether, if somewhat satisfactory, it could be further improved. If unsatisfactory or amenable to betterment, discomfort motivates a desire for change that, however vague and imprecise, generates an urge to overcome or improve the situation. This prompts us to imagine a better future that could be reached through deliberate intervention.

The initial approach should differentiate between circumstances, problems, and conditions. Circumstances refer to specific situations, usually ephemeral, which do not significantly affect the characteristics and performance of the social group, but which generate dissonance, disturbances, and, if repeated frequently, could become problems. They usually require specific interventions for which there are rules, regulations, and procedures established in advance.

Problems refer to situations whose impact on the social group is greater, affects performance and its future prospects, and requires broad, coordinated responses with a longer time dimension. Nevertheless, it is possible to visualize sets of decisions that configure one or more solutions to the problem in question within a certain period. To solve a problem, it is necessary to adopt policies that establish criteria for identifying interventions, choosing the most appropriate ones, and putting them into practice.

Conditions refer to complex situations with long antecedents that involve the entire system, require internal coordination processes, and demand a broad vision of the system's interrelations with the environment. To deal with them adequately, it is necessary to have an idea of the objectives and intentions of the entities with which the system interacts, to examine whether they are congruent and divergent with those of the system under consideration, and to respond quickly and flexibly to a series of challenges that arise incessantly from the turbulence in the environment.

A combination of circumstances can become a problem, and a concatenation of problems a condition. The reverse path is also possible, since conditions can be disaggregated by treating their components as problems and problems as circumstances. However, it is necessary to always keep in mind the original nature of the situations being faced.

Sir Geoffrey Vickers' notion of *acts of appreciation* which imbricate judgments of fact with judgments of value to define courses of action comes to play at this stage (Vickers, 1965). To complement his scheme, I have added judgments of reason and leadership styles to his scheme, articulating an expanded version of how acts of appreciation inform governance tasks.

Three streams of influence are involved in every act of appreciation: *mindset*, which includes the thought structures, the repertoire of concepts and ideas, as well as the rational procedures that link them; *evidence*, which comprises the data and information that provide the elements to construct perceptions of reality and are obtained through observations, measurements, and inferences; and *character*, which encompasses the values, principles, attitudes, emotions, behaviors and also the underlying cultural patterns that give meaning to what is thought and perceived (Sagasti et al., 2023; Sagasti, 2024).

The integration of the three streams of influence that shape the acts of appreciation leads to tentative *outcomes*, which after successive revisions arrive at a good-enough *closing outcome* that sets the course to be followed and guides decision-making in the planning and management processes. These three streams of influence interact with each other and are continually evolving; it is difficult to disentangle the influence and relative weight of each, especially in situations requiring individual and group decisions in complex settings. They also demand frequent adjustments in the way mindsets, character, and evidence combine in acts of judgment to lead to appropriate outcomes and effective decisions and management.

A final component of acts of appreciation is the different leadership styles that refer to the ways in which individuals or groups exercise power and authority to generate outcomes. They combine, to varying degrees, *disciplinary* or coercive elements (use of force, obedience, subordination, sanctions), *rational* elements (arguments, persuasion, reasoning, norms, institutions), and *emotional* elements (identification, empathy, affinity, aversion). All of these come into play, consciously or unconsciously, in the acts of appreciation that lead to outcomes in governance processes.[2]

Leadership styles may vary over time depending on the circumstance, problem, or condition faced by the system, but to exercise leadership in a reasonable manner it is necessary first to learn *followership;* this is how to follow. It is difficult to become an effective leader without having first some notion of what motivates those who support and suffer the exercise of power and authority.

These considerations figure, either consciously or unconsciously, in every situation we face and every decision we make, whether personal, professional, academic, political, or social, at all times. When facing any situation, we unwittingly put together the repertoire of ideas we have accumulated over time with the data and information we perceive and our values, preferences, and aversions.

Once we set a course of action with the final good-enough outcome of the acts of appreciation, it gives rise to planning, which involves taking anticipatory decisions in situations that have not yet occurred but are envisaged to occur, and to management, which transforms anticipatory into actual decisions as time passes and the future becomes the present. Planning and management produce results, impacts, collateral effects, and second-order consequences, which when examined and

[2] These types of leadership are derived from and partially overlap with what Max Weber called traditional authority, legal authority, and charismatic authority (Weber, 1967, p. 53).

reflected upon, allow learning about how governance, planning, and management should be conducted (Sagasti, 2024).

Rethinking progress and development, and embarking, both individually and collectively, toward a renewal of our value systems and of ways of realizing them at the twilight of Bacon's epoch requires a multiplicity of continuously evolving acts of appreciation, of enhanced approaches to governance at the personal, group, and social levels.

What Next?

The Baconian Program has run its course. Its components are being reassessed, and even though the fog of uncertainty that envelops our times allows only a dim and blurred vision of what may come after, we have some signposts for the transformations and adjustments it requires.

The scientific method is venturing beyond the limits of narrow instrumental rationalism to leave room, not only for cyberspace and virtual reality as a new realm for the exercise of human faculties, but also for other ways of "registering shadows on the screen," to quote Sir James Frazer once again. Ethical, moral, and aesthetic issues, among others, should be even more explicitly incorporated into scientific research methods; they are already present but must be much more than an afterthought, something added after research results have been obtained. Debates on the impact of Artificial Intelligence, in which science-based technologies are running well ahead of their prudent usage, provide an example of the urgent need to take into account their collateral effects and second-order consequences.

As advanced earlier, non-Western cultural perspectives, in particular ancestral and traditional forms of knowledge acquisition and utilization, are now increasingly being taken into consideration in fields like biodiversity conservation. Together with feminist viewpoints, these should inform a broader systemic appraisal of the scientific research process and of the ways their results are utilized. Beyond the utilitarian approach to the conduct of science, which prevailed unrivaled since the deployment of Bacon's program and its fusion with the international expansion of markets and capitalism, it is necessary to reemphasize the importance of curiosity-oriented "useless" research. Time and again it has proven to provide the knowledge that led to technologies that significantly improved the human condition (Hobsbawm, 2014, pp. 190–191; Flexner, 1939).

The purpose, direction, and focus of the Baconian Program need to be rethought from the perspective of what progress and development mean at the twilight of Bacon's epoch. We have begun, hesitantly, to redefine their significance, to revitalize existing, and create new values to reorient human activity in ways that reduce its negative impacts and forestall its threats to the survival of our species and countless others (Sanchez Perez, 2023).

The last component of Bacon's program, institutions, requires also a major restructuring. Institutional arrangements organize, codify, and steer knowledge-generation activities, and the work of scientific researchers, developers of technologies and innovators, in directions that have proven, in too many cases, harmful and inimical to improvements of the human condition. The settings in which research outfits operate—oriented primarily toward profit-making and largely disregarding environmental and social consequences—will be, later or hopefully sooner, reformed to incorporate notions such as knowledge as a public good, reorienting a sizable portion of their work in more positive directions and making research results widely available.

New institutional arrangements must prevent the total subjugation of the natural world to the folly of self-absorbed politicians, the voracity of self-indulgent entrepreneurs, and the self-centered whims of acquisitive consumers. All of these portend the destruction of the ecosystems that support life, and the subsequent ruthless cull of a world population that appears excessive because of the extremely unequal distribution of global wealth and consumption habits.

Whether we are aware or not, we are moving into the post-Baconian epoch. The crises, turbulence, instability, uncertainty, and bewilderment that characterize our times are symptoms of much more profound changes, of an epochal transformation. Wrenching adjustments in mindsets, conceptions, habits, and practices will be required from all of us, together with extraordinary efforts to open our minds and apprehend the human predicament as we move deeper into the twenty-first century.

The future of humanity over the next centuries will be determined by our success in overcoming the darkness that is encroaching on the world at the twilight of Bacon's epoch, which is dimming our collective capacity to envisage the dawn of a new period in the history of humanity. In contrast with the lone achievement of Sir Francis Bacon, should a new program emerge, it will not be the dream of a gifted individual. The complexity and interconnectedness of the world we live in demands a collective learning process arising out of a multiplicity of human interactions.

References

Bindé, J. (Ed.). (2004). *The future of values: 21st-century talks*. UNESCO.

Bohm, D. (2004). In L. Nichol (Ed.). *On dialogue* (Routledge classics ed.). Routledge.

Bohm, D., & Peat, F. D. (1987). *Science, order, and creativity: A dramatic new look at the creative roots of science and life*. Bantam Books.

Bok, S. (1995). *Common values*. University of Missouri Press.

Bronowski, J. (1953). *The common sense of science*. Vintage Books.

Bronowski, J. (1956). *Science and human values*. Harper Torchbooks.

Bury, J. B. (1932). *The idea of progress: An inquiry into its origin and growth*. Dover Publications.

Caws, P. (1967). *Science and the theory of value*. Random House.

Flexner, A. (1939). The usefulness of useless knowledge. *Harper's Magazine, 179*, 544–552.

Frankopan, P. (2023, March 3). Apocalypse then: Lessons from history in tackling climate shocks. *Financial Times*. Retrieved from https://www.ft.com/content/33e66ae3-dac2-4cc0-b859-79edc7dd07dd

Frazer, J. G. (1964). In T. H. Gaster (Ed.), *The new golden bough: A new abridgment of the classic work*. New American Library.

García Morente, M. (1980). *Ensayos sobre el progreso*. Dorcas.
Graeber, G., & Wengrow, D. (2021). *The Dawn of Everything: A New History of Humanity*. Penguin Random House UK.
Hobsbawm, E. (2014). *Fractured times: Culture and society in the twentieth century*. Abacus.
Jonas, H. (1984). *The imperative of responsibility: In search of an ethics for the technological age*. University of Chicago Press.
Kakkuri-Knuuttila, M.-L. (2025). David Bohm's philosophy of science in his causal interpretation of quantum mechanics. *Synthese, 206*(5), 223. https://doi.org/10.1007/s11229-025-05139-8
Kung, H. (1998). *A global ethic for global politics and economics*. Oxford University Press.
Morin, E. (2004). The ethics of complexity and the problem of values in the twenty-first century. In J. Bindé (Ed.), *The future of values: 21st-century talks*. UNESCO.
Naim, M. (2022). *The revenge of power: How autocrats are reinventing politics for the 21st century*. St. Martins.
Nisbet, R. (1980). *History of the idea of progress*. Basic Books.
Pylkkänen, P. (2025). Real consciousness in a real world: Interactionist monism. *Journal of Consciousness Studies, 32*(5–6), 62–81. https://urn.kb.se/resolve?urn=urn:nbn:se:his:diva-24969
Ravn, I. (1989). *Implicate order and the good life: Applying David Bohm's ontology in the human world* [PhD dissertation in Social System Sciences]. University of Pennsylvania.
Rostow, W. W. (1971). *The stages of economic growth: A non-communist manifesto*. Cambridge University Press.
Sachs, I. (2009). Revisiting development in the twenty-first century. *International Journal of Political Economy, 38*(3), 5–11.
Sagasti, F. (2024). *Decisiones en tiempos turbulentos: Medio siglo en ciencias de sistemas, planeamiento, gestión y gobernanza*. Fondo de Cultura Económica, Fondo Editorial Universidad del Pacífico.
Sagasti, F., Málaga, L., & Ugarelli, G. (2023). *Gobernar en tiempos de crisis: Política e ideas en el Gobierno de Transición y Emergencia, Perú 2020–2021*. Planeta.
Sanchez Perez, J. (2023, April 25). *The Quechua idea 'pacha' urges us beyond narrow self-concern*. Psyche. Retrieved from https://psyche.co/ideas/the-quechua-idea-of-pacha-urges-us-beyond-narrow-self-concern
Schmieke, M. (2022). Bohm's super implicate order and the quantum Zeno effect. *Dev Sanskriti Interdisciplinary International Journal, 19*, 01–10. https://doi.org/10.36018/dsiij.v19i.241
Val, A., Hirota, M., Encalada, A., Paez, B., Neves, E., Marcovitch, J., Cañas, J. S., Rezende, J., Moraes, M., Raimundo, R. L. G., Arieira, J., & da Mota e Silva, T. (2025). Chapter 8: Knowledge connectivity in the Amazon: Bridging scientific, indigenous, and technological perspectives for sustainable development. In *Amazon assessment report 2025—Connectivity of the Amazon for a living planet*. Science Panel for the Amazon (SPA). https://doi.org/10.55161/FNVX8547
Vickers, G. (1965). *The art of judgment: A study of policy making*. Basic Books.
Weber, M. (1967). *El político y el científico*. Alianza Editorial.
Wiedmann, T., Lenzen, M., Keyßer, L. T., & Steinberger, J. K. (2020). Scientists' warning on affluence. *Nature Communications, 11*(1), 3107. https://doi.org/10.1038/s41467-020-16941-y

Chapter 11
Into a Post-Baconian Epoch

In this epoch the goal is not to dominate nature,
but technology, irrational social force and institutions
that threat the survival of society.

Eric Fromm (2017, p. 188)

We have met the enemy, and he is us.

Pogo (Walt Kelly, 1970)

Sir Francis Bacon's program was ahead of its time; now the times are ahead of Bacon's program. He focused most of his intellectual work on what he called the rules of nature. This was the main subject of his implicit program, and he is justly recognized for the pivotal role he played in promoting the use of knowledge to dominate nature through understanding. Yet, he has also been questioned for the undesirable consequences of the relentless and unrestrained subjugation of nature.

Power over the fragile ecosystems that allow us to exist should be exerted with utmost care—our survival on the planet depends on the services they provide. Perhaps, we should remember that in Bacon's time the total world population was about 580 million people, 13 times less than the nearly eight billion in the twenty-first century. Moreover, current personal consumption and resource use levels now exceed by a large margin those of 400 years ago. The impacts of human activity on the environment in Bacon's time were mostly localized and could be contained or reversed; they became a worldwide concern with the emergence of the domain of the global in the late twentieth century.

Following its implicit formulation, unfolding, and deployment over several centuries, the extraordinary success of Baconian Program was a bittersweet achievement. Intertwining Bacon's implicit program with the expansion of capitalism and international markets led to viewing human activities through the narrow lens of economic efficiency. Environmental and social consequences were disregarded as externalities not worth including in economic calculations, and future consequences were ignored or sharply discounted.

F. Sagasti, *Knowledge is Power*, Innovation, Technology, and Knowledge Management, https://doi.org/10.1007/978-3-032-20668-8_11

Glimpsing the Future

Can we expect a luminous dawn after the twilight we are now living and the darkness of the impending night? Is it possible to dissipate the fog of uncertainty that envelops us at the twilight of Bacon epoch? Perhaps not, but we can at least imagine and explore what the future may hold.

Let us begin by considering extreme scenarios along three dimensions: the prospects for the human species, for the generation and utilization of knowledge, and for governing the conduct of human affairs.

Views on the future of our species diverge sharply. At one extreme are statements that envisage the extinction of our species through catastrophic events (Colebrook, 2012). A sober report prepared by the Homeland Security Agency of the United States listed several possible "global catastrophic and existential risk that hold the potential to threaten human civilization" (Homeland Security Operational Analysis Center, 2024, p. vii). Nuclear wars, sudden and severe climate change, the global spread of pandemics, the threats posed by synthetic biology, possible volcanic eruptions, the impact of artificial intelligence acting on its own or amplifying other catastrophes, and asteroid and comet impacts, to which global terrorism could be added. The demise of our civilization and the disappearance of humanity from the face of the Earth would leave free space for other species to emerge and thrive without our disturbing presence.

At the other extreme are those who anticipate a future in which biological and electronic enhancements will improve human beings. Transhumanists expect genetic engineering, prosthetic devices, and artificial intelligence will help our species transcend current biological limitations. Beyond preventing diseases and avoiding the ravages of old age, technological advances could take humanity to a new evolutionary stage and extend lifespans indefinitely. Some transhumanists envisage colonizing other planets to escape a possible Earth collapse, others favor uploading their brains into electronic devices to live forever in their circuits, and most foresee tinkering with our genetic makeup to design the type of descendants they would like to have.

Only a few rich or powerful people are likely to have access to these enhancements, exacerbating inequalities and presaging a possible divergence in the evolution of our species. As American political scientist Francis Fukuyama put it: "the posthuman world could be one far more hierarchical and competitive than the one that currently exits, and full of social conflict as a result. It could be one in which any notion of 'shared humanity' is lost" (Fukuyama, 2002, p. 18). This brings to mind H. G. Wells's science-fiction classic, *The Time Machine*, in which humanity has bifurcated into two species, the Eloi and the Morlocks, with the former ending up as prey for the latter.

Nonetheless, biological and other enhancements have their enthusiasts. American computer scientist and science-fiction writer Ramez Naam thinks that:

> We are not at the end point of evolution—there is no such thing. We are just an intermediate step on one branch of the tree of life. But from this point on we can choose the directions in

> which we grow and we change. We can choose new states that benefit us and benefit our children ... We will not all opt for the same changes. ...Different men and women, different communities, different ideologies will all select different goals to work towards. Some of us will choose to stay as we are, while other will choose to transform. Humanity will expand, splinter, and blossom (Naam, 2010, p. 198).

The future of scientific and technological knowledge is another source of divergence. Some envisage a reprisal of Middle Ages obscurantism, with superstition and religious dogmas, complemented by fake news, alternative facts, and conspiracy theories taking over the public discourse, informing political decisions and guiding decision-making. In this scenario, science stagnates; scientific evidence and findings are rejected by a significant part of the population and powerful leaders, prompting retreats into self-contained silos of prejudice that refuse to consider any views other than those they cling to.

There are signs that this possible future for the evolution of knowledge generation is not idle speculation. These include the rejection of time-proven scientific findings, such as the effectiveness of vaccines; the deep funding cuts for research, which have taken place in the world's leading science and technology power; the diminishing returns to investment in research; and the rise of religious fundamentalism that questions everything but divine revelation as a source of truth. In addition, as defense spending increases in a geopolitically unstable world, resource allocations for scientific research and technological development in high-income countries are likely to experience significant declines.

However, aiming to transform knowledge into power, several emerging and middle-income countries are investing heavily in the creation and consolidation of their own science and technology capabilities. In addition, large technology-based corporations and many technological start-ups are also allocating significant resources to research and development.

Cyberspace, virtual reality, and artificial intelligence, together with the recovery of ancestral knowledge, the upgrading of traditional techniques, and with alternative perspectives on the nature of research are transforming the process of knowledge generation and utilization. The scientific method is likely to evolve toward explicitly acknowledging and compensating for cultural biases, while maintaining strict standards of replication and validation of research results.

The future of governance presents another dichotomy: autocracy or democracy. Autocratic rulers seek to exercise political power without limits and for indefinite periods. They employ violence, money, ideology, propaganda, pressures, blackmail, and corruption to suppress dissent and silence criticism. While often wrapped in democratic trappings, such as elections and frequent contact with their followers, they manipulate electoral processes, make false promises, and distort facts to consolidate their hold on power. Inflexibility and a tendency to impose arbitrary decisions go hand in hand with a rejection of accountability and a disregard for the distinction between the public and private interests. These characteristics make it difficult to adapt in rapidly changing circumstances and to cope with uncertainty, ambiguity, and turbulence.

Democratic rulers abide by the rules established for the exercise of political power and authority, support the periodic renewal of political leadership through free and fair elections, listen to their constituents, and distinguish sharply between the public and private interests. Opting for dialogue and consensus, they seek to balance alternative viewpoints but are capable of enforcing agreements and implementing decisions taken after deliberation. These features make democratic regimes flexible and adaptive, capable of coping with change and volatility while maintaining course. Yet, they are also imperfect, can be coopted, and must be continuously reinvented.

These extreme scenarios regarding the future of humanity, knowledge, and governance are unlikely to emerge unalloyedly in the post-Baconian epoch; the times ahead will be messier and more complicated than any self-consistent or ideal vision. Yet, however blurred and imperfect they may be, alternative visions are useful to keep in mind, shifting as quickly as possible between combinations of their features, traversing the middle ground and muddled spaces in between, searching for interstices to move forward. In a paradoxical way, ideal visions are needed to effectively trundle through these middle/muddled spaces and the occasional interstices that may be laboriously found. Ideals can be indefinitely approached but never fully attained—yet they can make appealing and viable the partial and temporary compromises essential to gradually approach them.

American journalist and lecturer Kara Platoni provides an example of what may be in store for someone born in 2025:

> We imagine a world that has overcome the worst threats of our time: a creeping climate disaster; a deepening digital divide; our persistent flirtation with nuclear war; the possibility that a pandemic will kill us quickly, that overly convenient lifestyles will kill us slowly, or that intelligent machines will turn out to be too smart. We hope that democracy survives and these technologies will be the opt-in gadgetry of a thriving society, not the surveillance tools of dystopia. If you have a digital twin, we hope it's not a deepfake. You might see these sketches from 2024 as a blithe promise, a warning, or a fever dream. The important thing is: Our present is just the starting point for infinite futures. What happens next, kid, depends on you (Platoni, 2024, para. 71).

Understanding and managing discrepancies and contradictions requires a paradoxical approach to navigate through opposite viewpoints or states, shifting from one to the other as rapidly as possible, appearing to consider all simultaneously. A paradoxical approach attempts to discover and develop frames of reference capable of containing and dissolving inconsistencies, recognizes that contextual changes and deliberate interventions alter our perception of situations and modify their possible evolution, and accepts that our reasoning about ambiguous and contradictory situations evolves gradually.

As the American professor Mary C. Morrison explains:

> We stand in a turmoil of contradictions without having the faintest idea how to handle them: Law/Freedom; Rich/Poor; Right/Left; Love/Hate—the list is endless. Paradox lives and moves in this realm; it is the art of balancing opposites in such a way they do not cancel each other but shoot sparks of light across their points of polarity, It looks at our desperate either/ors and tells us they are really both/ands—that life is large than any of our concepts

> and can, if we let it, embrace our contradictions (Morrison, as cited in, Smith & Berg, 1987, p. 3).

In the highly interconnected, complex, and uncertain world at the twilight of Bacon's epoch, a paradoxical approach helps to explore options, to find cracks in seemingly impenetrable barriers through which to squeeze forward, adopting nuanced and tentative approaches to reconcile inconsistencies, building gradually a sequence of outcomes acceptable to most of the parties involved. It entails examining at the same time wholes and parts, simplicity and complexity, thought and action, long and short terms, strategy and opportunism, focalized and broad perspectives, and radical and incremental interventions.

Explorations of the future require a multiplicity of disciplined imagination exercises and of open-ended conversations, capable of accommodating a variety of provisional and partial conceptions, and of steering the conduct of human affairs through the middle and muddled grounds that are likely to provide favorable, or less harmful, paths for the evolution of humanity. The Russian political philosopher Piotr Kropotkin put it well: "although daring in thinking is no guarantee of daring in practice, mental timidity in constructing an ideal is certainly a criterion of mental timidity in practice" (Kropotkin, 1970, p. 46).

This is the task for governance during the coming decades of twilight. Perhaps it may be useful to go back to the origins of the Baconian Program, assessing what Bacon thought about the use of political power.

Bacon on Politics

As stated earlier, Sir Francis Bacon did not dwell only on how to use knowledge to exercise power over nature; he also mulled over what he called the rules of policy, the ways in which those who exercise political power should behave. Bereft of financial resources and continuously begging favors, his knowledge of how the courts of Elizabeth I and James I worked, the roles of favorites, the precarious balance between Parliament and royalty in a constitutional monarchy, as well as his close acquaintance with the behavior and mores of his peers, supporters, and rivals, allowed him to gradually rise and do well in the volatile and risky political atmosphere of the English court.

Referring once again to Bacon's writings, when discussing the union of England and Scotland, he argued "there is a great affinity and consent between the rules of nature, and the rules of policy: the one being nothing else but an order in the government of the world, and the other an order in the government of an estate" (Bacon, 2011a, vol. 10, p. 90). When recounting the myth of the Sphinx, he described two riddles in the conduct of human affairs: "one concerning the nature of things, another concerning the nature of man" (Bacon, 2011a, vol. 10, p. 373) which have different ways of solving them and different rewards. Regarding the second riddle, he concludes "whoever has a thorough insight into the nature of man may shape his fortune almost as he will and is born for empire" (Bacon, 2011a, vol. 10, p. 373).

Dispersed through his works, Bacon provided insights into how rulers should exercise political power and authority. These could be of help when attempting to put into practice whichever preferred policies may emerge from an examination of the middle and muddled ground between the extreme scenarios for the future of humanity.

As illustration, witness his musings, still current, about the burden of political leaders: "men in great place are thrice servants: servants of the sovereign or state; servants of fame; and servant of business. So, as they have no freedom; neither in their persons, nor in their actions, nor in their times. It is a strange desire, to seek power and to lose liberty; or to seek power over others, and to lose power over a man's self" (Bacon, 1985, p. 90). Furthermore, aware that political effectiveness requires sometimes unsavory companions, he counseled: "as for cunning and corrupt men, you must (I know) sometimes use them; but keep them at a distance; and let it appear that you make use of them, rather than that they lead you" (Bacon, 2011b, vol. 13, p. 7). First-hand experience made me realize the contemporary relevance of these warnings.

For Bacon, transparency should be a matter of policy decisions by rulers, who need to decide what to disclose and what to conceal: "for if a man has the penetration of judgement as he can discern what things are to be laid open, and what to be secreted, and what to be showed at half-lights, and to whom, and when" (Bacon, 1985, p. 76). The need to be watchful and ready to spot troubles and to be aware that these may be caused by himself was also one of Bacon's concerns: "and let men beware how they neglect and suffer matter of trouble to be prepared: for no man can forbid the spark nor tell whence it may come. The difficulties in princes' business are many and great, but the greatest difficulty is often in their own mind" (Bacon, 1985, p. 116).

He underscored the need for prudence when facing disputes in a government team and the importance of instilling hope when it takes time to address grievances: "for when the authorities of princes are made but an accessary to a cause … kings begin to be put almost out of possession. … And it is a certain sign of a wise government and proceeding when it can hold men's hearts by hopes, when it cannot by satisfaction" (Bacon, 1985, p. 102). Bacon also suggests that rulers should keep a neutral and skeptical stance when dealing with factions in government: "I say not the consideration of factions is to be neglected … but great men, that have strength in themselves, were better to maintain themselves indifferent and neutral. … When factions are carried too high and too violently, it is a sign of weakness in princes, and much to the prejudice both of their authority and business" (Bacon, 1985, pp. 211–212).

Caution and patience in negotiations with difficult opponents were another of his recommendations: "In dealing with cunning persons, we must ever consider their ends, to interpret their speeches; and it is good to say little to them, and that which they least look for. In all negotiations of difficulty, a man may not look to sow and reap at once, but must prepared business, and so ripen it by degrees" (Bacon, 1985, p. 204).

In his essay *"Of Counsel,"* he also highlighted the importance of advisors but warned about the potential shortcomings of receiving advice on how to govern, which included divulging secrets, receiving self-interested advice, and being perceived as a weak ruler. In his "*On Youth and Age*," Bacon also pondered on the relative advantage of young and old people involved in government tasks, arguing that "young men are fitter to invent than to judge, fitter for execution than for counsel, and fitter for new projects than for settled business" (Bacon, 1985, p. 187), but that the aged could add experience and knowledge to deal with past and current situations. In a similar vein, he also gave suggestions on how to deal with different types of supporters in his essay *"On Followers and Friends"* (Bacon, 1985, p. 205), and on what the prerogatives and obligations of rulers are in his proclamation about the *"Jurisdiction of the Council of Wales"* (Bacon, 2011a, vol. 10, p. 373).

As advanced in the preceding chapter, what Bacon called the rules of policy we now know as governance, the art of exercising power and authority in just, honest, moderate, and effective ways. Knowledge is power refers not only to the domination of or over nature, but also to power and authority in society. These ideas prompt an examination of the relations between legitimacy, knowledge, responsibility, and trust.

Legitimacy emerges from the consent of the governed, from leaders who seek the common good, and from respecting and strengthening institutional arrangements. The legitimate exercise of power and authority requires knowledge, responsibility, and trust.

While holding high office, I confirmed that, even in the direst circumstances, knowledge confers power. Combined with readiness to take advantage of the unexpected, determination to act boldly, and with a leadership style that empowers others, knowledge helps to shape the course of events and to prevail in difficult situations, however unlikely this may appear at first.

Knowledge about the characteristics, aims, intentions, and behavior of the governed; about the socioeconomic and biophysical context, together with the constraints they impose and opportunities they provide; and about the ways in which all of these interact with each other to open or close spaces for deliberate interventions and actions. Responsibility entails facing the consequences of past and current decisions and conduct, and the imperative of considering and weighing options, interests and implications of every choice. Trust, the capacity and sentiment that moves us to rely on others, underlies the interactions between knowledge, responsibility, and power. Leaders should be capable of generating trust and hope, which requires openness, moderation, and the capacity to create positive visions of the future. Incidentally, these are also some of the characteristics of democratic governance.

Toward a New Program?

While developing the components of his implicit program, Bacon had a genial intuition but only a vague conception of its prospects for success, and even less of an idea of what it would lead to. He was a transitional figure between two ages. He did not manage to garner royal support for his knowledge-generation proposals during his lifetime. As shown by his downfall from grace, uncanny and accurate foresight could not be expected of him.

It took more than 300 years for the idea of a Baconian Program—dominating nature through understanding to improve the human condition—to take shape, and nearly another century before it could be described in a more or less coherent way. A few more decades were required to tease out from Bacon's works the various components of his implicit program for humanity.

We have now, 400 years later, the responsibility of looking forward, of anticipating ways of judiciously reaping the benefits of the unfolding, deployment, and extraordinary but ambiguous success of the Baconian Program. We are also responsible for reversing the damage done and preventing further negative consequences.

In addition to rethinking the components of the Baconian Program, of redefining progress as the creation and realization of values, of conceiving development as the latest and last reinterpretation of progress at the twilight of Bacon's epoch, and of exploring how governance transforms knowledge into power, we must ask ourselves whether it makes any sense to think of a new program for humanity. Do we need a new program for the future of humanity? Does it make sense attempting to develop one?

When I began my forays into Baconland I thought this was the case; now, I am not sure. On the negative side, the world has become too complex, fragmented, unstable, ambiguous, and uncertain to pretend that an extraordinary individual or, more likely, an enlightened collective of worldwide talents could produce a set of prescriptions and proposals to guide future human endeavors. On the positive side, speculation about a possible post-Baconian Program for Humanity may inspire and lead to piecemeal actions and collective undertakings that could improve, in however slight, partial, and localized, but worthwhile way, the human condition. It could take several decades, or even longer, before a Program for the whole of humanity could be articulated with the coherence that we can now—400 years later—retrospectively attribute to the Baconian Program. This search must build on its achievements and enormous success—but at the same time acknowledge its fateful consequences.

Two indications suggest a possible direction for such a search. First, there is a need to expand what became a rather narrow range of considerations—referred almost exclusively to the exercise of our rational faculties—that were fully incorporated into the implicit design of the Baconian Program. Perhaps this calls for putting ethical, emotional, aesthetic, and transcendence aspirations—that is, feelings and the search for meaning—on equal footing with reason, integrating all of them into attempts at envisaging and outlining a new program (Damasio, 2018, pp. 15–32).

Second, in the process of putting the Baconian Program in practice, Western civilization took the world by storm. In just a few centuries, it altered all aspects of the human condition. Other cultures and civilizations had to absorb, adapt to, and respond to the advances of the Western worldview. Along the way, the potential contribution of the outlooks and mindsets of other civilizations were lost or ignored. The same can be applied to patriarchal cultures, which for centuries and millennia have obscured and belittled the contribution of women, half of humanity, to the improvement and maintenance of living standards everywhere. It is time to reconsider these states of affairs and begin to recover a diversity of civilizational, cultural, and gender perspectives on how knowledge can improve the human condition and its prospects.

Living in the uncertain times of the transition toward a post-Baconian epoch, we can only vaguely speculate about what may, or should, be in store for whatever humanity may become in the future. Perhaps it will take grounded speculation exercises during the rest of the twenty-first century before a new set of proposals to steer human efforts could be articulated with the clarity and coherence that we can retrospectively attribute to Bacon's program.

Yet, this should not stop us from engaging our intellectual, emotional, and aesthetic energies to anticipate what could eventually become a broadly encompassing set of shared concepts, facts, and values regarding the future of our species. Whatever emerges from these attempts should strike a paradoxical and precarious, but essential, balance between personal freedom and collective action. Respect for individual rights must be embedded in a renewed set of institutional arrangements, which must codify restraint and mutual respect while fostering effective cooperative behavior.

The key objective of these uphill efforts to articulate new guidelines should be to promote reciprocally fruitful interactions between increasingly diverse and differentiated groups, societies, civilizations and, maybe, even human subspecies, as well as with other species and the ecosystems that sustain living organisms. Each and all of these should have the opportunity to fulfill their aspirations, realize their expectations, and follow their own evolutionary path. This would mean going beyond the Baconian injunction to "improve the human condition," shifting toward "becoming responsible for the future of humanity and of life."

As we move to a new epoch, "knowledge is power" means that we are forced to become the authors of our own destiny. Even though the role of contingency, of unexpected events and of surprises, will always be present and must be acknowledged, we should remember what the French microbiologist Louis Pasteur said: "chance favors prepared mind" (Pasteur, as cited in Latour, 1988, p. 88).

Power to Control Power

As stated in one of my papers written quite some time ago, "amidst the confusion and turbulence, we may venture that the human predicament at the twilight of the Baconian epoch is a condition humanity will have to face time and again. Our knowledge and capacities advance relentlessly—but humanity continuously outpaces its own creations. By the time our understanding—let alone our habits, institutions and values—catch up with the products of our own intellect, we will have moved, once more, to uncharted territory. We do this by enlarging and transforming the realm of human experience; and also by creating new realities, generating new problems and discovering new mysteries to be unveiled. We may even consider this open-ended search for new interpretations of the human condition, for novel ways to solve the riddle of our contingent existence, as a unique attribute of the human species"—whatever it may become in the post-Baconian epoch (Sagasti, 2000, pp. 600–601).

Along the way, we reconstruct our own individual realities all the time and our collective realities every so often. We are living now in a unique period of human history in which reality is being reconfigured for all the members of our species and, incidentally, for other living organisms. We are transcendental beings searching for meaning in our individual and social lives, remaining unsatisfied with whatever we achieve, aspiring to better understand our contingent existence, and aiming to leave a legacy for the future. These drives have become more urgent now, in the transition toward an epoch whose outlines cannot be clearly discerned.

Yet, we can be reassured that knowledge is still power, perhaps more than ever, but knowledge of a different kind. Knowledge that complements the domination of nature in which our species has become proficient, so adept and masterful that we have ended up snaring ourselves with the twisted ropes of the means to do so. Paradoxically, as Hans Jonas argued, to release ourselves from this self-imposed bondage, we must use power to control power; we must improve governance. We now need knowledge about how to use knowledge to acquire power over power. Coping with the uncertainty, ambiguity, and turbulence of the twilight of Bacon's epoch requires mastery, not so much over nature—we already have acquired it—but mastery over ourselves.

Acts of appreciation, which integrate mindsets (repertoire of concepts and rules to link them), evidence (data and information), and character (values, principles and attitudes) may help in marshaling knowledge to exercise power not just over nature, but most importantly power to govern ourselves. Mindset and evidence are enabling conditions, necessary but not sufficient, for transforming knowledge into potential power; character gives meaning to knowledge and transforms potential into actual power. Values, attitudes, principles, beliefs, affinities, aversions, preferences, antipathies—character—shape the ways in which knowledge is used to wield power over power. Character configures the ethical frameworks that determine whether knowledge and power are used for good or bad, for improving or worsening the human condition, for enhancing our chances of survival or for hastening our possible demise.

The emerging period of history demands a renewal of behavioral norms and rules of conduct, of ethical and moral frameworks to align them with García Morente's redefined notion of progress—"the realization of the realm of values through human effort … for building goods and destroying evils" (García Morente, 1980, p. 45). Adopted and practiced by inner-prompted consent, by personal convictions and deep feelings, rather than by imposition and coercion, these frameworks should be capable of containing, assessing, and giving meaning to a multiplicity of interrelated initiatives that should gradually prevail to improve the human condition in the post-Baconian epoch.

Yet, there remains the thorny issue of reconciling values, not only between but also within individuals, for some of these may turn out to be inconsistent. British philosopher and historian Sir Isaiah Berlin argued this point forcefully:

> If these ultimate human values by which we live are to be pursued, then compromises, trade-offs, arrangements have to be made if the worst is not to happen. So much liberty for so much equality, so much individual self-expression for so much security, so much justice for so much compassion. My point is that some values clash: the ends pursued by human beings are all generated by our common nature, but their pursuit has to be to some degree controlled—liberty and the pursuit of happiness, I repeat, may not be fully compatible with each other, nor are liberty, equality, and fraternity (Berlin, 2014, para. 10).

Therefore, we must find ways of processing, aggregating, and integrating judgments of all types—moral, ethical, aesthetic, and among others—into coherent sets of values. We should do this first within ourselves, and then share them with others, gradually expanding their reach, seeking agreement and consent on the rules that should govern our collective actions and behavior.

To overcome, or at least skirt around, the difficulty of making choices between diverse preferences, it will be necessary to temporarily satisfy them to different degrees and extents. It requires searching for and wiggling through argumental fissures to surmount what appear as incompatible aims; paradoxically switching our regard between what seem to be, at first sight, contradictory stances; provisionally bowing to one and then to the other while continuing to explore options to reach the least unsatisfactory conclusions. This underscores the imperative of putting emphasis on achieving shared, provisional, and cumulative intersubjective agreements, embracing a sequence of temporal and partially acceptable outcomes that could gradually construct a better and more desirable future for most, if not all.

The concept of "intermediate area" or "transitional space," advanced by British psychoanalyst Donald Winnicott to account for the interactions between mother and child, and between the inner reality and the external life of an individual, provides a way of thinking about creative and practical imagination and a sequence of good-enough outcomes. This concept suggests that those fragile and temporary sequences of agreed outcomes may prove a fertile ground in which to find ways out of whatever stymies and constrains shared initiatives (Hollway, 2011).

Leadership and Trust

The gradual expansion of overlapping consensuses and evolved sets of shared values requires styles of leadership capable of creating the enabling conditions for moral dialogue. Responsibility, tolerance, knowledge, and effectiveness are essential to achieve this. Responsibility, in the sense of acknowledging and facing up the consequences of one's actions, and of taking care of whatever one freely accepts as an obligation; tolerance, understood as recognition, respect, and celebration of diversity, rather than just grudging acceptance of differences; knowledge, in the Baconian sense of a better understanding of natural and social phenomena to improve the human condition; and effectiveness, putting thought into action, linking ideas and practice, to accomplish the imagined, and to realize the values agreed upon (Vickers, 1980; Jonas, 1984; Gamio Gehri, 2006; Embree, 2006).

As advanced earlier, trust, a basic human emotional and cognitive disposition to rely on others, is the fundamental bond that holds societies together and underlies these enabling conditions for value reinterpretation, creation, and realization. The ability and disposition to generate and maintain trust is an indispensable prerequisite for good governance, for exercising leadership in ways conducive to improvements in the human condition.

Trust is based on the belief that individuals, collectives, and institutions will act in a benign and not in a harmful way, and that they will be reliable and behave as anticipated. Mediated by symbolic systems and institutions that create mutual interdependence, trust informs acts of appreciation, the cognitive, factual, and emotional decision-making capacities required for joint human action. A minimum level of trust is a necessary condition for the enablers of value change—responsibility, tolerance, knowledge, and effectiveness—to initiate and sustain the moral dialogues that could lead to a redefinition of progress development through the reinterpretation, creation, and realization of values (Hosking, 2014, pp. 27–28, 201).

Trust requires moderation and discipline. According to British historian Geoffrey Hosking, too little trust leads to "obstinately vicious circles of distrust, from which escape is extremely difficult," and excessive trust can be counterproductive, for "trust in the untrustworthy is at best unrewarding, at worst pernicious" (Hosking, 2014, pp. 200). Similarly, inordinate degrees of responsibility deprive others of agency, while the opposite extreme breeds callousness and indifference. Too much tolerance leads to extreme relativism in which anything and everything is acceptable, while too little fosters sectarian behavior and exclusion (Drummond, 2006). Aspiring to exceedingly high levels of knowledge may cause paralysis by analysis, while ignorance ensures counterproductive errors. Focusing intently on effectiveness may disregard human transcendental impulses; neglecting it leads to idle speculation, wastefulness, and frustration. Discipline is required to wield moderation, even in situations that may incline us to reject it.

Experience has taught me some ways of generating trust, particularly in politics: telling things as they are, not as we or others would like them to be; never promising what cannot be done and doing what is promised; being transparent and avoiding conflicts of interest; recognizing errors and correcting them quickly; and giving trust, trusting others to generate trust in ourselves.

This is what the paradoxical art of governance is all about: transforming knowledge into social and political power, generating trust to steer individual and collective actions toward the common good, doing so while being fully aware of the collateral effects and noxious second-order consequences of overwhelming the natural ecosystems, of glaring human inequalities, and of authoritarian and arbitrary political rule.

At the twilight of Bacon's epoch, this is a task for all, not just for the authorities in any domain, at any level. Each of us can and should exercise power for the common good in our own settings and in our own ways; each and every one of us can make a difference through education, communication, and, most importantly, through example; each of us can improve the art of governance, starting with the way we govern ourselves. The ripple effects of doing so may be, at first, imperceptible, but history and experience have shown they can become significant and meaningful in the medium and long run.

However, we must be aware that the tide has been turning against attempts to move in the direction of gradually building a new consensus for whatever humanity may become in the coming decades. The proliferation of social networks and online communications is creating a cacophony of blurred messages that make us cling to the known, to the tried, to the past. They are devaluing live human interactions and propitiating some sort of widespread electronic solipsism, which could make seeking agreement and consensus a more elusive pursuit as we wade further into the post-Baconian epoch.

As American novelist Lydia Millet put it, "ordinary emotions let us blunder through the onslaught of information in the slow befuddlement of a stubborn belief that the familiar is bound to persist. But without a swift, far-reaching, and cooperative global effort, the familiar will *not* persist" (her emphasis) (Millet, 2024). The arrival and widespread adoption of artificial intelligence chatbots, which cater to the whims, desires, and aspirations of their interlocutors, reinforcing their deeply held beliefs, prejudices, and delusions, have made reaching interpersonal agreements an even more difficult task.

Nonetheless, I do not believe it is naïve or wishful thinking to state that human renewal is possible. We have the power to do so; we can generate and expand trust. On a limited scale, in many places and for some times, I have seen this happen over and over again. More than half a century of academic, professional, policy, and political work, together with my brief experience heading the government of my country at a most critical time during the COVID-19 pandemic, has strengthened my conviction that there is a hidden reservoir of energy and goodwill that can be tapped when urgent needs arise. We should take heart from what American historian and social critic Lewis Mumford anticipated decades ago:

> When the moment comes to replace power with plenitude, compulsive external rituals with internal, self-imposed discipline, depersonalization with individuation, automation with autonomy, we shall find that the necessary change of attitude and purpose has been going on beneath the surface during the last century, and the long buried seeds of a richer human culture are now ready to strike root and grow, as soon as the ice breaks up and the sun reaches them. If that growth is to prosper, it will draw freely on the compost from many previous cultures (Mumford, 1969, pp. 433–434).

References

Bacon, F. (1985). In J. Pitcher (Ed.), *The essays*. Penguin Books.

Bacon, F. (2011a). in J. Spedding, R. Ellis, & D. D. Heath, (Eds.), *The works of Francis Bacon: Vol. 10: The letters and the life 3* (Digitally printed version). Cambridge University Press.

Bacon, F. (2011b). In J. Spedding, R. Ellis, & D. D. Heath, (Eds.), *The works of Francis Bacon: Vol. 13: The letters and the life 6* (Digitally printed version). Cambridge University Press.

Berlin, I. (2014, October 23). A message to the 21st century. *The New York Review*. Retrieved from https://www.nybooks.com/articles/2014/10/23/message-21st-century/

Colebrook, C. (2012). Introduction: Extinction. Framing the end of the species. In *Extinction living books about life*. Open Humanities Press. Retrieved from https://www.livingbooksaboutlife.org/books/Extinction/Introduction

Damasio, A. R. (2018). *The strange order of things: Life, feeling, and the making of the cultures*. Pantheon Books.

Drummond, J. J. (2006). The good and negative obligation, the tolerable and the intolerable. In R. Rizo-Patrón de Lerner (Ed.), *Tolerancia: Interpretando la experiencia de la tolerancia / Toleration: Interpreting the experience of tolerance* (pp. 27–40). PUCP Fondo Editorial.

Embree, L. (2006). La tolerancia analizada reflexivamente. In R. Rizo-Patrón (Ed.), *Tolerancia: Interpretando la experiencia de la tolerancia*. PUCP Fondo Editorial.

Fromm, E. (2017). *¿Tener o ser?* (C. Valdes, Trans.). FCE.

Fukuyama, F. (2002). *Our posthuman future, Consequences of the biotechnology revolution*. Picador.

Gamio Gehri, G. (2006). El liberalismo y la sabiduría del mal. La búsqueda de consensos prácticos y las figuras políticas de la tolerancia. In R. Rizo-Patrón (Ed.), *Tolerancia: Interpretando la experiencia de la tolerancia*. PUCP Fondo Editorial.

García Morente, M. (1980). *Ensayos sobre el progreso*. Dorcas.

Hollway, W. (2011). In between external and internal worlds: Imagination in transitional space. *Methodological Innovations Online, 6*(3), 50–60. http://dx.doi.org/doi:10.4256/mio.2011.006

Homeland Security Operational Analysis Center. (2024). *Global catastrophic risk assessment*. Retrieved from https://www.fie.undef.edu.ar/ceptm/wp-content/uploads/2024/11/RAND_RRA2981-1.pdf

Hosking, G. A. (2014). *Trust: A history* (1st ed.). Oxford University Press.

Jonas, H. (1984). *The imperative of responsibility: In search of an ethics for the technological age*. University of Chicago Press.

Kelly, W. (1980). "We have met the enemy…" reprint of 1970 poster, Toni Mendez Collection, Billy Ireland Cartoon Library & Museum, The Ohio State University. Retrieved from https://library.osu.edu/site/40stories/2020/01/05/we-have-met-the-enemy/

Kropotkin, P. A. (1970). *Selected writings on anarchism and revolution*. MIT Press.

Latour, B. (1988). *The pasteurization of France* (A. Sheridan & J. Law, Trans.). Harvard University Press. Retrieved from https://archive.org/details/pasteurizationof0000lato_e1l2

Millet, L. (2024, August 20). A future beyond the climate crisis. *The MIT Technology Review*. Retrieved from https://www.technologyreview.com/2024/08/20/1096053/climate-change-future-for-future/

Mumford, L. (1969). *The pentagon of power: The myth of the machine*. Harcourt Brace.

Naam, R. (2010). *More than human: Embracing the promise of biological enhancement*. Broadway Books.

Platoni, K. (2024, August 15). Happy birthday, baby! What the future holds for those born today: An intelligent digital agent could be a companion for life—And other predictions for the next 125 years. *MIT Technology Review*. Retrieved from https://www.technologyreview.com/2024/08/15/1096178/125-years-predictions-babies-digital-agents/

Sagasti, F. (2000). The twilight of the Baconian age and the future of humanity. *Futures, 32*(6), 595–602.

Smith, K. K., & Berg, D. N. (1987). *Paradoxes of group life: Understanding conflict, paralysis, and movement in group dynamics*. Jossey-Bass Publishers.

Vickers, G. (1980). *Responsibility: Its sources and limits*. Intersystems Publications.

Chapter 12
Epilogue

Perhaps the best illustration of the way in which different civilizations have conceived the origin of human capabilities and the ways in which knowledge confers power, is contained in various versions of the myth of a hero stealing the fire from the goods and giving it to humanity. In his survey of the myths and traditions on the origin of fire, Sir James Frazer referred to Bacon's metaphor of "first vintage approximation" to characterize his own work, inviting others to discover the hidden meanings concealed in the vineyards of intellectual pursuits. His comprehensive study listed dozens of myths on the origin of fire, found all over the world since ancient times, showing that they exhibit similar patterns (Frazer, 1930, pp. 2, 201). The theme of theft of fire is a recurrent one in ancient mythologies, although not in all cases was it stolen from the gods.

Along the same lines, American writer and comparative mythology expert Joseph Campbell identified analogous cosmogonic mythical cycles of "separation-initiation-return" in a great diversity of cultures. These followed a common sequence: "a hero ventures forth from the world of common day into a region of supernatural wonder: fabulous forces are there encountered and a decisive victory is won: the hero comes back from this mysterious adventure with the power to bestow boons on his fellow." Giving a concrete example, he pointed out that "Prometheus ascended to the heavens, stole fire from the gods, and descended" (Campbell, 2004, p. 47).

The Greek myth of Prometheus, the titan who took the fire from the gods and gave it to humanity, is the best known of these myths. Its evolution over two- and one-half millennia has captured like no other the changing conceptions of the place of knowledge in human affairs.

At the end of the eighth and beginning of the seventh centuries before Christ, Hesiod saw Prometheus as the deceiver of Zeus, the supreme god, deserving punishment for his theft and because his interventions always ended up harming humanity. Two centuries later, Aeschylus viewed him as a benefactor who sacrificed himself for the salvation of humanity. In the following century, Diogenes blamed

F. Sagasti, *Knowledge is Power*, Innovation, Technology, and Knowledge Management, https://doi.org/10.1007/978-3-032-20668-8_12

Prometheus for providing the knowledge and techniques that would allow urban life and lead to the corruption of social mores. In *Protagoras*, Plato would present him as a benefactor who taught technical skills to humanity, but whose gift had to be complemented by Zeus bestowing morality and justice to underpin the civilized coexistence of human beings.

During the Roman and Middle Ages, Prometheus was seen as the shaper and animator of man and other living creatures. A variety of interpretations were provided by Lucien, Ovid, Horace, Cicero, Plutarch, Isidore of Seville, Tertuliano, Lactantius, and Fulgentius, among others. The philosophers and literary figures of the Renaissance—including Boccaccio, Ficcino, Pomponazzi, Bovilius, Conti, and Calderón de la Barca—viewed Prometheus as the symbol of creative capacities, as a sage who undertakes the task of civilizing humanity, and as a philosopher who steals the fire of superior knowledge from heaven and brings it down to earth.[1]

At the beginning of the seventeenth century, Sir Francis Bacon, in his *Wisdom of the Ancients*, provided an account that expresses the view of the myth that has prevailed since then. Prometheus creates humanity and, because of love for his creation, steals the fire from the gods and gives it to his creatures. Far from being grateful, humans denounce Prometheus before Zeus, then known by his Roman name as Jupiter, who decides to bestow the stolen fire and other gifts to humanity as a reward for betraying its benefactor. Incensed, Prometheus commits further affronts against Jupiter, offering a bogus sacrifice and attempting to ravish the goddess Pallas; in retaliation, the supreme god punishes both Prometheus and his creatures.

To chastise humanity, Jupiter orders Vulcan, the god of fire and metal working, to make beautiful and graceful Pandora as a gift to humanity, equipping her with a box full of evils but with hope ensconced at the bottom. When offered the box, Prometheus (forward looking) being prudent, does not open it, but his brother Epimetheus (backward looking) does and all sorts of calamities are set loose throughout the world, with only hope remaining at the bottom of the box. To further punish Prometheus, Jupiter chained him to a pillar on the top of Mount Caucasus, where an eagle ate his liver day after day, following its regrowth during the night. The titan's torment ended after a long time, when Hercules, crossing the sea in a flimsy vessel, shoots the eagle with an arrow and liberates Prometheus.

Bacon provides a detailed interpretation of the myth at many levels. For him "Prometheus clearly and expressly signifies Providence … the special and peculiar work of Providence was the creation and constitution of Man." As advanced in chapter three, Bacon uses his recounting of the Promethean myth to make explicit his view of the centrality of human beings in the order of things. He also argues that the myth indicates that the arrogance of Prometheus and of humans deserves to be punished:

> For they who break into extravagant praises of human nature, and the arts in vogue, and who lay themselves out in admiring the things they already possess, and will needs have the

---

[1] For historical accounts of the evolution of the myth of Prometheus, see: Raggio (1958), Rossi (1970, 1974), García Gual (1979), Landes (1969), Dougherty (2006), and Flahault (2013).

> sciences cultivated among them, to be thought absolutely perfect and complete, in the first place, show little regard to the divine nature, whilst they extol their own inventions almost as high as his perfection. In the next place, men of this temper are unserviceable and prejudicial in life, whilst they imagine themselves already got to the top of things, and there rest, without further inquiry. On the contrary, they who arraign and accuse both nature and art, and are always full of complaints against them, not only preserve a more just and modest sense of mind but are also perpetually stirred up to fresh industry and new discoveries. Is not, then, the ignorance and fatality of mankind to be extremely pitied, whilst they remain slaves to the arrogance of a few of their own fellows …? (Bacon, 1985, p. 272).

In late eighteenth century, young Wolfgang Goethe saw Prometheus as a symbol of self-reliance and the creative mind, but later in his life, with *Dr. Faustus* and *Pandora*, Goethe would take a darker view of the Promethean myth. Mary Shelley's 1818 novel *Frankenstein, or the Modern Prometheus* warned against the evil consequences of attempting to emulate the Greek titan, while her brother Percy Shelley's 1820 poem *Prometheus Unbound* would depict him as embodying the highest moral and intellectual perfection.

At the end of the nineteenth century, André Gide's satire *Prometheus Misbound* saw humanity receiving a "devouring belief in progress" as gift from Prometheus and depicted the gnawing eagle as the human conscience that is eventually silenced when Hercules kills it. Albert Camus wrote *Prometheus in Hell* in the aftermath of World War II and described the Greek titan as "the model for contemporary man," as the hero who loved humanity enough to give it the fire of freedom, technology, and the arts. But he adds that if he were to return, men would treat him as the gods did: "nail him to a rock, in the name of the very humanism he was the first to symbolize." In spite of this betrayal, Camus believes that Prometheus would retain "his quiet faith in man" (Camus, 1946/1947, p. 1).

The successive reinterpretations of this myth can be seen as mirroring the evolving concerns of leading Western intellectuals through the ages, with the central place awarded to humanity largely remaining constant. However, challenges to the Promethean centrality of humanity have multiplied at the twilight of Bacon's epoch. As indicated in the preceding chapters, the assumption of humanity's superiority and uniqueness has both come under attack on many fronts.

As a consequence, we are now being compelled to regard ourselves in a new light, to reposition ourselves in an ex-centric manner in relation to other living organisms and to the world that surrounds us. Bacon's interpretation of the myth of Prometheus requires updating in more uncertain and ambiguous terms, discarding his view that "Man is the center of the world." A retelling of this myth should also take into account that only a small portion of humanity benefited from the bounty of the Baconian/Promethean quest for knowledge.

We could thus argue that the gods punished Prometheus because he gave the fire of knowledge to a just few men, not to all. Also, because he gave humanity the knowledge and means to destroy itself, both with lethal weapons and by fouling his life-sustaining nest. He was also castigated for giving humans the means to consciously alter their own evolution, allowing them to use knowledge to change their own biological makeup and physical constitution, thus usurping a godly prerogative.

Moreover, Prometheus gave humanity the fire of knowledge, but he did not look forward enough to anticipate the negative consequences of stealing it from the gods and giving it to humanity. In this sense, we could say that Prometheus had some of the traits of his brother Epimetheus who opened Pandora's box and unleashed evil all over the world. The gift of fire prompted an unceasing and destructive quest for material progress, which ended up undermining its accomplishments. The limited foresight of Prometheus deserved punishment.

In spite of the calamities spread when Pandora's box was opened, humanity could always rely on the gift that remained, nurturing hope as last resort. Hope to alleviate the anguish of humanity's awareness that is capable of destroying itself.

The eagle eating at Prometheus' liver during the day represents the negative consequences of the unfolding, deployment, and triumph of the Baconian Program. Its regrowth during the night represents the confidence that it is possible to overcome the drawbacks of unrestrained scientific and technological advances; that knowledge can and will be used to restore nature and improve the conduct of human affairs; that new conceptions of progress and better governance are possible.

However, until the time comes for a contemporary or future version of Hercules that kills the eagle, liberating humanity from its self-imposed Promethean torments, we shall have alternating periods of hope and despair. Nonetheless, adding trust to hope—Pandora's remaining gift in the box—I am confident that there will be longer periods of recovery not only at night, as was the case for Prometheus, but also at the dawn of a post-Baconian epoch. As French American writer Marguerite Yourcenar put it clearly in the words of her fictional emperor Hadrian:

> Life is atrocious, we know. But precisely because I expect little of the human condition, man's periods of felicity, his partial progress, his efforts to begin over again and to continue, all seem to me like so many prodigies which nearly compensate for the monstrous mass of ills and defeats, of indifference and error. Catastrophe and ruin will come; disorder will triumph, but order will too, from time to time. Peace will again establish itself between two periods of war; the words *humanity*, *liberty*, and *justice* will here and there regain the meaning which we have tried to give them (her emphasis) (Yourcenar, 1963, p. 293).

References

Bacon, F. (1985). In J. Pitcher (Ed.), *The essays*. Penguin Books.

Campbell, J. (2004). *The hero with a thousand faces*. Princeton University Press.

Camus, A. (1946/1947). *Prometheus in the underworld* [Essay]. The Philosopher Network. Retrieved from https://thephilosopher.net/camus/wp-content/uploads/sites/94/2024/11/Prometheus-in-the-Underworld-Albert-Camus.pdf

Dougherty, C. (2006). *Prometheus*. Routledge.

Flahault, F. (2013). *El crepúsculo de Prometeo: Contribución a una historia de la desmesura humana* (1st ed.). Galaxia Gutenberg.

Frazer, J. G. (1930). *Myths of the origin of fire*. Macmillan. Retrieved from https://archive.org/details/MythsOfTheOriginOfFire
García Gual, C. (1979). *Prometeo: Mito y tragedia*. Ediciones Peralta.
Landes, D. S. (1969). *The unbound Prometheus, Technological change and industrial development in Western Europe from 1750 to the present*. Cambridge University Press.
Raggio, O. (1958). The myth of Prometheus: Its survival and metamorphoses up to the Eighteenth Century. *Journal of the Warburg and Courtauld Institutes, 21*(1–2), 44–62. https://doi.org/10.2307/750486
Rossi, P. (1970). *Los filósofos y las máquinas 1400—1700*. Labor.
Rossi, P. (1974). *De la Magia a la Ciencia*. Alianza Editorial.
Yourcenar, M. (1963). *Memoirs of Hadrian*. Straus & Giroux.

Index

F. Sagasti, *Knowledge is Power*, Innovation, Technology, and Knowledge Management, https://doi.org/10.1007/978-3-032-20668-8

K

L

M

N

W

Y

MIX
Papier aus verantwortungsvollen Quellen
Paper from responsible sources
FSC® C105338

If you have any concerns about our products,
you can contact us on
ProductSafety@springernature.com

In case Publisher is established outside the EU,
the EU authorized representative is:
Springer Nature Customer Service Center GmbH
Europaplatz 3, 69115 Heidelberg, Germany

Printed by Libri Plureos GmbH
in Hamburg, Germany